A Passion for Steam

Small scale steam locomotives and how they work

Marc Horovitz

Atlantic

Atlantic Publishers

PUBLISHERS

Atlantic Editions Limited
83 Parkanaur Avenue, Southend-on-Sea,
Essex SS1 3JA

ISBN: 978-1-902827-18-6

British Cataloguing in Publication Data
A catalogue record for this book is available
from the British Library

All photographs and illustrations by
Marc Horovitz unless otherwise noted

Designed by Juliet Arthur,
Atlantic Editions Limited

Printed in China,
by Printworks International Ltd.

A Passion for Steam

This book is dedicated with heartfelt thanks to all those who came before and who, by having come before, made this book possible.

Acknowledgements

I'd like to sincerely thank the following for their help in this endeavour: Jeff Young for reading my rough manuscripts and providing valuable insights; Dave Pinniger for putting me in the way of engines and shipping many of them to me over the years; Juliet Arthur for her fine design work on this book; Trevor Ridley for coming up with the initial concept for this tome; and all of the others who have helped me in one way or another through the years with information, either technical or historical.

Marc

Marc Horovitz

Preface

Perhaps the most hackneyed phrase ever to be employed when writing about the steam locomotive (in all its myriad forms) is 'the romance of steam' – and in any publication containing these words one expects to see the usual endlessly recycled photographs and information designed for purchase by the well meaning for a husband, grandfather, or favourite uncle who 'likes trains.' As with all clichés however, this one contains more than a grain of truth in that there are a huge number of people around the world for whom the steam-worked railway is a subject of perennial interest. Maybe it is just the drama of a passing steam train or perhaps it is because the steam locomotive, which has been described as the nearest thing to a living beast that man has ever made, is an elemental machine that uses metal, fire and water to produce power and movement.

Over the last thirty years there have been an increasing number of people who have actually yearned to run their own steam operation – albeit on a scale that they can manage in their own garden or yard. Now these small sized, garden-scale locomotives run, even the most basic of them, in just the same way as the real thing, and the sight and sound of a busy steam locomotive hauling a train in one's own working railway is something that is always a rewarding experience for those of us who have a passion for steam.

Now, one of the problems for steam romantics such as myself is that while one may take up this rewarding hobby, perhaps with the purchase of one of the many commercial live-steam offerings available today, it is a step taken often with only the very vaguest of ideas about how a steam locomotive actually works. Indeed, when I took my first faltering steps into the garden with radio controlled, narrow-gauge steam power some twenty-five years ago, there seemed to be little technical information available other than in publications aimed firmly at the pragmatic model engineer, rather than the more artistic model-railway builder who just happened to be using real steam locomotion rather than high revving electric motors in a steam-outline shell.

For myself, I learned most of my stuff the hard way – over many years and with many mistakes but, within these pages, acknowledged small-scale-steam expert Marc Horovitz employs his definitive collection of steam locomotives in the garden scales to provide an enjoyably accessible overview of all the types of live-steam locomotive that you are likely to come across in your garden-railway adventures. From a simple, single-cylinder oscillator to a sophisticated miniature version of the full-sized locomotive – all is simply explained with the aid of clear and effective colour diagrams combined with pertinent photography.

The gallery pages, themselves a large proportion of this book, present a highly visual museum of reference with over eighty steam locomotives in the various garden-railway scales, with each delightfully framed photograph enhanced with full description and technical details of the model concerned. This book is destined to be both a voyage of discovery for the newest of live-steam enthusiasts and a well-thumbed reference for the grizzled garden-railway veteran.

Tag Gorton
Editor, *GardenRail* Magazine
www.atlanticpublishers.com

Contents

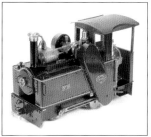

Bibliography

You sometimes have to dig for information about model steam locomotives. Books on this subject are not the stuff of mainstream book sellers. Much of what has been written is now out of print, but can often be found in used-book stores and on used-book sites on the Internet. These books, especially the old ones, make fascinating reading and there is a wealth of knowledge in them. Here, in alphabetical order by author, are some that I have found to be particularly useful over the years.

Bassett-Lowke Railways: A Commemorative Edition, Bassett-Lowke Railways and Steam Age, 1969

Carlson, Pierce, *Toy Trains: A History*, Harper & Row, 1986

Coles, Tim, *A Beginner's Guide to Model Steam Locomotives*, Patrick Stephens, 1986

Cooke, Eddie, *7mm Live Steam: The Eddie Cooke Articles*, Gauge 0 Guild, 1997

Ellis, Hamilton, *Model Railways 1838-1939*, George Allen & Unwin Ltd., 1962

Evans, Martin, *Manual of Model Steam Locomotive Construction*, Percival Marshall, 1960

Evans Martin, *Model Locomotive Boilers*, Model & Allied Publications Ltd., 1969

Evans, Martin, *Model Locomotive Valve Gears*, Percival Marshall, 1962

Fuller, Roland, *The Bassett-Lowke Story*, New Cavendish Books, 1984

Greenly, Henry, *The Model Lomotive: Its Design and Construction*, Percival Marshall, 1904

Greenly, Henry, *Model Steam Locomotives*, Cassell and Company, Ltd, 1922

Harley, Basil, *Toyshop Steam*, Model and Allied Publications, 1978

Harris, K.N., *Model Boilers and Boiler Making*, Argus Books Ltd., 1967

L.B.S.C, *Shop, Shed, & Road*, Perdival Marshall, 1929 (reprinted 1969 in expanded form). Also, any of L.B.S.C.'s locomotive-construction books are worth reading

Levy, Allen, *A Century of Model Trains*, Crescent Books, 1974

Malins, P.S., *Mamod: The Story of Malins Models*, Mamod Sales & Service, 1996

Minns, J.E., *Model Railway Engines*, Octopus Books Ltd., 1973

Reder, Gustav, *Clockwork, Steam, and Electric*, Ian Allan, 1972

Van Riemsdijk, John, *Modelling in Gauge 1: Book 2: John van Riemsdijk's Contribution*, Gauge 1 Model Railway Association, 2005

Whitehouse, Patrick B. and John Adams, *Model and Miniature Railways*, Chartwell Books Inc., 1976

Introduction

A freelance 2-6-2, built by Don Mason, takes its train around a bend on the Ogden Botanical Railway (OBR). The locomotive, which is based on Roundhouse Engineering parts, has a single flue, gas-fired boiler.

When Trevor Ridley first approached me about doing this book I immediately agreed, then just as quickly forgot all about it. When next I saw him, a year or so later, and he asked, "How's the book coming?," I had no idea what he was talking about. After he patiently refreshed my memory and made it plain that he was actually serious about it, it was evident that I had better make a start. So, after many, *many* months, you hold the result before you.

One does not lightly undertake a project like this. When you write about something close to your heart, you want to present it in just the right way. It's not the same as writing about diseases of dogs' innards or some other purely dry, technical matter. Although there *is* much technical about steam locomotives, this is also a subject that brings us much joy. Otherwise, why would we pursue it? So the topic must be approached in a way that conveys both the technical information as well as that sense of profound pleasure that these little engines provide us. I hope that I have done that here.

While writing and illustrating the book has been a long, hard slog, at no time have I regretted undertaking it or loudly and colourfully cursed the muse that inhabits me, as I have been known to do with other projects. On the contrary, I've enjoyed every minute of it, with the possible exception of all those minutes spent dragging eighty-plus locomotives up the stairs and out to the garden for photographs, then back down

again. But, as P.G. Wodehouse says, "You have to take the roughs with the smooths."

It sometimes happens that, after intensively delving into a topic for an extended period of time, you come away loving that topic a great deal less than you did when you started out. Happily, that was not the case for me with this book. In fact, I think the opposite happened. My affection for these little engines is stronger than ever.

This is an exceptionally broad and deep subject that cannot possibly be covered in its entirety in any single volume. And, even at this late day in its evolution, it is still an organic subject that continues to change and grow over time. I have tried to fairly deeply scratch the surface here, but there is still much exploration for you to do, if you've a mind to pursue it. If you do, you'll be amply rewarded.

I have also tried to convey a sense of the wonderful diversity that can be found in our little locomotives and, perhaps, to get you to look at them as something more than just tiny, though fascinating machines. Every engine out there – from the one-off scratchbuilt models to those that come off the production line in hundreds or thousands – was designed and built by a real person (or several real persons) and each embodies the designer's and maker's personalities in one way or another. So the miniature steam locomotive, like everything else in our lives, represents a connection between you, the end user, and other human beings.

7

Chapter 1

A passion for railroads

Why does one love railways? This is a question I've asked many people over the years and I have yet to receive a good answer. Nor is it a question that I can answer myself. Some people come from railway families. Some were given trains at an early age. Some lived near railways when young. All of these factors may have had something to do with it, but none of them addresses the arcane reason why railways became a passion. After all, countless other people came from railway families, had model trains as children, or lived near the tracks, and they think no more of railways than they do of the sidewalks beneath their feet.

And what about people like me? My family were not railroaders and I didn't grow up near railroads. As a child, I was given trains, not because some adult thought I should have them, but because, even at an early age, I wanted them. I suspect that this will always remain one of life's minor mysteries.

Early days

I've read countless accounts of people's early days with model railways, and they take on a dreary sameness. My own early days followed the well-trod course, so I won't bore you with the details. In brief, I had trains as a child (Marx clockwork, then Lionel electric), graduating to HO as a teenager. I had an indulgent father who would often take my sisters and me to Union Station in downtown Denver on Sunday mornings in the 1950s to witness the exciting departure of the *Texas Zephyr*, one of Burlington's crack passenger trains.

There were two seemingly minor incidents in my youth that I recall as being seminal to my ultimate journey into garden railroading and live steam. The first was the discovery at the main branch of the Denver Public Library of an old Bassett-Lowke catalogue. This was one of my first introductions to British railways, both full size and model, and I was captivated. I was amazed to learn that the same model locomotive was often offered in three flavours – clockwork, steam, and electric – and that the electric versions were often the most expensive in those days. I pored over this treasure for hours on many occasions.

The second event occurred one afternoon in the mid 1960s at Caboose Hobbies, a frequent haunt. In those days, they carried a lot of foreign model-railway magazines. On the cover of one was a picture of a steam-powered train running in a garden railway. The locomotive was a tram engine, which was something new to me. I've always been attracted to the odd and unusual, and I thought that tram engine a most wonderful thing, especially so because it actually ran on its own steam power. In addition, this single photograph, at a stroke, opened to me the concept of the garden railway.

Lapses and renaissance

I entered architecture school in 1967 and railways went by the board. Upon graduation in 1972, I took a job in Houston, Texas, and railways experienced a brief resurrection in my life in the form of HOn3 and Sn2 modelling. A year later, though, I entered graduate school in Austin, Texas, and railways once again faded from view.

In grad school in 1973 I met Barbara Lilly, who was later to become my wife and life's companion. She and I enjoyed going to garage sales (what the British would call jumble or car-boot sales). At one, probably in 1975, I found one of Kalmbach's slim volumes on HO railroading, which didn't interest me much. However, on a whim, I asked the lady if

An Aster 'King Arthur' with a train of six Aster Southern Railway coaches, crosses the Harris Viaduct on the author's railway. The 'King Arthur' was one of Aster's first locomotives and, with its slip-return-crank valve gear and Smithies boiler, owes much to 1930s British model-locomotive technology.

Right: This Bassett-Lowke 'Super Enterprise' from the 1930s was the author's first live-steam locomotive.

Lower: Archangel engines have always occupied a special place. *Sgt. Murphy* was the first engine from Cock Lane acquired.

she had the trains to go with the book. She said that she did not, but that her husband had some he wanted to sell.

An appointment was duly made and the trains were brought out. This turned out to be one of those life-changing moments. The trains were Lionel's from the 1930s, and they were made *entirely of metal.* Although they bore little resemblance to full-size trains, their inherent charm, physical heft, and strong nostalgia component was overpowering. I was transfixed. I'd never seen anything like them before and they spoke to my heart. A deal was struck and the trains were mine (I still have them). As a result of this transaction, I made the conscious decision to become a collector. I joined the Train Collector's Association (TCA) in 1976. Also in 1976, I graduated from the University of Texas with a Master of Architecture degree, moved back to Denver, and Barb and I got married.

At a TCA show not long after, I acquired my first live-steam locomotive, a Bassett-Lowke 'Super Enterprise.' This rekindled my interest in steam, as well as the desire to build my own engines. I signed up for a machine-shop class at the local trade school and learned to use a lathe and mill.

A visit to Archangel
In 1979, Barb and I made our first trip abroad. I had begun acquiring books and reading everything I could get my hands on about garden railroading and live steam, especially the garden-size engines. I had read a little about Stewart Browne and Archangel Models, so made it a priority on this trip to pay him a visit. I didn't know where he was located or how to contact him and, at this long remove, I don't recall how I figured it out, but I did.

I rang him up and was grudgingly (it seemed to me) given permission to stop by. Barb and I took the train to High Wycombe, then walked the two or three miles to his house on Cock Lane, where he had his workshop in an outbuilding in the back. We were met at the door by a nice lady who showed us through the house into the back garden, where we were met by Stewart, who escorted us into a small shed where

he kept his finished engines. This turned out to be another of those life-changing moments that I vividly recall.

The engines were magical and they evoked feelings of both excitement and longing that are difficult to describe. They were big, colourful, and beautiful beyond words. There was a wonderful smell in the air that I would ever after associate with Archangel locomotives, although I later realised that it was nothing more than the odour of paint drying on a damp day. When Stewart discovered that his only sale that day was to be a catalogue for £1, which was all I could afford at the time, we were quickly ushered out, but the damage had already been done. I was well and truly hooked.

Also on this trip I discovered the evocative writings of Jack Wheldon and Dave Rowlands, which further paved the road I now found myself on. And I also discovered Beck engines from Germany, which were being advertised in the British press at that time.

Sidestreet Bannerworks, Light Railway Division
To digress a little, back home I had set myself up in the graphics business, designing and producing architectural graphics in textiles – banners. In our college days, Barb and I

9

sold our artwork in a little public market on a side street off the main 'drag' (as it was called) in Austin. We called ourselves the Sidestreet Studio. When I set up the banner business, I kept the name, which became Sidestreet Bannerworks.

In the US, in the late 1970s, there was virtually nothing happening in garden-scale steam. Aster engines were being imported, but those were only for rich dilettantes, or so I thought. That was it. No work-a-day engines for those building garden railways were available.

It occurred to me that someone should import Beck engines into the US, and I could think of no one better for the job than myself. So, I invented the Light Railway Division for my company, designed a letterhead, and wrote to Beck in Germany, proposing that they make me their sole US agent. I was astonished (and still am to this day) to receive a reply in the affirmative. So, with a grubstake from my mother, I ordered two *Annas* – one green and one black – and took out a small ad in *Model Railroader* magazine. I was off and running.

It didn't take long for Beck to realize that I was not to be their path to riches in the New World and, after a year, they gave the agency to a larger company, who, ultimately, did little better than I. But by that time I had a mailing list and the beginnings of a following. I offered similar, related products, became an Aster dealer, and, eventually, Roundhouse Engineering's US agent. It took a while, but the market slowly grew.

Garden Railways magazine

Mine was a mail-order business. Whenever I had a new product, I would send an announcement to everyone on my list. However, if I didn't have anything new for six months, my public forgot I was alive. I needed a way to keep my company name fresh in their collective mind.

I decided that a bimonthly company newsletter was what was wanted. The idea was that it would not only announce new products, but I could use it to discuss pertinent topics, chat about engines, and generally keep interest going. Thus, in 1982 the *Sidestreet Banner* was born.

This fledgling newsletter had a much longer reach than I ever imagined it would, even from the first issue. It instigated correspondence from such luminaries as Dave Rowlands, Jack Wheldon, Dave Pinniger, and John Wenlock, then president of the 16mm Narrow Gauge Modellers Association. By the second issue, articles by these people and others were appearing in the *Banner*. Peter Jones' 'Scribblings on a Workshop Wall' appeared in Volume 2, Number 4, and today, over twenty-five years later, still appears in every issue of *Garden Railways*. This was heady stuff.

The *Banner* continued to grow for a year and a half, while my interest in real banners continued to wane. By this time, we had been back to Britain and met the people with whom we had been corresponding. I had also become a member of the 16mm Narrow Gauge Modellers Association and the Gauge 1 Model Railway Association. Both of these organisations supplied wonderful newsletters that provided hours of enlightening reading.

Around this time I began to write a regular column for *Live Steam* magazine, called 'Small Scale Steam.' This focused on the various aspects of garden-scale steam locomotives, which had heretofore been widely ignored by the live-steam press. This helped to further the cause.

By the end of 1983 I thought I could tell which way the wind was blowing. I made the decision to turn the *Banner* into a real magazine that would contain articles on all subjects pertaining to garden railroading, not just steam. The first issue of *Garden Railways* appeared in January of 1984 – sixteen pages in sparkling black-and-white.

Barb became active in the magazine, becoming *Garden Railways'* first horticultural editor. The magazine and the hobby of garden railroading continued to grow in the US. In 1985, in conjunction with the Denver Garden Railway Society, *Garden Railways* magazine co-sponsored the first National Garden Railway Convention. In addition to proposing the initial idea of the convention to the club, I was active on the planning committee. The first convention was deemed a success, so we had three more in Denver before throwing it open to the world. From there the convention took on a life of its own and has been held annually in various parts of the US ever since.

Things with the magazine progressed until the fall of 1986, when we thought that perhaps *Garden Railways* alone could provide us with a living. We decided to put all of our energies into it and produced the magazine's first colour cover on the last issue of that year. We let the banner business die a quiet and well-deserved death and passed the Roundhouse agency on to Peter Olson at West Lawn Locomotive Works. We were out of the graphics and engine business and into the publishing business full time.

Not long after this, we received a call from Kalmbach Publishing Company, who inquired as to whether we had ever considered a distributor for *Garden Railways*. This came at a fortuitous time and we signed on. They distributed the magazine to hobby shops, which greatly boosted circulation. The magazine continued well and, in 1996, we sold it to Kalmbach. I stayed on as editor while Barb retired to the garden.

The Ogden Botanical Railway: Mark I

When we started *Garden Railways* magazine, we lived in a small double (semi-detached property) in an older part of the city. We had no railway. A year or so into publication, Barb suggested that, since I was the publisher of a magazine that dealt with garden railroading, it might bolster my credibility if I had one of my own. So, thus shamed into action, I began planning our first railway.

Unfortunately, we shared our backyard with our neighbours in the other half of the double. They had two large, friendly dogs who pretty well took over the property, so the backyard was pre-empted. The only other available option was a small space in the front yard, between the sidewalk and the street. Barb had already built a tiny garden in an eight-foot by twelve-foot plot. This, then, would host the first Ogden Botanical Railway (OBR), so named because we lived on Ogden Street.

A trackplan evolved and was duly staked out. It was nothing more than a simple loop, as that's all we could get into that space. The track was GarGarves dual-gauge flex (0 and 1),

which had rails of folded stainless-steel sheet pressed into slots in wooden ties. The roadbed was a course of bricks laid on sand in the existing garden, with the track literally strapped to it.

I was concerned about vandalism, as our neighbourhood at the time was perhaps not the best. I needn't have worried, though – most passersby didn't even notice it. Those who did – women mostly – were intrigued. The only damage ever done was during one winter when the track, invisible under the snow, was inadvertently stepped on.

On open days we'd set up our lawn chairs, run trains, and converse with pedestrians. This railway lasted until we moved into our first real house.

The OBR: Mark II

We moved, I think, in 1986. It took about three years before we had another railway, as the yard required a lot of work before one could be built.

The second incarnation of the Ogden Botanical Railway had proper track. It, too, was dual gauge, but hand-laid on redwood ties using LGB's code-332 brass rail. Switches were scratchbuilt to suit the lay of the land, an idea that I had always liked better than the constraints of store-bought switches. The garden that attended this railway was purpose made and nicely complemented the line.

Minimum radius was seven feet, which accommodated all but the largest of engines. This was the widest radius that we

A steamup in 1984 on the diminutive Ogden Botanical Railway, Mark I. The entire line was placed in an 8ft x 12ft existing garden in the front of the house. Passersby mingle with participants.

Left: The Ogden Botanical Railway, Mark III. A train crosses the tall Harris Viaduct, so named because Mike Harris provided the materials for it. The locomotive is by Don Mason.

Lower: The station area of the OBR, Mark II. The platform was cut from a piece of pool-table slate. This garden was made for the railway. Across the brick path is the full-size garden. The picture was taken in the late 1980s.

could fit in the available space. Track was level and the west side, which was on land that fell away a little, was supported by redwood trestles. On the east side it was at ground level and ran in planter boxes in between.

A station platform hugged the slightly curved platform tracks. This was made from a chunk of thick slate salvaged from an abandoned pool table. I cut it to size using a hand-held circular saw with a stone-cutting blade. It was a horrible job, producing clouds of slate dust that went everywhere, but the end result was most satisfactory. This railway served us well until we moved to our current residence in 1992.

The OBR: Mark III

We had discovered an empty half-acre lot in the city – a rare find – and decided to design our own house. We positioned the house on the lot to give us a small front yard and an exceptionally large backyard. The property was essentially an enormous weed patch when we moved in and it took a long time to bring even a semblance of order to it.

Fighting the weeds was a constant struggle. The first year we had a magnificent crop of dandelions. It occurred to me that if I were able to dispose of all the seeds, next year's crop would be much diminished. I waited until all of the flowers had gone to seed, which was a risk as, should the wind come up, there would go the seeds. My luck held, though, and one fine day I went out with the shop vacuum and sucked up every one of the seed heads that I could see. As I had hoped, the next year we had few of that particular weed.

It again took about three years to bring the yard under control, build stone walls to contain the dirt that would form the backbone of the railway (which came from the house's foundation), and to come up with an acceptable trackplan.

This railway would be a raised, level loop of approximately one hundred and fifty feet in length. It would serve two important stations, Ogden and Lizard Westen, plus an inter-mediate halt, Gatorbone. Engine facilities and passing tracks would be provided at the larger termini, while a siding would serve Gatorbone Halt. I wanted everything on this railway to ultimately be scratchbuilt – track, trains, buildings, etc. – with no commercial products anywhere. I'm still working towards that goal.

I hand laid the track again, this time with code-250 brass rail. It took a couple of years before the loop was complete. There are seven switches, each different from the others, and each made for its particular spot on the railway. All switches

Right: OBR Nº2 with a train of empty cane wagons. The engine and stock was scratchbuilt by the author specifically for the railway.

Lower: The station at Gatorbone Halt, made of indigenous stone and wood from a privet hedge, is a small example of 'National Park' architecture.

are manual, controlled by scratchbuilt switch levers. The track skirts the periphery of the railway's area, which is an island in the yard. Minimum mainline radius is thirteen feet.

On the south side, the land drops away and the railway is supported by a long bridge, the Harris Viaduct. This comprises steel girders resting on concrete piers. Wind can be a hazard when crossing this bridge. On one blustery day a train crossing the viaduct was actually blown off, dragging its engine after it. Fortunately, the only casualty was a scratched buffer beam.

A lesser concrete bridge was provided over a small valley on the east side. This has since self destructed due to ignorance on the part of its builder (me), and has been replaced by a temporary bridge made of privet branches. A concrete retaining wall supports the track as it rounds the southeast curve.

Structures

I wanted to use two distinctly different types of architecture on this railway. Although the railway is fanciful in many respects, I envision the line as existing in the 1930s. Art deco has always appealed to me and I have (so far) constructed a pair of art deco engine houses out of concrete. The one at Lizard Westen has one stall while the one at Ogden has two. These were made from similar components, though, and have a family look about them. There's also a tunnel with art deco portals. More about that anon.

The other type of architecture I wanted is known in

One of two art-deco engine houses on the line, still awaiting doors. The structure is made of cast concrete.

the US as 'National Park' style. This involves the use of a lot of natural materials, primarily rough-cut wood and stone. The station structures at Gatorbone and Lizard Westen are of this style, using real wood and red sandstone. There is no station yet for Ogden. All stations have concrete platforms.

The only other structure at present is a small, concrete tool house that is in the process of self-demolition, again due to my ignorance. All part of life's rich pageant, I guess. It will be replaced eventually.

Engines and rolling stock

As I mentioned above, I wanted everything on this railway to be scratchbuilt specifically for it. This did not preclude visiting engines, of course, but the trains that belonged to the railway itself had to be its own.

The first (and so far only) rolling stock constructed was a string of seventeen cane cars. Why cane cars? Because I like them, and for no other reason.

Although I've scratchbuilt half a dozen or so engines over the years, only two locomotives to date have emerged that were designed specifically for the OBR. These are both tram

The monorail, with engine unpainted, waits with its train of coaches at Lizard Westen. The twin portal, art-deco tunnel is another concrete structure.

engines. One has one, single-acting oscillator and the other, of similar external appearance, has a pair of double-acting oscillators. More engines will most likely be forthcoming, but time is a precious commodity and, at this juncture in my life, far too little of it is spent in the workshop. I also have plans for more passenger and freight stock, but they are hidden in an obscure future.

The Lizard Valley Steam Monorail

I have always been fascinated by the famous Listowell & Ballybunnion monorail in Ireland and decided to have something like it. I didn't want to build scale models of that railway's stock, but I did use the same Lartigue monorail system.

Rolling stock consists of four identical maroon coaches and one, earlier green one. These were built for the railway in 1996. There is no freight stock. The locomotive I built from my own design and, much to my surprise, it performs very well indeed. You can read more about it elsewhere in this book.

Track was problematic. I had some code-197 rail on hand, so I made up a short test section with scratchbuilt A-frames. This worked fine, but took too long to build. I ultimately asked Larry Herget at Ozark Miniatures if he would cast some A-frames in white metal for me if I supplied a pattern, and that is what happened.

I plotted a point-to-point route for the monorail – about sixty or seventy feet – between Lizard Westen and Ogden, bypassing Gatorbone. This would be the 'Inland Route' and would figure heavily in the railway's advertising. I built the track on the bench and installed it in sections. Near Lizard Westen, the track passes under the hill through the northern portal of the aforementioned two portal, art-deco tunnel. A wooden road passes through the other opening. In due time, the track was complete.

The monorail was in place for about three years, I think, before disaster struck. It was always in peril, just because of what it was, but damage came from an unexpected source – Mother Nature. The winter of 2006-07 was one of the worst ever. We had weeks of snow. In the Lizard Valley, the snow accumulated and did not melt for months. With each successive storm, the snow on the bottom became more compacted. When it finally melted in the spring thaw, I found that about a third of the length of the monorail track had been neatly and evenly crushed. As this is being written it has not been rebuilt.

The 'Locomotive of the Month'

My interest in miniature steam locomotives has grown stronger over the years. As a result of this, my collection of locomotives grew well beyond my early expectations.

I have always had a passing interest in museums, ever since I designed one as a thesis project for my architecture degree. The preserving, documenting, and display of artefacts is an engrossing subject, especially when applied to one's personal interests. Most of my engines are out where I can at least see them, although the manner in which they are displayed and lit is something less than ideal. And, since they are at my house, sharing them is often difficult, given the confines of available space. However, I did want to share them and the Internet ultimately supplied the solution.

I had had my web site up and running for some years when it occurred to me that I could post the engines online and share them in that way. However, given the number of loco-motives available to post, it would take forever before a web site could be built that would contain them, and I didn't want to wait forever. Then I had a brainstorm – why not just post them one at a time? I could develop a mailing list and send out a notice when each was posted, all through the magic of the World Wide Web. So, the 'Locomotive of the Month' (LotM) was born on my Sidestreet Bannerworks web site.

Each month I take an engine from the collection and photograph it from various points of view. I write about its prototype, if it had one, then describe the model itself, noting anything odd or unusual about it. Then, if the engine is runnable, I give it a go and discuss the run, including any problems (and solutions) that were encountered. Along with each review is a list of basic specifications for each locomotive. There are only two rules regarding what appears on LotM: it has to be in my collection and, if it is a commercial model, it has to be out of production.

This has proven popular and has become a resource for me as well. I can go back and read about a run of a particular engine to refresh my memory about how it performed and behaved. As this is written, I'm up to number 91. All previous locos are on the site as well and are available for anyone to view. I enjoy hearing from people around the world regarding the engines, several of whom have been kind enough to point out errors in my text. (One of the joys of the Internet is that mistakes can be instantly corrected and are not perpetuated, as they are in print.) It's also a way to get me out to the track at least once a month for a run.

Chapter 2

Basics

All steam locomotives (with the exception of turbines), regardless of size, work in fundamentally the same way. They are an aggregation of separate but integrated systems. These systems include the boiler, the heating system, the control system, and the cylinders.

How it all works (generally)

A steam engine, locomotive or otherwise, converts the energy from burning fuel into power and motion (figure 1). It does so by first burning the fuel to heat water. Water, when heated sufficiently, turns into steam. At sea level, in open air, the boiling point of water is 212° Fahrenheit or 100° Celsius. But when that same water is confined in a pressure vessel (the boiler), the boiling temperature rises as the pressure inside increases. There are complex formulas that are used to determine the boiling point/pressure relationship.

Heat is energy. As the water is heated, its energy-carrying capacity increases. At the boiling point, water undergoes a phase change from liquid (water) to gas (steam). Steam carries more energy than does water; the less water there is in steam, the more energy is carried. Superheated (dry) steam carries the most energy.

When the water in the boiler has been heated enough and the pressure within it has risen high enough for the steam to do some useful work (called working pressure), the steam can be gradually released into the cylinders. If the steam is not released, or the fire lessened, the pressure in the boiler will continue to rise until the safety valve (a necessary fitting on *all*

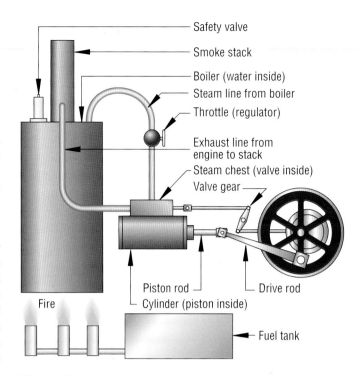

Figure 1
Basic steam-engine
The essential parts of a steam engine are illustrated here

boilers, regardless of size) opens (called blow-off pressure), releasing the excess pressure to the atmosphere.

Steam is controlled by a throttle or regulator. This is simply a valve of one type or another that releases the steam in a controlled manner.

The steam cylinder is what converts the energy contained in the steam to motion. Inside it is a piston. The steam, when

This engine is a *Cranmore* Peckett, built by David Hick. It's an example of an accurate and faithful scale model of a specific prototype.

Left: While *Robin*, made by John Prescott, is a freelance model representing no specific prototype, it is nevertheless a plausible engine that follows prototype practice.

Lower: This Bowman 0-4-0 tank engine could be considered nothing but a toy. However, it runs on steam using the same principles as the most sophisticated of locomotives.

admitted into the cylinder, is under pressure and it pushes on the piston. It will push it in either one direction only (called single acting) or it will push it, alternately, in both directions (called double acting). Attached to the piston is the piston rod, which carries the motion outside the cylinder. And attached to the piston rod is another rod that connects the piston rod to the wheel, thus causing it to rotate.

When released, the steam doesn't go directly to the cylinders. If it did, nothing would happen, as the system would just lock up. It has to go through a valve, or valving mechanism, that allows the steam to enter the cylinder, push the piston, then exhaust (i.e., get out of the way), as the piston returns to its position before it was pushed. This valve, in the case of fixed cylinders, is controlled by valve gear, which in turn is controlled by the wheels. The relationship between the piston and the valve is critical to the engine's performance.

Steam, when it is admitted to the cylinder, continues to expand, unlike, say, compressed air. This expansion is how it gives up some of its energy to the pistons.

Most of a steam engine's energy, however, just goes straight up the stack. Steam engines are notoriously inefficient, which is what ultimately led to their demise. This is due to a variety of factors, including losses in combustion and heat transfer to the water, heat losses in the cylinders, and mechanical losses. However, that needn't overly concern us. In our little engines, the steam era lives on. It is alive and well in countless gardens throughout the world.

Types of Engines

Since all steam engines work in basically the same way, what's the attraction? If you've seen one, you've seen them all, right? Not at all. Although they all do basically the same job, there is endless variety, ingenuity, and interest in how they get that job done.

Little locomotives fall broadly into three categories: prototypical models, freelance models, and toys. Prototypical models are those that represent, to a greater or lesser degree, specific full-size locomotives. Freelance models are engines that do not represent any particular full-size engine (prototype). They might follow prototypical practice and be plausible 'might have been' engines, or they might be completely fanciful, or something in between. Toys are the simple engines that were intended for youngsters, either as demonstrators of scientific principles or as model-railway locomotives that were simple to make, run, and maintain. They may or may not resemble full-size engines.

Some people take the rather narrow view that if a miniature steam locomotive is not a representation of a full-size engine, then it has no merit. Others feel that any machine that propels itself by steam, regardless of size, is a viable steam locomotive, as it functions in the same way as any other steam engine, regardless of size. I tend to take this latter view. To build a working model of a full-size locomotive in all of its particulars is a virtual impossibility. Some things just can't be scaled down, and steam is one of them. If it were possible to build an exact replica, internally and externally, of a full-size engine, it wouldn't function. Compromise must be made somewhere, usually in the boiler design and controls. And, having made this compromise, the model, all of a sudden, becomes not an exact replica. The best one can hope for is a model that closely resembles the prototype in its external characteristics and, perhaps, in some of its performance characteristics.

On the other hand, if one embraces all of steamdom as valid and viable, the possibilities expand exponentially. Some of my favourite little engines are those that were designed specifically for use in the garden. Some of these are representative of full-size engines but many are not. However, all were designed to satisfy a stated set of parameters for use on little railways in the backyard. For example, they must be controllable, able to haul a train of reasonable length, and run for a minimum amount of time without attention. Or, they must incorporate as many features of a full-size locomotive as possible and be operated in much the same way, demanding nearly constant attention from the driver or engineer to make sure that it is performing at its peak. There are many approaches to this end of our hobby, which is a great part of its charm and appeal.

In the following chapters you will be introduced to the mechanics of how these engines work and a lot of the variety that can be built into them. I hope that you enjoy it as much as I have over the years.

Chapter 3
Cylinders

Asteam engine's cylinders are one of its distinctive visual characteristics – the things that make it recognizable as a steam engine. Of course, there are lots of locomotives that have the cylinders hidden between the frames and elsewhere, but everyone likes to see the cylinders and their attendant motion. Cylinders come in two basic varieties: oscillating and fixed. Let's start with oscillating cylinders.

Oscillating Cylinders
'Oscillate' means to move to and fro, which is what an oscillating cylinder does. It is mounted on a pivot pin, or trunnion, and it oscillates up and down about this pivot as the engine moves.

An oscillating cylinder can be either single or double acting. In a single-acting cylinder, the steam pushes the piston in only one direction, relying on the momentum of the engine to return the piston to the top of the power stroke. With a double-acting cylinder, the steam pushes the piston in both directions.

What causes the cylinder to oscillate is the fact that the piston rod is not jointed and is attached directly to the crankpin on the wheel. As the wheel goes around, the rigid piston rod and piston cause the cylinder to wobble about its trunnion. There is an intimate relationship between the cylinder, the piston/piston rod, and the wheel.

Refer to figure 1. Steam is admitted to the cylinder at one or both ends (depending on whether it is single or double acting) through holes called ports. The cylinder has a flat face on its backside that butts up to the port block, through which the trunnion passes. A spring over the trunnion, bearing against the port block, keeps the cylinder's flat face snugly against the port block. The mating surfaces between the cylinder and the port block must be very smooth to ensure steam tightness.

In the port block are two carefully positioned steam passages. One is called admission (steam in) port and the other is exhaust (steam out) port. As the wheel rotates and the cylinder oscillates, the steam port in the cylinder will alternately align with the admission and exhaust ports. The entire system is set up so that when steam is admitted into the cylinder, it pushes the piston to the other end, causing the wheel to rotate half a

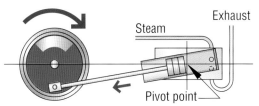

1. Steam from the boiler is admitted to the cylinder through the admission port.

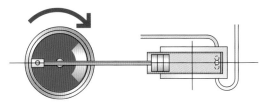

2. The piston is forced to the end of its stroke, driving the wheel.

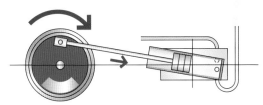

3. As the cylinder oscillates, the cylinder port becomes aligned with the exhaust port and the steam is exhausted

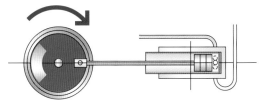

4. Momentum carries the piston to front dead centre, and the cycle repeats.

Figure 1
Steam cycle of a single-acting oscillating cylinder

This elegant, old (circa 1906), gauge-1 Carette 2-2-0 'stork leg' has two, single-acting oscillating cylinders. The rod reaching forward from the cab is linked to the reversing valve.

17

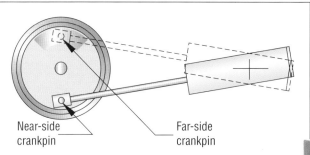

Near-side crankpin   Far-side crankpin

Single-acting cylinders have crankpins that are positioned 180° apart on opposite wheels. This balances the power strokes, but still causes dead spots when the pistons are at dead centre.

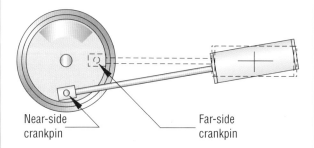

Near-side crankpin   Far-side crankpin

Double-acting cylinders have crankpins that are positioned 90° apart on opposite wheels, usually with the right-hand wheel leading. This not only balances the power strokes, but ensures that there is power to the wheels in any position.

Figure 2
Crankpin positions on single- and double-acting cylinders

The ubiquitous Mamod is powered by two, double-acting oscillators. This particular gauge-1 example is a rare bird, having been specially produced by Mamod for the Gauge 1 Model Railway Association before gauge-1 engines were a standard part of their line. This red engine was produced with a straight stack; production red engines had diamond stacks.

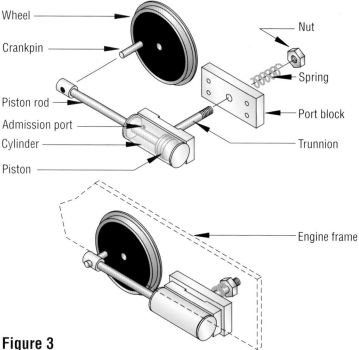

Wheel — Crankpin — Piston rod — Admission port — Cylinder — Piston — Nut — Spring — Port block — Trunnion — Engine frame

Figure 3
Double-acting oscillating cylinder

turn. By then the cylinder will have oscillated to the exhaust port and, as the wheel completes its revolution, the steam is forced out, or exhausted, through the exhaust port. If the cylinder is double acting. The opposite sequence is taking place at the other end of the cylinder, giving it twice the power.

Toy locomotives often used oscillating cylinders. They are easy to make and assemble and are simple and reliable in use. The most primitive of these toys often had just one, single-acting oscillator, mounted in the cab or the smokebox and geared to an axle. The gear reduction gave the single cylinder, which operated at a fairly high speed, enough power to drive the engine and pull a train.

One step up from this was the engine that had two, single-acting oscillators, often driving a single large driver. This big wheel, coupled with the necessarily long piston rod, gave these engines the nickname of 'stork leg.' For an engine with two, single-acting cylinders to run properly, the crankpins on the far-side driver had to be positioned 180° apart from the crankpin on the near side (figure 2). Between the action of the two cylinders, the wheel would receive a power stroke through most of its revolution. There would still be two dead spots, 180° apart, as the cylinders each reached their respective front-dead-center (FDC) positions. However, the momentum of the engine easily got them past FDC. What it meant, though, was that this sort of engine was generally not self starting, unless the cylinders happened to be in an optimum position. They had to be given a gentle push to get them going.

I knew of these engines for many years before I saw one run for the first time. This was at the legendary steam up at Diamondhead, Mississippi, one year, when Murray Wilson, who always brought a handful of ancient engines, ran an old Carette or Bing stork leg with a train of equally aged tinplate cars. It was magical. I'd expected the thing to race around like crazy, flying off the end when it hit the curve. Instead, it moved around gracefully, pulling its train in a stately manner for lap after lap in a most impressive and unexpected manner.

A locomotive that has two, double-acting cylinders (figure 3) is a step up in sophistication. This engine, with cranks spaced 90° apart (figure 2) instead of 180, will be self starting under all conditions, since the power cycle will have no dead spots. Perhaps the best-known toy locomotive with this setup is the venerable Mamod locomotive, first introduced in 1980. This engine was responsible for introducing thousands of people to the joys of small-scale live steam.

One of the main objections to oscillating-cylinder locomotives is the very fact that the cylinders oscillate. Except for one or two notable exceptions, full-size engines didn't work this way, and those cylinders bobbing up and down look funny, offending the sensibilities of some people. However, there was prototypical precedent for this type of cylinder in locomotives. Filer & Stowell, an American company founded in 1856 (and still in existence today!) produced a logging locomotive with oscillating cylinders. The Dewey Brothers, another US company, also produced an oscillating-cylinder locomotive.

Some people hide the oscillating cylinders on their engines with with sheet-metal covers that suggest fixed cylinders. However, if you take the viewpoint that a miniature steam locomotive is a locomotive in its own right and that the railway that it runs on is, in fact, a real railway, only writ small, then every locomotive becomes its own prototype and you needn't worry about your engine being 'unprototypical.' Although oscillating-cylinder locomotives are less efficient than fixed-cylinder engines, and they lack sophistication, they have a lot going for them. As mentioned above, they're relatively easy to construct if you're scratchbuilding one. They're easy to maintain, too, and it's almost impossible for them to go out of adjustment. They can be exceptionally sweet running and, with a proper throttle, can easily be operated at realistic speeds while hauling long trains. I like them.

Fixed Cylinders with D-valves

Almost all full-size locomotives use cylinders fixed to the frames, with steam admission and exhaust controlled by valves of one sort or another. The most common type of valve, particularly on earlier engines, is known as the 'D-valve,' as the valve resembles the letter D lying on its back.

Typically, a full-size locomotive will have at least two cylinders. Fixed cylinders, on conventional, full-size locomotives, come in three general arrangements. Perhaps the most common is for both the cylinders and the valves to be mounted outside the locomotive's frames, with the valves

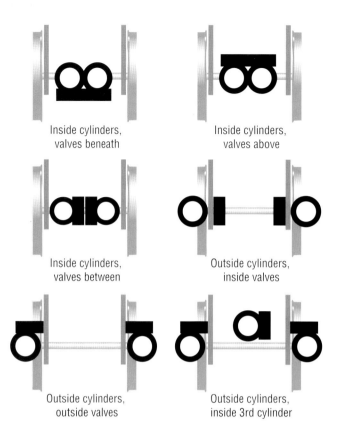

Inside cylinders, valves beneath

Inside cylinders, valves above

Inside cylinders, valves between

Outside cylinders, inside valves

Outside cylinders, outside valves

Outside cylinders, inside 3rd cylinder

Figure 4
Various cylinder/valve arrangements

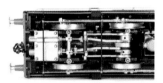

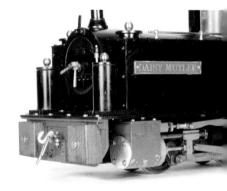

Right: Aster's pannier-tank 0-6-0T has two D-valve cylinders between the frames. The valves, clearly visible in this photo, are beneath the cylinders. The cylinders directly drive the cranks on the second axle, while the valves are controlled by eccentrics next to the cranks.

Centre: Jack Wheldon's *Daisy Mutler*, a 'Pooter' class engine, has outside cylinders with valves on top.

Lower: This 16mm-scale Peckett by David Hick has outside cylinders with inside valves controlled by slip eccentrics on the second axle.

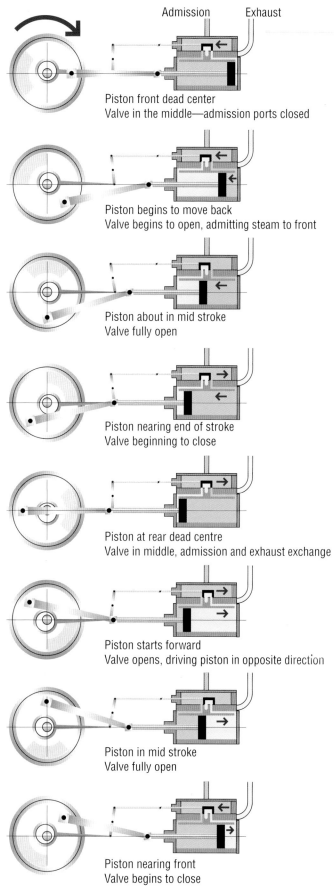

Admission   Exhaust

Piston front dead center
Valve in the middle—admission ports closed

Piston begins to move back
Valve begins to open, admitting steam to front

Piston about in mid stroke
Valve fully open

Piston nearing end of stroke
Valve beginning to close

Piston at rear dead centre
Valve in middle, admission and exhaust exchange

Piston starts forward
Valve opens, driving piston in opposite direction

Piston in mid stroke
Valve fully open

Piston nearing front
Valve begins to close

Figure 5
Steam cycle of a D-valve cylinder

arranged atop the cylinders. In Britain, many locomotives carried their cylinders outside the frames and the valves and their attendant gear inside. And finally, especially in the earlier days of steam, both valves and cylinders were carried between the frames, which made for a much cleaner looking locomotive, but vastly complicated maintenance and repairs (figure 4). In later days, three-cylindered and four-cylinder compounds carried two cylinders (and valves) outside the frames, with the third (and fourth) carried between.

A fixed cylinder has a drive rod between the piston rod and the wheel or axle, hinged at the end of the piston rod. As the wheel rotates, the piston goes back and forth via the motion of the rod (of course, it is the piston that is pushing the wheel around). The valve is controlled via a separate but integrated system, in sync with the piston, but cycled (usually) 90° out (figure 5). There are various ways of controlling the valve, which we'll look at later.

The cycle, in its simplest form, works like this. When the piston is at the front-dead-centre position, the valve is just ready to open. As the wheel rotates, the valve begins to open, admitting steam to the cylinder, which drives the piston back, giving the wheel a power stroke. Meanwhile, the steam that was on the other side of the piston, and that had driven it to FDC, is allowed to escape, or exhaust, by the same valve. As the piston approaches rear dead centre, the valve closes. When the piston reaches rear dead centre, the cycle reverses and the piston is pushed the other way.

The beauty of a valve controlling the piston is that, unlike an oscillator, the valve's action can be varied. For one thing, the valve should close early, sometimes well before the piston finishes its stroke. The reason for this is that the steam that has just been admitted to the cylinder continues to expand, even after the valve is closed. If the valve closed just as the piston reached the end of its stroke, a lot of steam would be wasted. If the valve closed when the piston was at, say 85% of its full stroke, the steam in the piston would continue to expand, pushing the piston even though the valve is closed. This closing of the valve is referred to as 'cut-off.' You'd say, "The engine has 85% cut-off." On full-size engines, at higher speeds, the cut-off can be increased, making the engine run even more efficiently. On our model engines, while this is possible, it is usually not done, and can only be practically done with radio control and a sophisticated, well-made locomotive.

The D-valve resides in a box either on top of or next to the cylinder it controls. This box is known as the 'steam chest.' A

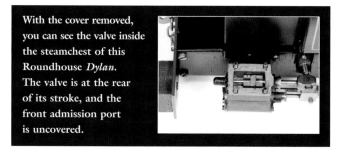

With the cover removed, you can see the valve inside the steamchest of this Roundhouse *Dylan*. The valve is at the rear of its stroke, and the front admission port is uncovered.

Beck's *Anna* uses piston valves, unusually driven by outside slip eccentrics. In the second photo, the valve has been removed and you can see the hole in the side of it that communicates with the longitudinal passage through the valve.

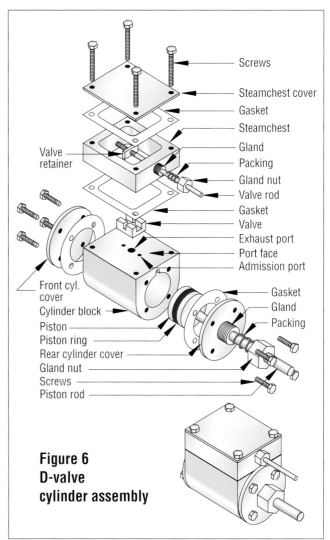

Screws
Steamchest cover
Gasket
Steamchest
Gland
Valve retainer
Packing
Gland nut
Valve rod
Gasket
Valve
Exhaust port
Port face
Admission port
Front cyl. cover
Gasket
Cylinder block
Gland
Piston
Packing
Piston ring
Rear cylinder cover
Gland nut
Screws
Piston rod

**Figure 6
D-valve
cylinder assembly**

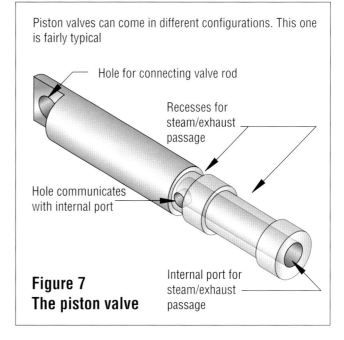

Piston valves can come in different configurations. This one is fairly typical

Hole for connecting valve rod

Recesses for steam/exhaust passage

Hole communicates with internal port

Internal port for steam/exhaust passage

**Figure 7
The piston valve**

rod attached to the valve, appropriately called the valve rod, protrudes from the chest and is connected to the mechanism that controls it, called the valve gear, which is discussed later in the book.

The valve, which is free to move up and down slightly, has a flat, smooth face on its underside. This slides back and forth along the flat floor of the steam chest. This floor is called the port face. In it are two steam-admission ports, with a larger exhaust port in between them (figure 6).

Steam enters the steam chest through the line from the throttle. Its pressure forces the valve onto the port face, making a steam-tight seal. As the valve moves towards one end of the steam chest, the admission port in the opposite end is uncovered (opened). This port communicates with a steam passage to the end of the cylinder, admitting steam into the cylinder. At the same time, a cavity in the underside of the D-valve encompasses both the other steam port and the larger exhaust port, thus creating a passage for the escaping steam from the other end of the piston to depart. The exhaust port is larger than the admission ports so as to not impede the exhaust steam's exit. As the valve begins to travel in the other direction, the process is reversed, *ad infinitum.*

One of the advantages of the D-valve system is that as the valve wears, it wears in. That is, it wears against the port face, which will wear correspondingly, creating a more steam-tight seal as the valve ages. In well-cared-for model engines of our size, a D-valve will almost never have to be replaced. A disadvantage is that they comprise a fair number of pieces, all of which have to be precisely machined for the locomotive to function properly. That's one reason an engine with D-valves is significantly more expensive than an oscillating-cylinder locomotive. One way of partially getting around some of this manufacturing difficulty is by the use of piston valves.

Piston Valves

By the end of the steam era, virtually all locomotives utilized piston valves. However, the piston valves of a full size, mainline

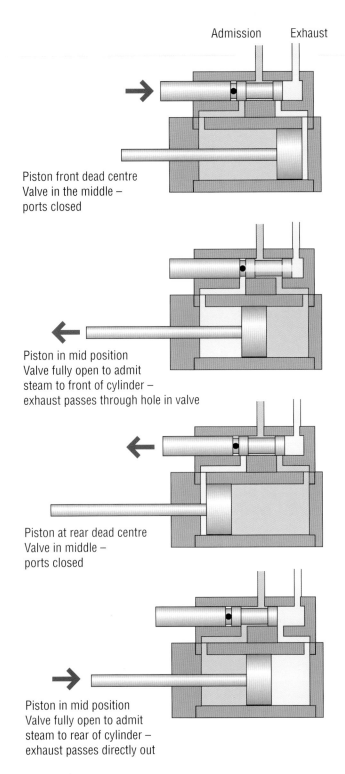

Piston front dead centre
Valve in the middle –
ports closed

Piston in mid position
Valve fully open to admit
steam to front of cylinder –
exhaust passes through hole in valve

Piston at rear dead centre
Valve in middle –
ports closed

Piston in mid position
Valve fully open to admit
steam to rear of cylinder –
exhaust passes directly out

Figure 8
Steam cycle of a piston-valve cylinder

not tightly) onto a carefully bored hole in the cylinder block. It has steam passages machined into it (figure 7). Steam is admitted into the cylinder by the valve in much the same way as a D-valve (figure 8). However, there are some differences.

Most (but not all) piston-valve locomotives are reversed by exchanging the admission lines with the exhaust. (You can't do this with D-valve cylinders. If you put steam into the exhaust line, you'd blow the valve off the port face and the engine wouldn't function.) This means that the valve and the way it functions inside the cylinder has to be absolutely symmetrical as regards forward and reverse. Thus, the steam events of a piston-valve cylinder are much like those of an oscillator, with the same inefficiencies.

Another drawback to the piston valve is that, unlike the D-valve, when it wears, it wears out, not in. With a well-made and maintained engine this could take many years, but eventually the valve will get sloppy in its hole, lose steam, and cause the performance of the engine to gradually diminish. Be warned.

How many cylinders?

As mentioned above, model locomotives can have as few as one cylinder. Not only toy engines run on single cylinders, but some fine and otherwise sophisticated models do, as well. These engines were designed as runners, rather than engines that would see prototypical operation, with a lot of to-ing and fro-ing. A well-designed locomotive with a single cylinder

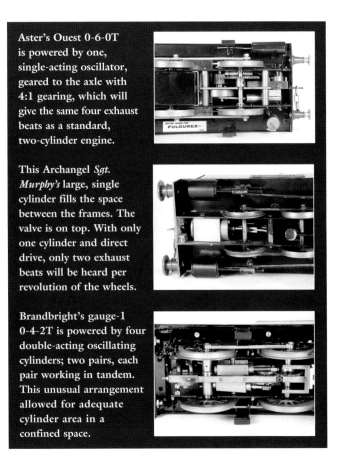

Aster's Ouest 0-6-0T is powered by one, single-acting oscillator, geared to the axle with 4:1 gearing, which will give the same four exhaust beats as a standard, two-cylinder engine.

This Archangel *Sgt. Murphy's* large, single cylinder fills the space between the frames. The valve is on top. With only one cylinder and direct drive, only two exhaust beats will be heard per revolution of the wheels.

Brandbright's gauge-1 0-4-2T is powered by four double-acting oscillating cylinders; two pairs, each pair working in tandem. This unusual arrangement allowed for adequate cylinder area in a confined space.

locomotive bear little resemblance to those used in toy and model engines.

With model piston-valve cylinders, the cycle of events is similar to that of D-valve cylinders. However, the valve that accomplishes this is quite different. A piston valve, as the name implies, is a cylindrical valve that fits very snugly (but

Right: Steam is up at the roundhouse prior to the day's work on Jack Verducci's Crystal Springs Railroad. This is one of the few garden railways in the world where steam locomotion is used to actually operate the railroad in a prototypical manner.
Jack Verducci

Centre & Lower: When single-acting oscillators are paired with side rods, strange things happen. The cylinders must be 180° out of phase with each other, while the side rods must be only 90° out. One side of the engine looks pretty conventional, but look at the odd crank arrangement on the other.

between the frames, controlled by slip-eccentric reversing, can be a thing of beauty.

LBSC, the pen name of one of the pre-eminent British model-locomotive designers and builders in the mid-20th century, designed single-cylinder locomotives at least up to 2½in gauge. In more recent times, Archangel Models made good use of a single cylinder in many of their locomotives. And the well-known 'Project' locomotive of the Gauge 1 Model Railway Association also has but one cylinder. All of these engines are excellent runners, can pull long, heavy trains, and run at realistic speeds, both fast and slow. The biggest disadvantage to a single cylinder is that the engine cannot be considered self-starting and must always be given a push. This also precludes the use of radio control, except to maintain speed and stop the train, once it is rolling.

Two single-acting cylinders, as mentioned above, can also be used on model locomotives. Together, they function in much the same way as one double-acting cylinder. The crankpins on the wheels must be placed 180° apart to get equal power strokes. If the locomotive has more than one powered axle, like Aster's 'Old Faithful,' for instance, this leads to trouble. Side rods connecting the wheels cannot be spaced at 180°, as they run the risk of getting 'crossed' at dead-centre positions. They must be at 90°. So, if the cylinders must be at 180° and the side rods at 90°, what's to be done? The solution is to have an odd crank arrangement on one side of the locomotive that allows this to happen.

Most full-size locomotives, of course, had two, double-acting cylinders. This made them self starting and fully controllable, as it does with model engines. A two-cylindered model engine

Left: While compound engines in model form are rare, they do exist. Charles Mynhier's scratchbuilt 2-10-10-2 'Virginian,' in 0 scale, is a working compound. Note the size difference between the high-pressure cylinders (rear) and the huge low-pressure cylinders in front. *Charles Mynhier*

Lower: Three cylinders are uncommon. This Accucraft Shay has three vertical cylinders on one side of the engine. The three cranks are 120° apart from each other, making for exceptionally smooth running.

with valve gear that can be reversed from the cab can be run pretty much in the same way as a full-size locomotive, either manually or via radio control. This means that, theoretically anyway, the engine is capable of working in the yards, shunting cars back and forth, just like any full-size engine. It can back its train into a siding, stop at stations or for signals, and pull slowly into the roundhouse at the end of the day.

In practice, I can think of exactly one person who actually runs his garden railway in the same manner that a full-size railroad is run, using steam power. That is Jack Verducci of California. On Jack's railroad, an engineer is assigned a locomotive and it is his responsibility to not only take care of the engine's needs, but to follow orders regarding the picking up and dropping of loads and getting his train to its proper destination on time. If he runs afoul of Murphy's Law, he must communicate his distress to the dispatcher. All of this is made possible by two-cylindered locomotives.

Some locomotives, both full size and model, have more than two cylinders. Shay locomotives often have three, mounted vertically in a row on one side of the engine. Some large, mainline steam engines also have three cylinders, with the third residing between the frames. Accurate models of these engines will also have three cylinders. And some locomotives have four cylinders, as well. Sometimes these are arranged to drive a single set of driven axles and sometimes they are split so that each pair drives a separate set of wheels, as on a Beyer-Garratt or conventional articulated engine.

One thing that must be touched on here is compound locomotives. Compound engines can have two, three, or four cylinders. A compound engine uses its steam twice. Instead of exhausting the steam (which still has a lot of latent energy) up the stack, it is diverted to another cylinder or cylinders and used again to extract more energy from the lower-pressure steam. The first cylinder is the high-pressure cylinder, and is the smaller of the two. The low-pressure cylinder will be much larger. The difference between the two is a matter of strict proportions.

On a three-cylinder compound engine, the two outside cylinders are usually the high-pressure cylinders, exhausting to a large low-pressure cylinder inside the frames. On a Mallet articulated locomotive, there are two high-pressure cylinders on the rear engine, exhausting to the larger, low-pressure cylinders on the front engine.

Successful model compound locomotives, even commercial models, have been built, which function in the same way as full-size engines, but these are beyond the scope of this book.

Chapter 4
Pistons and lubricators

The piston, which resides inside the cylinder, is what the steam pushes against to convert thermal energy to mechanical energy. There are several variations that are used in garden-size models. Let's begin with the simplest.

Oscillating cylinders

In a single-acting oscillating cylinder, there is no rear cylinder cover to help support the piston rod. The piston alone must oscillate the cylinder. Because of this, there needs to be a fair amount of surface area acting on the cylinder walls to accomplish this feat without the piston becoming cocked in the cylinder and also to prevent it wearing prematurely. This is done with a piston that is longer than normal, say one-and-one-half to two times longer than its diameter.

These pistons are most often made of brass, precisely machined to fit the cylinder with very little slop. The low pressure, highly saturated, 'warm fog' type of steam that these engines usually generate is often enough to keep them lubricated, as they rely on a thin film of water between the cylinder wall and piston to create a steam-tight seal. Many times, these engines did not have a separate lubricator (see below). The cylinders could be physically pulled away from the port faces and a drop of oil inserted in between to help keep them slippery.

A variation on this theme is the piston that Bowman used on their locomotives. This incorporated a blob of felt on the piston rod, behind the brass piston. The idea was that you soak

the felt with oil and it would meter the oil out to the cylinder during the run. There's a certain amount of controversy as to whether lubrication on this sort of engine is even necessary.

When you get into double-acting oscillators, the sophistication level can vary greatly. Since, by definition, a double-acting cylinder must have a rear cylinder cover upon which the piston rod acts to oscillate the cylinder, the piston itself can be a more normal size. It can be like the one described above – a mere brass plug – or it can have one of the refinements described below.

The most basic of the double-acting oscillators can be found on the original Mamod locomotives. There was no rear-cover gland to make a steam-tight seal; the engine relied on a close fit between the cover and the piston rod for that

Above: This piston from a single-acting Bowman oscillating engine has a felt pad at the rear end that, when oiled, provides lubrication for the cylinder. The oil rings are more pronounced on this piston than is usual.

Left: This Archangel coal-fired *Russell* has standard D-valve cylinders and a displacement lubricator. Because of its tiny firebox, it's a difficult engine to keep in steam.

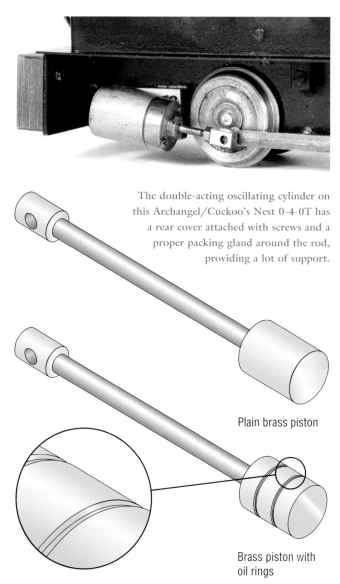

The double-acting oscillating cylinder on this Archangel/Cuckoo's Nest 0-4-0T has a rear cover attached with screws and a proper packing gland around the rod, providing a lot of support.

Plain brass piston

Brass piston with oil rings

Figure 1
Oscillating-cylinder pistons

purpose. The piston was a plain piece of brass with a tiny ring or two – called oil rings – cut into it circumferentially to trap a little oil or water for lubrication (figure 1).

The opposite end of the sophistication spectrum for this type of cylinder is one that has proper cylinder covers, screwed in place, with a gland and packing at the rear end to ensure steam tightness. An oscillating cylinder made to this standard will last for ages. I have even seen high-end oscillators that incorporated crossheads and crosshead guides, although this might be considered overkill.

Fixed cylinders
Between fixed cylinders and double-acting oscillators, there's not much difference, piston-wise. Pistons of similar proportions can be used. At the lowest end, in toy engines

and basic models, simple brass pistons with oil rings cut into them will suffice.

As the engine becomes more sophisticated, better pistons are called for. In the old days, a groove was cut around the piston, which was then carefully packed with oiled graphite yarn. This method is still in fairly wide use today and, if done properly, provides a good, steam-tight seal that will last a long time.

In lieu of graphite yarn, I have heard of the use of Teflon plumber's tape to pack pistons, and also for use in glands as packing (for which graphite yarn was also used). There is some controversy about the wisdom of this. The tape, which is about a half-inch wide and very thin, is twisted until it forms a string. It is then carefully wrapped around the piston groove until it is just proud of the piston, at which time it can be inserted into the cylinder. Some people feel that the tape will shred inside the piston, shedding bits of Teflon to cause problems elsewhere in the locomotive. However, the people I've spoken with who have tried this method have not reported any problems of this nature. I've tried it on the pistons of a couple of engines with poor results, and I'll not be using it again for that. However, I've had better results using it in packing glands.

In more recent years, the use of high temperature, oil-resistant O-rings has become common, especially in commercially produced locomotives. When the groove for the O-ring is accurately cut, according to the specifications of the O-ring manufacturer, the ring is forced against the walls of the piston, which makes for a very good seal. O-rings will wear out in time, requiring replacement. Smaller examples are used to pack glands.

In a full-size locomotive, and even in the riding sizes, pistons are often iron castings machined slightly smaller than the cylinder's inside diameter, with an accurately machined groove to take two or more iron piston rings that function in much the same way as the rings in your car. They are slightly sprung to bear positively on the cylinder walls and maintain a steam-tight seal. I have seen this approach taken with model

Right: Hugh Saunders incorporated a mechanical lubricator on his Alco 2-6-2T. Note the linkage to the expansion link, the motion of which powers the lubricator.

Centre: This large, in-line displacement lubricator sits in the door of an Archangel *Snowdon Ranger*. It has a big, fat, convenient drain plug at the bottom.

Lower: A dead-leg lubricator clings to the smokebox of the Salem Steam Models 0-4-0T.

pistons, particularly by Aster, which has substituted a fibre material in place of the cast-iron rings. Cast iron is a tricky material from which to machine such small, delicate parts without breaking a lot of them.

One final wrinkle, which was used by Beck in their locomotives and also by Aster in its Baldwin 0-4-2T, is to form each piston out of two Teflon cups placed back to back. The section of the piston cups is very thin, so that when the steam presses against it to drive the piston, the cup will expand slightly to form a good seal. However, if the slightest bit of grit gets into the cylinder, there is risk of damaging the piston. On the other hand, it might be argued that it is better to damage an easily replaced piston cup than to have the cylinder wall scored by the grit, necessitating reboring.

Lubricators

I can't close this chapter without discussing lubricators. While they are not actually part of the cylinder, they are critical to its function. Only very low-pressure engines – those that run at about ten pounds – are built without lubricators.

All of the locomotive's external parts can be lubricated from without. But what about the concealed parts that work inside the cylinder? They need lubrication, too. Enter cylinder lubricators.

Cylinder lubricators are devices that are designed to introduce a little oil into the steam line while the engine is running. They are generally fitted between the throttle and the cylinders. Steam-cylinder oil is not just any oil, but is specially formulated to work well in the hostile environment of steam cylinders. Steam oil is usually thick, brown, and sticky. Don't be tempted to use lightweight machine oil – it will quickly disappear, leaving your cylinders high and dry. And don't use motor oil, either. It contains detergents and other additives that could build up in the cylinders, harming them.

There are two basic types of cylinder lubricators used on miniature steamers – mechanical and displacement. Due to their complexity, mechanical lubricators are rarely used on our little locomotives, although you'll occasionally find them on more sophisticated engines. Mechanical lubricators have little reservoirs that are filled with steam oil. Inside the reservoir is a tiny pump that works slowly via a ratchet driven by a pawl. The pawl usually gets its motion from a link to the valve gear. As the wheels spin, the pawl goes back and forth, driving the ratchet, which slowly causes the pump to force oil into the

steam line. The advantage to this type of lubricator is that it is a positive action, so you know that the oil is getting to where it will do the most good. Also, this lubricator can be easily refilled while the engine is in steam. Its disadvantage, mentioned above, is that it is a complex bit of machinery.

The displacement lubricator is the type fitted to most garden-size locomotives. It works on the principle that water is heavier than oil. As steam passes through the line on the way to the cylinders, a tiny amount will condense into water inside the lubricator. This tiny drop, being heavier than the oil, will

Regner, on their Stainz 0-4-0T, use a Roscoe lubricator disguised as an air pump. It sports both a control valve and a drain plug. This is a dead leg lubricator, in which oil and water mysteriously pass one another in opposite directions through the same pipe.

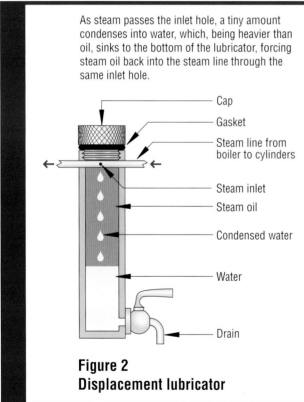

As steam passes the inlet hole, a tiny amount condenses into water, which, being heavier than oil, sinks to the bottom of the lubricator, forcing steam oil back into the steam line through the same inlet hole.

- Cap
- Gasket
- Steam line from boiler to cylinders
- Steam inlet
- Steam oil
- Condensed water
- Water
- Drain

**Figure 2
Displacement lubricator**

line actually passes through the lubricator. The line will have a tiny hole drilled into the side of it, inside the lubricator. It is through this hole that the exchange of fluids takes place.

The dead-leg, or Roscoe lubricator (named after Englishman James Roscoe, who patented it in 1862) works in a similar manner, except that the lubricator is on a 'T' or dead leg off the steam line. Steam somehow manages to enter the lubricator in one direction while oil simultaneously passes through the same line in the opposite. Strange, but it works. Roscoe lubricators will sometimes have a small valve on them to control the rate that the oil flows out.

At the end of the run, there should be a significant amount of water in the lubricator. If it's all water, that means that too much oil is getting through and, possibly, the cylinders will not have been lubricated throughout the entire run. If you find the lubricator completely filled with oil at the end, then no oil is getting through and the cylinders are running more or less dry. However, it doesn't take a great deal of oil to keep the cylinders happy, so if there is any water in the lubricator, oil is getting to the cylinders.

There are several things that can affect the flow of oil, including the size of the oil hole in the steam line and the proximity of the lubricator to the fire. If too close, the oil softens up and will flow more freely. If too far away, the opposite may happen.

A good lubricator will have a drain on the bottom. This is opened at the end or beginning of a run (with the cap off) and the water is drained off. Then the lubricator is refilled and is ready for the next run. If there is no drain, the water must be sucked out with a syringe, which is often messy. However, a lot of otherwise fine locomotives have lubricators without drains.

sink to the bottom, forcing (displacing) an equal amount of oil into the steam line, where it is carried along to the cylinders to lubricate the valves and pistons (figure 2).

There are two types of displacement lubricators: in-line and dead-leg, or Roscoe. With in-line lubricators, the steam

Chapter 5
Reversing mechanisms and valve gears

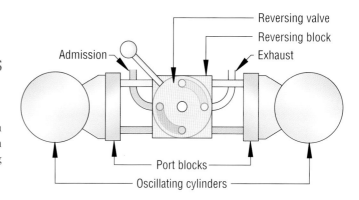

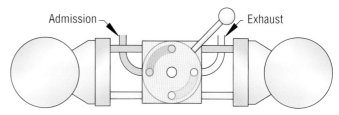

Figure 1
Rotary reversing valve

Only the simplest of toy engines are designed to go in one direction only. In this chapter some of the common – and a few – uncommon – mechanisms for reversing a miniature steam locomotive will be examined.

Oscillating Cylinders

An oscillating cylinder is generally reversed by exchanging its admission for its exhaust. In fact, that's about the only way to reverse them without needless complexity, and simplicity is the primary reason for employing an oscillating cylinder. There are two ways of doing this, both with valves.

The most common method of reversing admission and exhaust is via a rotary valve, such as those used on the Mamod and other locomotives of its type. The valve itself is a circular, flat piece, with two sausage-shaped slots milled into its face, each encompassing 90°. Figure 1 shows this. The

valve is held tightly to the reversing block by a spring so that no steam can escape.

The valve is mated with a port face on the reversing block in which are drilled four holes, each 90° apart around its centre. One hole, say at three o'clock, is the steam-admission port, and is connected by a pipe to the boiler. This may be via a throttle and lubricator, as on more sophisticated locomotives, or directly from the boiler, as on a stock Mamod. The hole in the nine o'clock position will be the exhaust port. The holes at twelve o'clock and six o'clock each communicate with both cylinders.

Referring back to the chapter on cylinders, you'll remember that the port block against which the cylinder rides has two holes for a single-acting cylinder, and four for a double acting. Either the upper or lower hole(s) can be the steam or exhaust port(s), as the operation of the cylinder is absolutely symmetrical. These ports are plumbed into the reversing block as shown in the drawing.

By simply rotating the valve 90°, the position of the sausages is changed, rerouting the steam from the lower holes to the upper, and vice-versa for the exhaust, thus reversing the engine.

This valve is also commonly used as a throttle on the more primitive species of locomotive, but it is usually very touchy, and not nearly as effective as a proper regulator.

The other way of accomplishing this steam/exhaust reversal is through the use of a piston valve identical to those used in

Top left: The rotary reverser on Maurice Cross's deWinton controls one, single-acting oscillator.

Lower: The Mamod engine, like most oscillators, uses a rotary valve for reversing. A typical valve is leaning against the buffer beam.

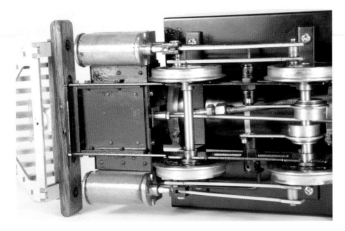

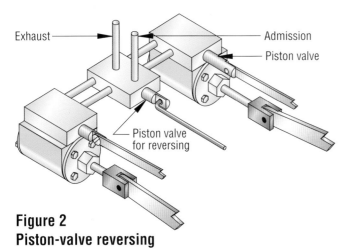

Figure 2
Piston-valve reversing

Exhaust

Admission

Piston valve

Piston valve
for reversing

This page –

Left: A piston-valve reverser is used on Accucraft's *Ruby.* The reversing valve is identical to the cylinder valves.

Lower: Another application of a piston-valve reverser, this one on Aster for LGB's *Frank S.*

Opposite page –

Top: Slip eccentrics run the valves on this HB Models Taff Vale 4-4-0.

Centre: A set of robust slip eccentrics actuate rocker arms that bring the motion through the frames on Aster's *Reno.*

Lower: Beck used an unusual outside slip eccentric on its *Anna.*

with these engines, it makes logical sense to just add a third valve between the cylinders, with a linkage to a reversing lever in the cab, to reverse the locomotive (figure 2). Piston-valve cylinders, like oscillating cylinders, are perfectly symmetrical in their action, so reversing them in this manner is quite feasible.

Aster's *Frank S.* for LGB, as well as several of Accucraft's locomotives, starting with the *Ruby*, are reversed this way. Of course, with piston-valve cylinders, other types of valve gear can be used as well, like the outside slip eccentric that Beck used on its engines. Both the rotary valve and piston valve are considered by some to be toy reversers, not worthy of a real locomotive.

D-Valve Cylinders

With few exceptions, if one of our garden-scale engines has fixed cylinders and does not use the toy-like piston valves, it uses D-valves. Even scale models of modern, full-size engines will have D-valves disguised as piston valves. The D-valve is the mainstay of our hobby as well as being the same mechanism used by countless thousands of full-size locomotives and other types of steam engines.

While it's not the intention of this book to get into valve and valve-gear design (there are lots of other books out there that cover that ground well), it is important that you understand how the valve works and its relationship to the valve gear.

'Valve gear' is simply the rods, levers, cranks, links, or what-have-you that controls the action of the valve. There are many well-known valve gears as well as some more obscure varieties. The simplest valve gear that can control a D-valve is the simple eccentric (which does not offer reversing capability) and its variant, the slip eccentric (which does).

In the chapter on cylinders, the steam cycle was briefly discussed. There, the concept of *cut-off* was mentioned. This refers to the admission of steam to the cylinder being cut off before the piston has reached its full stroke, using the expansion of the steam to push the piston the remainder of the way. In this way, the steam is used more efficiently. On a full-size locomotive, a skilled engineer will vary the cut-off depending on the engine's speed, the weight of

piston-valve cylinders. Again referring back to the cylinder chapter, in the same way that the valve in the steam chest alternately admits and exhausts the steam from either end of the cylinder, an identical valve plumbed into the steam line can reverse the admission and exhaust to oscillating cylinders. However, this device is rarely used for oscillators because it adds complexity.

Piston-Valve Cylinders

However, the piston-valve reverser is often used with engines that have fixed cylinders controlled by piston valves. Since the piston-valve technology is already in use

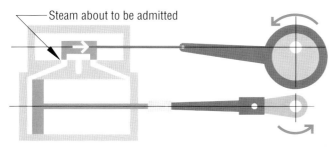

1. A valve with no lap will perform the same in forward or reverse with the eccentric set 90° ahead of the crank, but can only offer 100% cutoff.

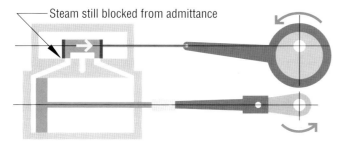

2. A valve with lap (shown in red) will not perform at all well with the eccentric set 90° in advance of the crank. It will neither open nor close the valve on time.

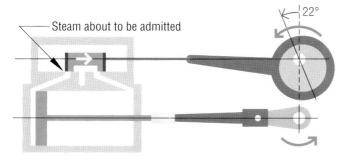

3. However, by advancing the eccentric 90° + the lap (in the case of the diagram, about 22°), the valve is set to admit steam when the piston is at front dead centre, while at the same time offering early cutoff for steam savings.

Figure 3
Lap and advance

the train, the gradient up or down, and other factors. Running at speed on level track, the necessary cut-off might be only 25% to keep the train running, while starting a heavy train might require the cut-off to be closer to 100% of the piston's travel.

Cut-off is controlled by *lap* in the valve. Lap can be defined as extra length of the valve that causes it to close the port early (cut-off). Virtually all D-valves have some lap.

Lead refers to the opening of the valve to admit steam to the cylinder slightly before the piston reaches dead centre. This was used on high speed, mainline locomotives to get the absolute most out of the steam. Lead was only introduced

when the engine was at speed. For the purposes of garden steam, it can be generally disregarded.

If the device controlling the valve (say, an eccentric) is set symmetrically – that is, 90° in advance of the driver's crankpin – the valve events for admission and exhaust will be identical. However, that's not what's wanted. We want the steam to begin to be admitted to the cylinder just as the piston hits dead centre, but we want the valve to close before the piston reaches dead centre at the other end. For this to happen, the eccentric must be *advanced* a little bit. This can be determined mathematically or empirically. The eccentric must be advanced the usual 90° in front of the crank *plus* the lap of the valve. Figure 3 illustrates

There are several different ways of implementing slip-eccentric reversing. This is just one of them.

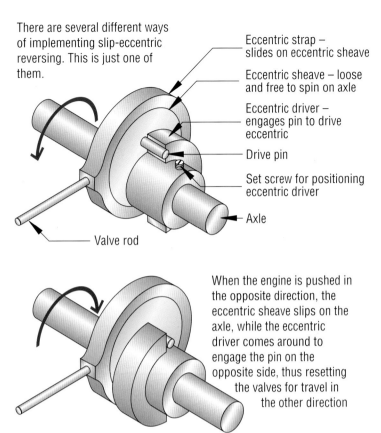

Eccentric strap – slides on eccentric sheave

Eccentric sheave – loose and free to spin on axle

Eccentric driver – engages pin to drive eccentric

Drive pin

Set screw for positioning eccentric driver

Axle

Valve rod

When the engine is pushed in the opposite direction, the eccentric sheave slips on the axle, while the eccentric driver comes around to engage the pin on the opposite side, thus resetting the valves for travel in the other direction

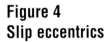

Figure 4
Slip eccentrics

Above: Vertical rocker arms bring the motion from inside valve gear through the frames to the outside valves on the Aster's C&S Mogul.

Right: Early Roundhouse engines, like this 'Old Colonial', employed unusual horizontal rockers to bring the motion outside the frames.

this principle. The diagram shows a cylinder controlled by a simple, non-reversing eccentric. In a slip-eccentric setup, the eccentric driver must be designed in a way to supply equal advance in both directions.

Slip-eccentric valve gear is popular because it is relatively easy to make but still functions much like other valve gears. Its disadvantages are that it is unprototypical (with some minor exceptions) and you must physically move the locomotive in the opposite direction to reset the valves. Once that's done, the engine will continue on in that direction, no matter how many times the throttle is opened and closed. Slip-eccentric gear can be used on locomotives with one, two, or more cylinders and can be found on any number of commercial and semi-commercial models.

With slip-eccentric gear, there is one eccentric per cylinder, usually mounted on the axle between the frames (figure 4). However, instead of being fixed to the axle with a set screw, the eccentric sheave is loose on the axle and is free to rotate. Next to the sheave is the eccentric driver, which is fixed to the axle. The eccentric sheave will have a pin (usually) protruding from it that the driver engages. As the axle rotates, the eccentric driver will hit the pin on the eccentric sheave, forcing it to revolve. When the locomotive is pushed in the opposite direction, the eccentric driver rotates with the axle, but the eccentric does not, until the driver comes around to engage the pin from the opposite side, thus driving the sheave in the other direction. The space between the driving surfaces on the eccentric driver are designed so that, when set up properly,

correct valve timing is achieved in both directions. A slip eccentric is almost always used on single-cylinder locomotives, as those usually must be pushed to get them going anyway.

If the valves of the locomotive are inside the frame, they will most likely be driven directly by the eccentrics. However, if they are outside the frames, atop the cylinders, then the motion must be brought through the frames. This is usually accomplished by rocker arms through the frames. However, the rocker arm will reverse the direction of the motion. To counteract this, the eccentrics must be set 180° out from their normal positions. Most engines use vertical rockers, but early Roundhouse locomotives used interesting horizontal rockers.

For locomotives with outside valve gear, a neat variation on the slip eccentric is the slip eccentric crank, or return crank. When the engine is pushed, the crank changes position relative to the axle, thus resetting the valves for reverse travel.

After slip eccentrics, we move into the realm of miniature versions of valve gears used on full-size locomotives. The quest for the perfect valve gear was never ending during the reign of steam. That Holy Grail was never fully realized. Every valve gear invented had flaws of one sort or another. The best ones made the least compromises.

In the full-size world, the most popular valve gear for modern steam locomotives is probably *Walschaerts*, named after its inventor, Egide Walschaerts of Belgium. This valve gear (figure 5) is entirely outside the engine and is driven primarily by a crank attached to the main crankpin. In the middle is a curved link (the expansion link) that pivots in the middle, in

Right: Although the valve gear on Mike Gaskin's 4-8-2 resembles Walschaerts, it actually uses a slip return crank for reversing.

Lower left and right: Note the position of the return crank in the two photos. It functions like a slip eccentric.

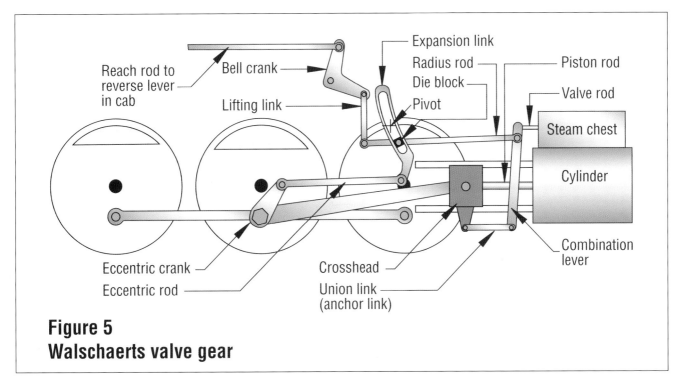

Reach rod to reverse lever in cab

Bell crank

Lifting link

Expansion link

Radius rod

Die block

Pivot

Piston rod

Valve rod

Steam chest

Cylinder

Combination lever

Eccentric crank

Eccentric rod

Crosshead

Union link (anchor link)

Figure 5
Walschaerts valve gear

Left: Full Walschaerts gear, shown here in the reverse position, on an Aster USRA 2-8-2.

Centre: This Archangel Darjeeling & Himalaya 0-4-0T has working Walschaerts valve gear.

Lower: Buffalo Furnaces (*sans* cab) by Jack Wheldon uses an unusual variation of Walschaerts. The expansion link has been placed at the rear of the engine. The distance from there to the valve is so long that the actual radius can be disregarded, allowing the expansion link to have a straight slot.

which the end of one of the rods (the radius rod) can slide up and down. This controls the direction of the engine.

A lever in the cab controls the radius rod via linkages. With the radius rod down, the engine goes forward. With it up, it reverses. As the (model) engine runs, the valve gear can theoretically be 'notched up' – the radius rod is brought closer to the centre of the expansion link. This changes the cut-off, causing the engine to run more efficiently. I say 'theoretically' because if your engine is running free, you have no way to notch it up. It can only practically be done with radio control, and very few people that I know of actually do this (although there are some!).

There's another important component to Walschaerts gear, though, and that is the combination lever. It takes its motion from the crosshead, via the union link (anchor link). It is the combination lever that snaps the valve open and closed.

There is a valve gear that is often used on more generic garden locomotives, commonly called 'modified Walschaerts.' It might better be called 'gelded Walschaerts.' This gear has a dummy combination lever, and would perform the same without it. It's just there for show. If you are unsure about your engine, look at the combination lever. A working one will have one connection at the bottom and two near the top – one for the radius rod and one for the valve rod. On the bogus gear, there is only one at the top where radius rod, valve rod, and dummy combination lever all come together. This valve gear is just a variant of eccentric-driven gear.

The next most popular gear might well be **Stephenson's**, also called **Stephenson's** *link motion* (figure 6). Invented by Robert Stephenson, this was one of the earliest successful locomotive valve gears. It is usually, but not always, inside the frames, being driven by eccentrics on the axles. There are two eccentrics per valve, one for forward and one for reverse. This

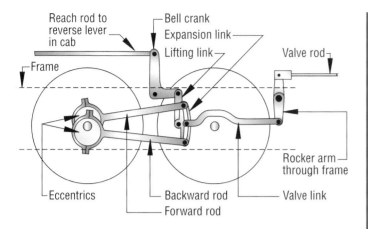

Reach rod to reverse lever in cab — Bell crank — Expansion link — Lifting link — Valve rod — Frame — Rocker arm through frame — Eccentrics — Backward rod — Valve link — Forward rod

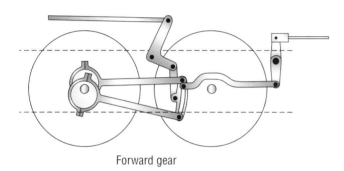

Forward gear

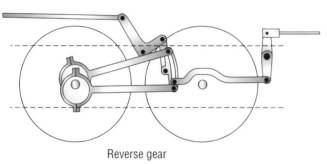

Reverse gear

Figure 6
Stephenson's valve gear

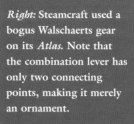

Right: Steamcraft used a bogus Walschaerts gear on its *Atlas.* Note that the combination lever has only two connecting points, making it merely an ornament.

Lower: Cyril Clarke used some components of Walschaerts gear on his C&M 0-6-2T *Atlantic,* but the gear is essentially eccentric-crank driven.

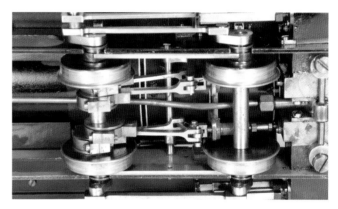

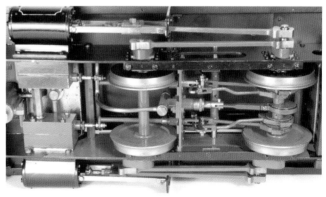

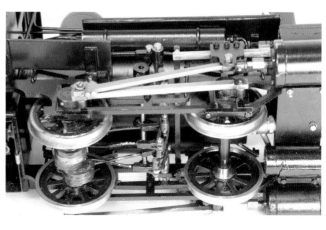

Top left: An amazingly small and finely crafted set of Stephenson gear adorn this 16mm-scale Peckett by David Hick.

Centre: Martin Sheridan used Stephenson gear on this ⅝in-scale Hunslet. The middle eccentric powers the axle pump.

Lower: On this Sandy River Forney by Argyle, rocker arms bring the motion from the inside Stephenson gear out to the outside valves.

can make things under the engine pretty crowded. Each of the two eccentrics is connected by a rod to one end of a curved expansion link. Sliding in this link is one end of the valve rod. The link can be raised or lowered by a lever in the cab

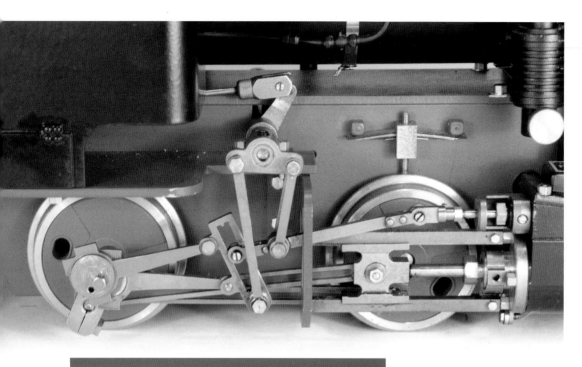

Allan gear, a variation of Stephenson's, is used outside the frames on Regner's 'Stainz' 0-4-0T. Note the straight expansion link.

Top: Hackworth gear, seen here on a Prescott Engineering *Robin*, is a relatively simple gear often used on full-size industrial engines.

Centre: Roundhouse Engineering used Hackworth gear on its first 'Pooter' class engines.

Lower: Fine, delicate Hackworth gear operates the valves on Wrightscale's tiny 'Wren'.

to engage either the forward or reverse eccentric. By partially raising or lowering the link, you get some motion from each eccentric, with which the cut-off can be varied. This gets into some exceedingly complex geometry.

Stephenson's gear is used on model locomotives primarily for historical accuracy. It is difficult to see while the engine is running, but it's comforting to know that it's there doing its job all the same. Usually only the most sophisticated models will be blessed by working Stephenson's gear. Lesser beings must be content with slip eccentrics. Also, if made to scale, Stephenson's gear can be somewhat delicate and subject to damage.

There have been variations on Stephenson's gear. One of the most notable is **Allan** valve gear, designed by Alexander Allan. On this gear, the expansion link is straight, not curved. When the gear is reversed, both the link and the valve rod move, which saves space.

Baker valve gear is rarely used on model engines in our scale, although Aster has produced one or two that use it. It was popular with many full-size railroads in the US, the Southern Railway being a notable one. In function, it is similar to Walschaerts gear except that, instead of using an expansion link with sliding die block, it uses a complex series of moveable links and cranks that achieved a similar result.

Hackworth gear (John Wesley Hackworth) is often found on smaller, industrial engines. This gear takes vertical motion from a crank on the driver's crankpin. This motion is converted to horizontal motion (to control the valve) through a die block moving in a slide, the angle of which can be changed to affect cut-off. When the slide is rotated past centre, the engine is reversed. With this gear, valve events can be affected by the springing of the locomotive, since the axle can move vertically in the frame, but the slide block does not. For our little engines, whose wheels are more or less rigid in

Right: For his locomotives, John Turner devised his own valve gear that has components of both Joy and Koppel. Cheddar later used this gear on their engines.

Centre left: Joy gear takes its motion from the main rod. The engine as a DJB Lynton & Barnstaple 2-6-2T *Taw*.

Centre right: Inside Joy gear is not often seen on models, but was used on this Carson for Bassett-Lowke *Experiment* 4-6-0 in gauge 3.

Lower: Rarely seen on models (or full-size engines, for that matter), but correct for Archangel's *Eigiau*, is Koppel valve gear. It is similar to Hackworth, but has no sliding parts.

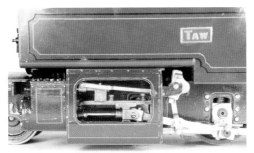

the frames anyway, this is not cause for concern. If you *are* concerned, one dodge (on an 0-4-0, anyway) is to simply spring the first axle while mounting the second rigidly. If the springing is right, this will still ensure that all four wheels are on the rails all the time.

Joy valve gear, designed by David Joy, is an improvement on Hackworth gear and sometimes found on model locomotives. This gear takes its motion primarily from the vertical motion of the drive rod (main rod, in British parlance). This is translated to horizontal motion to the valve via a slide block similar to that used in Hackworth gear. Joy gear can be inside or outside the frames – wherever the main rods are.

Koppel valve gear is rarely seen on models, but I do have one engine with it – Archangel's *Eigeau*. As in Hackworth's gear, vertical motion is taken from a crank on the crankpin. However, instead of a slide block, the motion is made horizontal via a series of links whose position can be changed to effect reversing. With this gear, there are no sliding parts to wear out.

Reversing with gears is sometimes used on model steam locomotives. John van Riemdijk, in the Gauge 1 Model Railway Association's *Newsletter and Journal*, described an elegant valve gear based on the use of gears. This is essentially an eccentric-driven valve gear, where the eccentric itself is on a secondary shaft or axle. There is a fixed gear on the main

axle and another on the eccentric's axle. Two 'floating' gears connect them. The position of these floating gears can be changed via a lever in the cab to change valve timing and direction of travel.

Another method, rarely used, relies on the cylinders driving a secondary axle that is geared to the main axle through a single idler gear. In this case, a simple gearbox can be made wherein, by moving a lever, an additional idler gear is introduced into the gear train, thus reversing the final output motion in same way that clockwork motors are reversed.

Chapter 6
Mechanisms other than traditional

On a Shay, small bevel gears that take their power from
the engine's drive train engage larger bevels on the wheels,
as on this Accucraft locomotive.

Up until now, almost everything covered here has been pretty traditional. However, the typical locomotive layout is not the only way of accomplishing motion via steam. In this section we'll look at alternatives, some prototypical and others possible only on garden-variety engines.

Models of Full-Size Geared Locomotives
Full-size geared locomotives are geared because, through gear reductions, they are able to haul much more than direct-drive locomotives, this at the expense of speed. (This reduction of speed is often a good thing in garden-size engines.) Also, because of the gearing and the way the locomotive's components are arranged, these engines can traverse very bad track and steep grades. Successful models have been built of all types of geared engines.

Shays, perhaps the most common of the geared locomotives, have a two- or three-cylinder steam motor mounted vertically on one side of the boiler, usually the right. The

This tram engine, built by the author, has a twin-cylinder steam motor. The double-acting oscillating cylinders and their associated steam ports form a single unit that can be removed intact. The steam motor is geared around 4:1 to the driven axle, providing slower speed and more power for this small locomotive.

Right: This unusual vertical-boiler Shay was made by Robins Springs in France. Pinion and crown gears take the place of the usual bevel gears. Cylinders are single-acting, so are positioned 180° apart.

Centre: A close-up of the Aster Climax's gearbox (cover removed). You can see the Stephenson's valve gear. The bevel gears just behind the jackshaft power the engine's water pump.

Lower: The complex gearing on Aster's Climax. Cylinders power a jackshaft, upon which is a helical gear that transmits power to the drive shaft. Hypoid gears (offset bevel gears) power the wheels.

boiler is offset a little to the left to counterbalance the cylinders. The output shaft is at the bottom of the motor. Flexible drive shafts connect the motor and the trucks. On each drive shaft is a pair of small bevel gears that engage larger bevel gears on the wheels.

The Climax has twin cylinders, one on either side of the boiler, inclined towards a jackshaft under the boiler, which they power. A helical gear on the transverse jackshaft engages another on a longitudinal shaft. This longitudinal shaft is

Above: Jim Hadden's Heisler is typical in that it has a pair of cylinders in a 'V' configuration beneath the boiler that drive swivelling power bogies.

Left: The cylinders are positioned 90° apart. They drive the wheels through a series of rotating shafts and gears.

Right: This charming tram engine, kitbashed by Hung Viet Ta, switches a stock car in front of the Lizard Westen station on the OBR. The locomotive started life as a Regner 'Willi,' which has one, double-acting oscillator and a gear-reduced chain drive to the wheels.

Centre: Belt drives are uncommon on live steamers, but Maurice Cross used one as part of the drive train on his deWinton. On the same shaft as the belt's pulley is a pinion that drives the crown gear on the axle.

Lower: Another crown-and-pinion arrangement, this on Larry Herget's 0-6-0T. There is one, double-acting oscillator in the smokebox that drives the pinion. Gears are from a fishing reel.

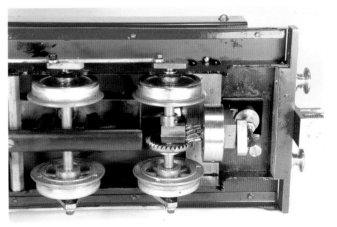

connected to the trucks via a flexible drive shaft similar to that of a Shay. Motion is transferred to the locomotive's axles from the drive shaft via hypoid gears.

The third most common type of geared locomotive is the Heisler. This engine has two cylinders arranged in a 'V,' with the legs 90° apart, under the boiler. This drives a longitudinal, flexible shaft that transmits power to the outboard axle of each truck through bevel gears. Power is transmitted to the other axle on each truck through conventional side rods.

Belt Drives

Belts are not often used on steam locomotives. When I say 'belt,' I refer primarily to the spring belts used with stationary engines to power toys and accessories. This type of belt involves a fair amount of friction, which sucks up power.

I have seen only a couple of examples of belt-driven locomotives, and have only one in my collection. This is Maurice Cross's deWinton, where a spring belt is used with pulleys as a speed reducer.

Crown and Pinion Gears

A pinion is a tiny gear, often with only six or eight teeth. It is usually used in conjunction with a larger gear to reduce the speed of the output shaft. This larger gear can be a spur gear or a crown gear, the latter having teeth that stand up around the edge of the gear as the gear lies flat. A crown is used instead of

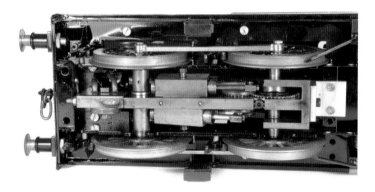

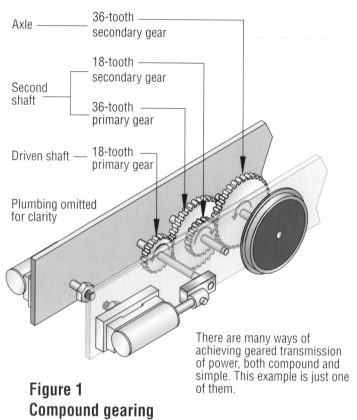

Axle — 36-tooth secondary gear

18-tooth secondary gear

Second shaft — 36-tooth primary gear

Driven shaft — 18-tooth primary gear

Plumbing omitted for clarity

There are many ways of achieving geared transmission of power, both compound and simple. This example is just one of them.

**Figure 1
Compound gearing**

Top left: Fred Freeman put dummy outside cylinders on his 16mm-scale Hunslet. One double-acting cylinder drives a gear on a jackshaft that powers the driving axle via a 2:1 reduction. Reversing is via slip eccentric.

Centre: Aster's GER 0-6-0T, based on a design by John van Riemsdijk, has one, single-acting oscillator that drives a large gear on the axle. If the locomotive didn't have large drivers, this arrangement wouldn't be possible.

Lower: Another interesting example of gearing, this on a Brandbright 0-4-2T in 1:32 scale. There are four double-acting oscillators, paired, each pair acting in unison. They drive a small gear, which drives a larger one on the axle. Note the thinness of the gears.

a spur where the motion needs to change direction 90°. The same deWinton engine mentioned above also uses pinion-and-crown gearing to get its motion to the wheels.

Crowns and pinions were used more commonly in the early days of toy engines, where a small oscillating cylinder in the cab might turn a pinion that would, in turn, power a crown gear.

Spur Gears

Spur gears are often used in model locomotives. They are sometimes used in representations of locomotives that, in full size, were not geared. One example of this is a 16mm-scale model of a Hunslet, built by Fred Freeman. This engine utilises a single cylinder between the frames, with dummy cylinders outside for cosmetics. The single cylinder is geared to the axle via a 2:1 reduction. This gives the engine the requisite four exhaust beats per driver revolution as well as making the engine more docile. Being a single cylinder, however, it will not self start.

Another good example is Aster's GER 0-6-0T. This engine has one, single-acting oscillating cylinder that drives the axle through 4:1 gearing, again providing the correct number of chuffs per revolution of the drivers.

Gearing can be single stage – where the engine drives one gear, which drives another on the axle – or it can be

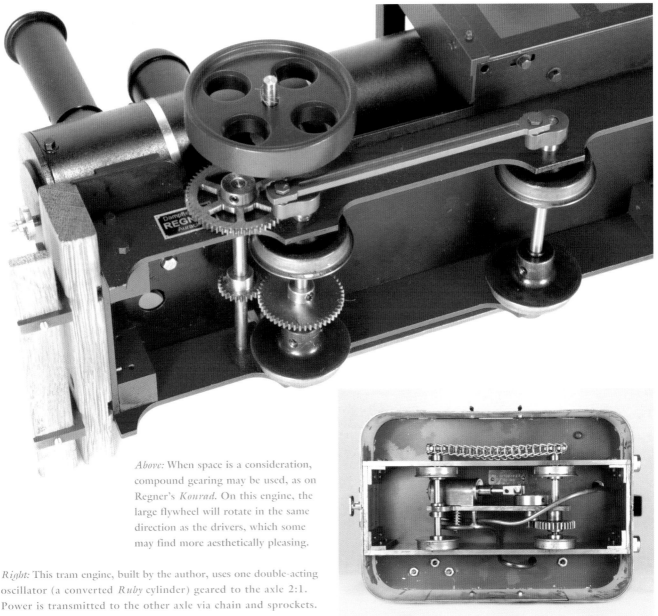

Above: When space is a consideration, compound gearing may be used, as on Regner's *Konrad*. On this engine, the large flywheel will rotate in the same direction as the drivers, which some may find more aesthetically pleasing.

Right: This tram engine, built by the author, uses one double-acting oscillator (a converted *Ruby* cylinder) geared to the axle 2:1. Power is transmitted to the other axle via chain and sprockets. The steam motor is hung from the axles.

compound. Compound gearing involves one or more intermediate axles with additional gears on them. This is often done because of space limitations. For instance, if you have a single-acting cylinder, but you want four exhaust beats per revolution of the wheels, you'll need a gear reduction of 4:1. However, you might be hard pressed to find room for a gear that is four times the diameter of your primary gear. To get around this problem, you can have compound gearing of 2:1 and 2:1, which will achieve the same result (figure 1).

Another thing to consider is direction of rotation. If your steam motor is geared directly to the axle, the motor will rotate in the opposite direction to the axle. If this offends your aesthetic sense, an option is to introduce another gear

into the line, called an idler. You can use any size gear. This gear does no other work than changing the direction of rotation of the output shaft.

Tram engines – regular steam locomotives that were boxed in for use on street railways – are fair game for all sorts of innovation, as the works are mostly hidden. All sorts of liberties with the drive system can be taken without anyone being the wiser. The tram engine, like a primitive logging engine, is an ideal platform for all types of simple-but-effective mechanics in steam locomotion.

Overtypes

The overtype locomotive is not a common beast. It is called this because the cylinder(s) is atop the boiler, like a traction

engine. Indeed, the few prototype overtype locomotives were evolved from traction engines.

Model-wise, Peter Angus made several attractive over-types. On the one I have, a single, D-valve cylinder drives a jackshaft on which there is a sprocket. A roller chain links to another sprocket below, on whose shaft is a small gear. This gear engages a larger gear on the rear axle, which, in turn is tied to the front axle via side rods.

Another overtype is the *Denver*, a project locomotive developed by Ken Orme, Jim Reyer, and myself for beginner loco builders. On this engine, a single-acting oscillating cylinder drives a jackshaft with a sprocket on it. A ladder chain transmits power to the rear axle, which has a second sprocket on it. Another chain transmits power to the front axle.

Whimsical Locomotives

When dabbling in the realm of garden-scale steam locomotives, there's no reason that a sense of humour, or even a sense of the outlandish, cannot be applied. Over the years, I have run across several examples of whimsical-but-functional steam locomotives. Graham Stowell in the UK is well known for his.

In the US, Dr Ralph 'Chip' Rosenblum has turned the steam locomotive into an art form. Using a combination of commercially available components and found objects, his fanciful creations never fail to amuse and delight as they perambulate down the track under their own power.

There are undoubtedly lots of other odd, unusual, and/or out-of-the-way methods of transmitting power to the wheels, both prototypical and otherwise. However, if you adopt the sensible attitude that anything that powers itself by steam is justifiably a locomotive in its own right, regardless of size, then everything becomes prototypical.

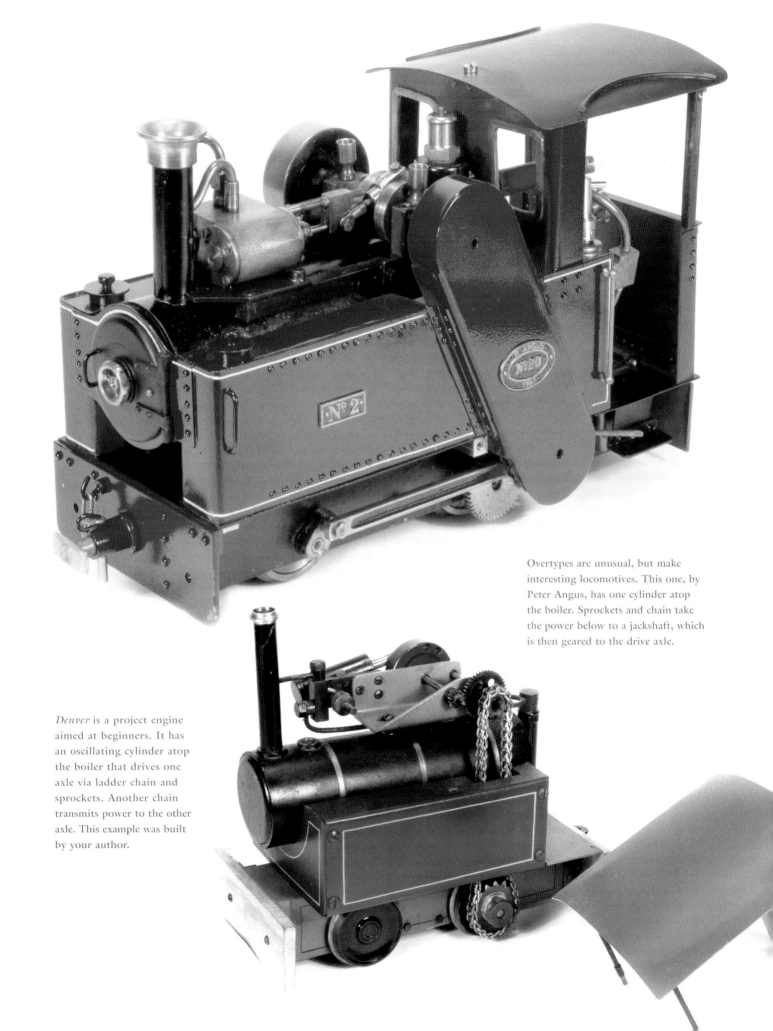

Overtypes are unusual, but make interesting locomotives. This one, by Peter Angus, has one cylinder atop the boiler. Sprockets and chain take the power below to a jackshaft, which is then geared to the drive axle.

Denver is a project engine aimed at beginners. It has an oscillating cylinder atop the boiler that drives one axle via ladder chain and sprockets. Another chain transmits power to the other axle. This example was built by your author.

Chapter 7

Boilers

The boiler is the heart of any steam engine. It doesn't matter how well designed or finely crafted the rest of the locomotive is, if the boiler is a poor steamer, the engine will never be any good. Conversely, a really good boiler can overcome, or at least disguise, a multitude of sins elsewhere. A good boiler will be designed to make maximum use of its fuel; provide as much surface area (heating area) for the fire to act upon as possible, given the volume of water contained within; and provide plenty of steam to power the cylinders in their intended way. A good-steaming boiler will produce just enough steam to run the locomotive with its maximum designed load in the worst conditions, but little more. A boiler that produces an overabundance of steam is just wasteful.

Boilers on little steamers are almost always made of copper, silver-soldered together. Earlier engines often had brass boilers that were soft-soldered. Mamod engines still have brass boilers. Brass contains zinc, which over time, can leach out, causing porosity in the metal. I've read accounts of such things happening, but have never encountered it myself. Bushings for fittings are often made of brass, although bronze (an alloy of copper and tin) is better, though harder to work.

Boiler pressure is measured in pounds per square inch (psi) in the imperial system, and kilograms per square centimetre (kg/cm²) in the metric system. You'll run across pressure gauges for either system. One kg/cm² equals 14.22psi. Most people, for the sake of estimation, call it 15psi. So, an engine that's running at 4 kg/cm² is running at just under 60psi.

In little engines, there are many more types of boilers in use than there are with larger locomotives. These are divided into two broad groups: internally and externally fired. Let's begin with externally fired boilers.

Pot boilers

An externally fired boiler has its fire entirely outside the boiler. These are commonly referred to as 'pot' boilers, as the boiler is really little more than a pot with a fire underneath. There

Above: This Bing engine from the 1930s has an unprotected pot boiler, making it susceptible to the slightest breeze.

Right: Jack Wheldon was an innovator in developing higher-efficiency pot boilers with his 'Pooter' class locomotives.

Opposite: Rob Lenicheck's Accucraft K-27. This engine has a large gas-fired boiler with twin flues, side by side.

are several variations to the pot boiler, which I'll get into later. A pot boiler is not self regulating like an internally fired boiler (see below). You light the fire and it makes steam. The fire is a fixed entity – it cannot be regulated while the engine is in motion. If there isn't enough steam, the engine slows. If there's too much, the safety valve is constantly going off, which is wasteful. As mentioned above, a good pot boiler will produce enough steam to run the engine with a good train and no more. Alas, this is not always the case. There are ways to increase or retard the output of a pot boiler, which will be discussed later.

There are good pot boilers and bad. The ratio of heating area to water volume must be correct or the water will never heat up sufficiently to make steam. The boiler must also have a suitably designed burner. Pot boilers on early, toy engines had unprotected fires or fires that were minimally protected with metal screens. Because of this lack of protection, even the slightest breeze or coolish weather would rob the boiler of heat, thus making the engine sluggish at best and inoperative at worst. It wasn't until later years that the pot boiler was taken more seriously and a lot of work and study went into making it more efficient (figure 1).

Jack Wheldon, with his 'Pooter' class engines, was one of these pioneers. Jack developed a firebox in which the boiler shell sat, which protected the fire from the elements, caused it to burn efficiently, and directed most of the heat around

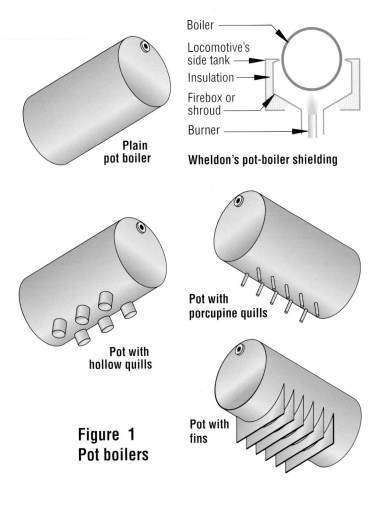

Boiler

Locomotive's side tank

Insulation

Firebox or shroud

Burner

Plain pot boiler

Wheldon's pot-boiler shielding

Pot with hollow quills

Pot with porcupine quills

Pot with fins

**Figure 1
Pot boilers**

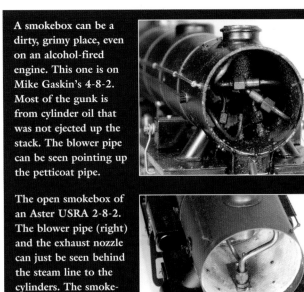

A smokebox can be a dirty, grimy place, even on an alcohol-fired engine. This one is on Mike Gaskin's 4-8-2. Most of the gunk is from cylinder oil that was not ejected up the stack. The blower pipe can be seen pointing up the petticoat pipe.

The open smokebox of an Aster USRA 2-8-2. The blower pipe (right) and the exhaust nozzle can just be seen behind the steam line to the cylinders. The smokebox is lined with insulating material.

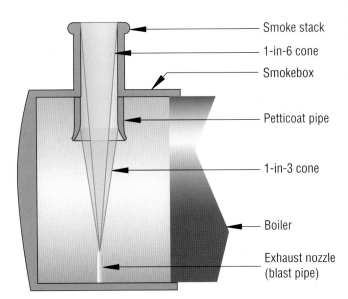

Smoke stack

1-in-6 cone

Smokebox

Petticoat pipe

1-in-3 cone

Boiler

Exhaust nozzle (blast pipe)

The blower and exhaust nozzles must be arranged in the smokebox so that a theoretical 1-in-3 cone will fill the bottom of the petticoat pipe and a 1-in-6 cone will fill the top of the stack. The stack and petticaot pipes must be sized accordingly.

**Figure 2
The smokebox**

the boiler where it would do the most good. His engines are a joy to run. They perform well in virtually any weather, from sub-freezing Colorado winters to the tropics, and even in a howling gale.

Jack also did work to increase the surface area of the boiler. He developed a 'porcupine' boiler that has copper quills in the bottom. Half of each quill extends into the fire while the other half resides inside the boiler. The idea here is that the quills increase the surface area of the boiler, transferring more heat to the water. A variation of that is the 'hollow quill' boiler, where the quills are actually stubby tubes containing water that extend into the fire. The surface-area-to-volume ratio of each tube is quite large, making them efficient mini-boilers.

Another way to increase the effective surface area is to solder fins to the bottom of the pot. Again, the fins extend into the fire, gathering heat. Rob Van Dort of Holland used this technique on at least one engine that I know of, a steam tram.

Pot boilers are the simplest boilers to construct as well as being the least efficient. They are used on locomotives designed for long duration with minimal messing about. They carry a lot of water, so don't have to be refilled often. Archangel engines equipped with pot boilers routinely get forty-five minutes duration or more, pulling heavy trains, with only the occasional addition of fuel.

Internally Fired Boilers

An internally fired boiler contains its fire within. Generally, an internally fired boiler will be more efficient than a pot, but it has its own drawbacks. It is more difficult to construct, has more components, and usually has less water space, which means a shorter run time before the boiler needs refilling. Also, it requires the fire to be drawn through it, which means (in the case of coal or alcohol-fired boilers) that the engine must have a proper smokebox, blast pipe, and blower.

The smokebox (figure 2) must be made as airtight as possible, the only openings being the smokestack (chimney) and those that communicate with the fire. To get the fire going, a small fan, usually battery powered, is placed in the smoke stack and turned on. This creates a mild vacuum in the fire space within the boiler (firebox, tubes, smokebox). Once the fire is lit, this vacuum will draw the hot gases through the boiler and out of the stack as well as drawing air in from the outside to oxygenate the fire, causing it to burn hotter. Once steam has come up a little – usually to about 20psi – the engine's blower can be turned on and the fan removed. It's at this point that the engine becomes self sufficient and alive.

The blower is simply a pipe from the boiler with a control valve on it. The end of the pipe, or nozzle, is placed in the smokebox directly under the stack, pointing up it. When the blower is turned on, a jet of steam is shot up the stack, which creates and maintains the vacuum in the smokebox, which draws the fire and keeps the engine alive.

The blast pipe, which is the exhaust line from the cylinders, occupies a position in the smokebox similar to the blower pipe. On larger locomotives, the blast and blower nozzles are incorporated into a single assembly. On our little engines, they more often appear as a pair of pipes placed side by side in the smokebox. When the engine is in motion, the blower can usually be turned off, as the blast from the exhaust will keep the fire going. However, if the engine is running light, there might not be enough force in the exhaust to draw the fire, in which case the blower should be cracked while running. There are important relationships between the size and placement of the blower and blast pipes, and the smokestack and petticoat pipe. If these are incorrect, an otherwise fine boiler will not function properly.

One of the beauties of an internally fired boiler is that it tends to be self regulating. If the engine is running easy, the exhaust will be slight, drawing the fire little. Under heavy loads or up steep grades, the engine is working hard, the blast becomes more intense, and the fire is drawn more vigorously, becoming hotter and more energetic, thus producing more steam as needed.

In larger locomotives (the ride-on sizes up to full size) there are very few boiler types in use, the most common being known as the locomotive-type boiler. This (usually) has a coal-fired firebox at the back end, surrounded on five sides by water, and a series of tubes or flues (larger tubes) that run through the main barrel to the smokebox. The surface-area-to-volume ratio is quite high, making these boilers excellent, efficient steamers.

Our little engines, however, enjoy a wide variety of internally fired boilers. Some are better than others and each has its advantages and disadvantages. I'll discuss a few of the more common ones here.

The Smithies boiler (figure 3), designed by Fred Smithies in the early part of the 20th century, has somewhat fallen out of favour today. Basically, it is a boiler encased in an outer

Five tubes help to circulate water in this Smithies boiler. Unusually, the tubes connect to a wet-leg downcomer at the rear of the boiler. The engine is a Carson for Bassett-Lowke 4-6-0 in gauge 3.

Figure 3: Smithies boiler

Smokebox
Outer shell
Inner boiler
Water tubes extend into fire

Three water tubes suffice in this gauge-1 engine's Smithies boiler. It was built by an anonymous builder to an LBSC design.

shell of larger diameter. The inner tube, which holds the water, is attached to the outer tube, or casing, at the top. The outer casing incorporates a firebox at the back end. Extending down from the rear of the inner boiler are a number of water tubes that come straight down at the back, then slope up toward the front of the engine, rejoining the inner boiler at the front. These increase the surface area and improve circulation through the boiler. A big advantage to this boiler is that the heat entirely surrounds the inner shell, where the water is. It is also relatively simple to construct. A disadvantage is that the water space is diminished and, unless well insulated, the paint tends to burn off the outer shell.

The Wrighton boiler (figure 4) was the design of Freddie Wrighton, a builder of gauge-1 locomotives in Britain half a century ago. His boiler had a firebox with a single large flue

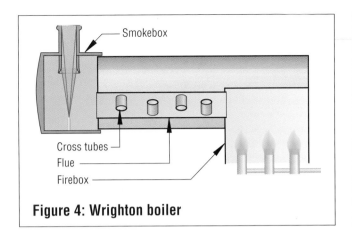

Figure 4: Wrighton boiler

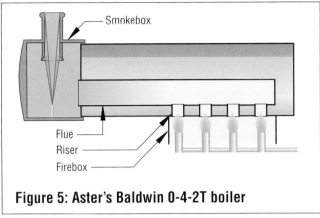

Figure 5: Aster's Baldwin 0-4-2T boiler

communicating with the smokebox. In the flue were a number of cross tubes set at an angle to increase surface area and impede the draft a little. This was a high-functioning boiler with a lot of surface area and the fire was entirely contained within the water space. It was a little more difficult to construct than the Smithies and, should one of the cross tubes spring a leak, tough to repair. Aster used a variation of this boiler (figure 5) in their Baldwin 0-4-2T.

John van Riemsdijk (JvR), a mainstay of the Gauge 1 Model Railway Association and a man scientifically trained in things steamy, has developed a number of excellent boilers for small engines. The **JvR type B boiler** (figure 6) features a

plain boiler shell with an external firebox toward the rear. Several fire tubes within the boiler emerge at the rear from the bottom of the boiler into the firebox, and into the smokebox at the front. This is an efficient boiler that is relatively easy to construct.

The **JvR type C boiler** (figure 7) has met with great success amongst model engineers and at least one commercial builder. Aster has used it on several of its engines. There are one or two variations to this boiler. The way it normally appears is as a simple boiler tube with flues that pass all the way through it, from front to rear. A special external firebox, often made of stainless steel, is attached to the boiler as a

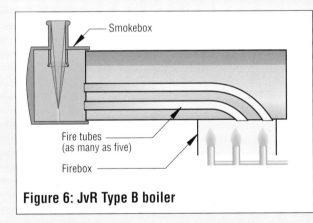

Figure 6: JvR Type B boiler

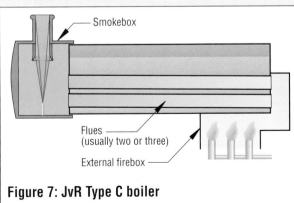

Figure 7: JvR Type C boiler

Top: Aster used a JvR type B on its small, freelance 0-4-0T *Old Faithful.* Here you can see where the firetubes emerge into the firebox.

Above: The JvR type C boiler has an add-on firebox that directs the fire into the firetubes, which emerge from the back of the boiler. This one, on an Aster 0-6-0T pannier tank, is made of stainless steel and extends back over the rear axle.

Right: The rear truck of *Firefly* has been removed and the ashpan dropped. The grate is in its working position.

Lower Right: With the grate dropped, the interior of the firebox is visible. The dry-back design gives more fire-grate area. Flue holes can just be seen on the tube plate on the right side.

Below: Hugh Saunders built this coal-fired Also 2-6-2T *Firefly*. It has a proper loco-motive-type boiler with a dry-back firebox.

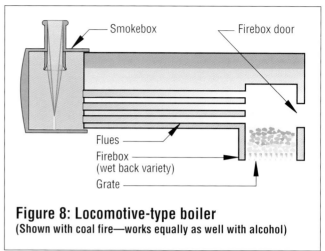

Figure 8: Locomotive-type boiler
(Shown with coal fire—works equally as well with alcohol)

separate unit. This directs the fire, which is under the boiler, through the tubes and into the smokebox. This may be the easiest-to-build internally fired boiler around.

All of the above-mentioned boilers are most suitable for alcohol fuel, although gas burners have been adapted to some of them. For coal burning, the **locomotive-type boiler** (figure 8) is almost a must. As the name suggests, this is an adaptation of the boiler type used on full-size locomotives. There is a firebox at the back with a grate in it for the coal. The firebox can be surrounded by water on five sides (called a wet-back firebox), or just on the sides and the crown sheet (called

a dry-back firebox), or a combination thereof. The wet-back firebox is the most difficult to build, but is the most efficient. However, it cuts down on combustion space within, which could be critical to a small locomotive's performance. The dry back is easier to build, but loses some heat via radiation through the dry back. In our small-scale engines, though, the difference in performance is minimal. In the back wall of the firebox is the fire door, through which the fire is fed.

From the front wall of the firebox, a number of fire tubes, or flues, communicate with the smokebox. These may include one or more larger superheater flues, through which the superheater pipe(s) pass.

As mentioned above, this is the most difficult type of boiler to build. It also has the highest ratio of heating area to water

Above: Martin Sheridan's beautiful Hunslet in ⅞in scale has a locomotive-type boiler.

Lower: Martin Sheridan's Hunslet was designed to burn coal or alcohol. The thick sides of the firebox are the water legs. There's a blowdown valve just above the mudring.

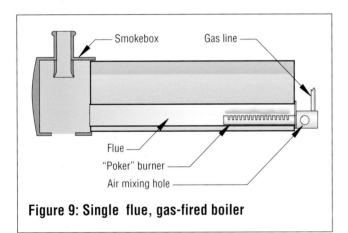

Figure 9: Single flue, gas-fired boiler

- Smokebox
- Gas line
- Flue
- "Poker" burner
- Air mixing hole

volume. The amount of water that this boiler can carry is relatively small, making some sort of feedwater system almost imperative. These are discussed elsewhere in the book.

The locomotive-type boiler is also well suited to alcohol firing. In fact, I have a couple of locomotives with this type of boiler that can be fired with either coal or meths. For alcohol firing, wick burners replace the grate and a fuel tank feeds the burner. The fire can be lit and checked through the fire door. Also, there is a relationship between the fire door and the draft. If the draft is too strong, threatening the fire, the door can be cracked a little to mitigate it.

The exception to the rule concerning internally fired boilers is the **single flue, gas-fired boiler** (figure 9). As its name suggests, it is a plain boiler with one relatively large flue through the water space (although there are variations on this theme as well). Into this flue goes a special gas burner (discussed in the 'Burner' section). Since this system is, in effect, self drafting (the pressure of the gas forces the fire through the flue), it requires no blower or even an air-tight smokebox, making them simple and economical to construct, as well as easy to use. This type of boiler has, in recent times, come to be a favourite with many commercial builders.

And, finally, come the **vertical boilers** (figure 10). While vertical-boilered locomotives in the full-size world were

Above: The vertical boiler in Maurice Cross's deWinton has a single flue up the middle. A suction fan is helpful in getting it going, after which the exhaust will draw the fire up the flue.

Right: On Larry Herget's logging engine, the boiler sits loosely atop the alcohol burner. It can be removed simply by undoing the steam line.

Below: With the boiler off, you can see the single flue. The boiler is encased in an outer shell, around which is fire space. In use, the boiler itself is surrounded by the hot gases. The twisted piece of metal in the foreground goes down the stack, acting as a retarder for the hot gases, getting a little more out of them.

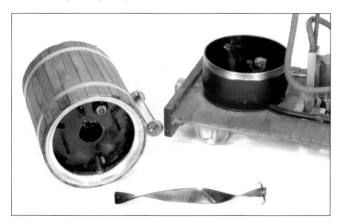

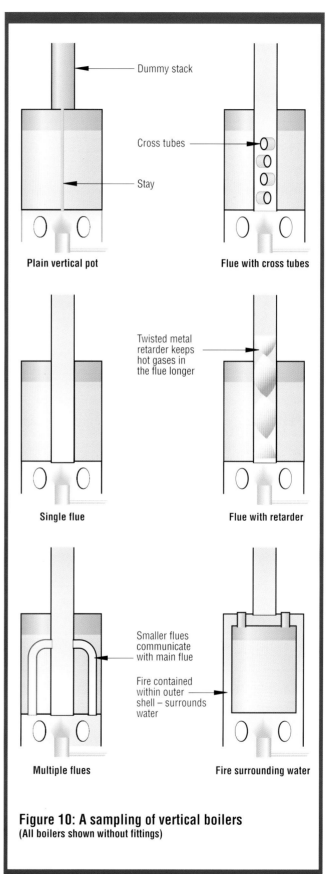

Figure 10: A sampling of vertical boilers
(All boilers shown without fittings)

relatively rare, and were most often used on industrial engines, they are fairly popular in the miniature world. There are a number of variations here, as with horizontal boilers. In some, the fire is allowed to pass entirely around the water barrel. Some have vertical flues of various numbers and sizes. Since the heat tends to go straight up (and out), retarders of

Aster, with the vertical boiler in their 'Grasshopper', used a four-wick burner. Above each wick is a boiler flue. All four flues converge at the base of the large smokestack.

one type or another can be used inside the flue(s). Cross tubes can also be used.

Also, since the heat rises, a vertical boiler may or may not have a blower, depending on its design. One engine I have, a tiny deWinton, gets steam up very quickly with the aid of a suction fan, and it relies on its exhaust blast to encourage the fire. However, it has no blower.

These are just a few of the ingenious solutions to the perennial problem of boiling water that have been thought of over the years. There are lots of little wrinkles that have been applied to them to improve efficiency, ease of construction, and aesthetics. The possibilities are virtually endless.

Superheating

Steam is a deep and complex subject. Most steam hobbyists know little about the scientific or mathematical workings of steam, nor do they particularly need to, to enjoy the hobby. In basic terms, as the pressure and temperature of steam rises, the more energy it contains and the more work it can do. In the full-size world, efficiency was always an overriding con-

cern in locomotive design. One way to be efficient was to conserve steam with properly designed valves and valve gear. Another was to produce the hottest, highest-pressure steam with the least amount of fuel possible. By the end of the steam era, there were locomotives that ran on steam in excess of 300psi. Our little engines normally run on pressures anywhere from 10psi to 100psi.

The steam itself is generally referred to in two ways: saturated and superheated (or dry) steam. Saturated steam is just a step above boiling water, both in temperature and consistency. Saturated-steam engines are often characterized by low-pressure boilers (under 20psi). These locomotives often run splendidly for long periods of time, pulling reasonable trains, with little fiddling.

Superheated steam, on the other hand, is produced by boilers running at high pressure, whose steam lines run through the fire one last time (the superheater) before entering the cylinders, receiving a last thermal boost (drying of the steam) before doing its work. On a pot boiler, this often means that the steam line simply passes beneath the boiler, through the

Right: In this Aster 2-8-2, the steam line forms a big coil in the smokebox, providing superheat from the hot gases coming through the engine's flues.

Lower: The coiled tubing under the pot boiler in this Archangel *Taw* (burner removed) are superheater coils. They are positioned above the wicks to get a final thermal boost before going to the cylinders.

flames, on the way to the cylinders. On internally-fired boilers, the superheater pipe will also pass through the flames, perhaps inside the outer shell of the boiler, as in a Smithies boiler, or through a special superheater flue within the boiler itself, depending on the type of boiler (figure 11).

Boiler Testing

Our little engines do present certain hazards. In realistic terms, though, the prospect of a boiler explosion isn't one of them. Copper is a very strong material in tension and the pressures we run at don't even approach one that would cause a catastrophic failure.

Having said that, though, every boiler must be tested. Testing will reveal leaks and flaws in design and/or workmanship. Boilers should never be constructed with soft solder – always with silver (not silver-bearing) solder. It is customary to test a boiler to twice its working pressure for a specified amount of time, often a half hour.

For safety's sake, boilers are always tested using water (hydraulic) pressure, not air or steam. When testing under hydraulic pressure, your only risk, in the event of a boiler failure, is getting a little wet. The way a boiler is typically tested is to remove all the fittings and replace all but one with plugs, making sure that the plugs are water tight. The boiler is then filled completely with water, with every attempt made to banish all air bubbles. With boilers of our size, it is easy to remove all the plugs, submerge the entire boiler in a sink or tub, then fit the plugs while the boiler is still under water. In this way, you have more assurance that all the air is gone.

Once the boiler is full of water, the test rig is screwed into the remaining bushing. This usually consists of a hand pump, a line to the boiler with a fitting for attachment (a banjo fitting is good), and a large pressure gauge tapped into the line. A large gauge will give a more accurate reading than a little one.

Make sure the exterior of the boiler is good and dry, so that if there's a leak, you can tell where it's coming from. The pump is then worked until the pressure gauge reads twice the working pressure of the boiler. The needle should remain steady for half an hour. If pressure cannot be maintained, there's a leak somewhere, either in the boiler or in the test system. If the leak cannot be found, it's possible that it might be in the clack valves in the hand pump!

Since water is incompressible, there is no danger of an explosion. Even in the unlikely event that the boiler fails catastrophically, all that would happen is that water would spurt out for a second and the pressure would instantly drop to zero. Once the boiler has passed its test, it's good to go.

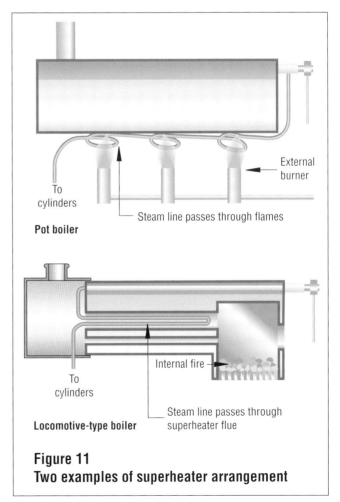

Pot boiler

To cylinders — Steam line passes through flames — External burner

Locomotive-type boiler

To cylinders — Internal fire — Steam line passes through superheater flue

Figure 11
Two examples of superheater arrangement

Chapter 8
Fuels and burners

Mamod engines, as they come from the factory, use solid-pellet fuel. Here is the burner tray from one, with a box of pellets.

When it comes to garden-size locomotives, several fuel options present themselves. All have advantages and disadvantages in greater or lesser number. There are four fuels in common use today. These include solid-fuel pellets, like Esbit or Mamod; alcohol, also called meths or spirits; gas (generally butane); and coal. Amongst commercial builders today, gas seems to be the fuel of choice, primarily because it is a relatively clean fuel and gas-fired boilers are easy to build in quantity. However, other options should be considered.

Solid pellets
This fuel was developed primarily for toy engines, both stationary and mobile. It's still supplied with Mamod and Wilesco engines. It's relatively difficult to light and doesn't put out a great deal of heat. This makes it attractive to manufacturers in our litigious world, but it does not endear itself to anyone who has used it for any length of time. Plus, it stinks. In certain circles, it is referred to as camel dung. Probably the best that can be said of it is that it provides an introduction to live steam for many people. I suspect that it might also be said that it has deterred a lot of people from live steam.

Pellet burners that are supplied as standard with some locomotives are soon replaced with those that burn other fuels. These often transform a balky, recalcitrant engine into a sweet running locomotive with lots of potential.

Alcohol or meths
Alcohol, or meths (short for methylated spirits), is the fuel of tradition. Thousands of locomotives, from the late 19th century

to the present, have been built to burn this fuel. It has a lot to recommend it and it's my personal favourite.

As fuels go, alcohol is relatively cheap, especially if purchased in larger containers. Different types of alcohols are available, but the ones we are primarily concerned with are ethanol and methanol. Ethanol has a slightly higher heat value than methanol, but either is satisfactory for use in locomotives. Isopropyl or 'rubbing' alcohol from the drug store or chemist is to be avoided, as it contains about 30% water. 'Denatured' alcohol is ethanol that has been rendered toxic and, thus, unfit for drink. These additives can include any number of chemicals, all of which burn, but some of which smell differently.

In a properly designed and adjusted burner, alcohol will burn cleanly, producing a slightly sweet odour. If there's a strong smell and your eyes water uncontrollably, there's something wrong, either in the wick adjustments or perhaps in the entire system. What you're smelling is unburned fuel. Despite this, your engine may still run just fine – you're just wasting fuel.

Your alcohol supply should always be kept covered, especially in moister climates. Otherwise, it can take on water from the atmosphere. I've experienced poor performance from engines that were just fine on previous runs. Upon investigation, I realized that I was using the dregs of fuel that had been in the can for who knows how long. A new supply of meths transformed the engine.

Because alcohol is clear (as is water) a colorant is often added to help distinguish it. Food colouring is good – just a couple drops of your favourite colour is all you need. You

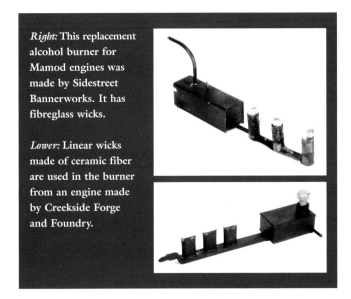

Right: This replacement alcohol burner for Mamod engines was made by Sidestreet Bannerworks. It has fibreglass wicks.

Lower: Linear wicks made of ceramic fiber are used in the burner from an engine made by Creekside Forge and Foundry.

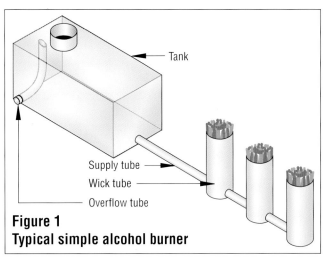

Figure 1
Typical simple alcohol burner

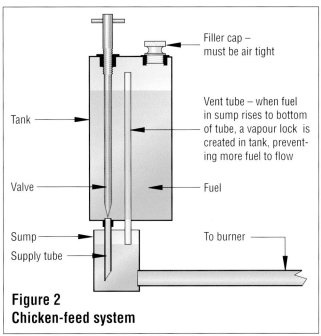

Figure 2
Chicken-feed system

may laugh – what idiot would confuse meths with water? Well, I've seen it happen. At a public, indoor steamup, a fellow whose name I conveniently can't recall accidentally filled his boiler with meths. Had he filled his meths tank with water, all would have been well, but he did not. It contained meths, too. He lit the fire and waited for pressure to rise, which it did with astonishing speed. Blow-off pressure was reached far more quickly than normal and, when the safety valve let go, the resulting plume of alcohol vapour instantly ignited. It was *spectacular!*

Another disadvantage to this fuel, and one you should be very aware of, is the fact that you can't see the flame in full sun. Many years ago, I had a Mamod locomotive that I fitted with an alcohol burner. I also fitted a servo in the cab so that I could radio control it. On one of its early test flights on a sunny day, I lit the fire and set the engine on the track. Before my eyes, the plastic case of the servo began to sag while the paint on the engine began to change colour, as if by magic. Being a little dense that day, I was absorbed by the spectacle for a while before coming to the realization that I had a fire – but couldn't see it! I was more careful thereafter, but the damage was done.

The most common type of alcohol burner is a simple wick burner, with a fuel tank attached (figure 1). The burner is usually composed of two to six wicks of varying diameter, connected to the fuel tank by a length of copper tubing. The tank will normally have a filler port – either a hole in the top or a small tube to which a filler syringe can be attached – and, if it's designed properly (not all are), an overflow tube. You simply fill the tank until fuel comes out the overflow. The overflow must be set at a level below the tops of the wicks, or the wicks will flood, causing a fire below.

Another wick burner involves a system called 'chicken feed.' The name comes from watering devices for chickens, where the water reservoir is above the receptacle the chicken drinks from. When the water in this receptacle drops, a vapour

lock in the reservoir is momentarily broken and more water is released into the bowl. And so it is with the alcohol system.

The fuel tank is above the level of the burner and situated directly over a small sump. There is a valve that releases fuel into the sump, and a vent tube that also extends into the sump (figure 2). When the valve is opened, fuel flows into the sump (and hence to the wicks) until it rises to the level of the bottom of the vent tube. This closes the system and creates a vapour lock in the tank to halt the flow of fuel. As the level drops, more fuel flows into the sump. To fill the tank, the valve must be closed or all the fuel will spill out the bottom immediately the filler cap is removed. It's a great system. On some engines, the fuel tank is entirely removable and can be refilled on the bench.

Another system, not much in use (and for good reason) is a simple drip system. This just involves a valve on the bottom

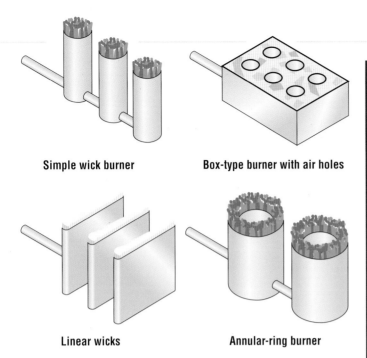

Simple wick burner

Box-type burner with air holes

Linear wicks

Annular-ring burner

**Figure 3
Different types of alcohol burner**

Right: An annular-ring burner from a vertical-boilered engine, *Usk,* made by Deryck Goodall. Air comes up the centre hole.

Lower: Hugh Saunders commonly used this box-type burner in his locos. It is filled with asbestos-wick material. The eight holes admit air to the fire.

of the raised tank which, theoretically, is opened to allow just enough meths into the sump for the engine to burn. The trick, obviously, is getting the adjustment right.

For any fuel to combust properly, it must have an adequate supply of oxygen. In an effort to supply this, designers have come up with a variety of wick shapes. These include simple, round wicks; oval wicks; annular-ring wicks (round wicks with an air hole in the middle); linear wicks; and box wicks, where there's actually a box filled with wick material and air holes coming up through it (figure 3). Hugh Saunders' burners were like this.

There is great controversy surrounding wick materials, which are plenty and varied. Cotton can be used as a last resort, but it quickly burns down and has to be frequently adjusted or replaced.

Asbestos yarn, if you can even find it anymore, is widely considered the material of choice for wicks. Those who have some tend to keep mum about it, jealously guarding their supply. If you're lucky enough to have some, a few simple precautions will render it harmless to use. Asbestos has gotten its well-deserved bad rap primarily because asbestos fibres, inhaled in quantity, can cause all sorts of nasty lung problems. If you are using it to pack wick tubes, wear latex gloves when handling, as well as a face mask. But, most importantly, wet it down with either water (preferred, because it doesn't evaporate so quickly) or meths. This will go a long way toward preventing airborne fibres.

Other, more modern wick materials currently in use include fibreglass and different forms of ceramic fibre. Each material has its own wicking characteristics. Because of this you'll have to experiment in packing your wicks to get optimum performance. I'm not a great fan of fibreglass yarn. In my

experience, it tends to crust over on top and not wick properly until the crusty part has been removed. Ceramic fibre seems to work better.

John Garrett has had great success in using wicks made out of brick! He uses a soft, porous firebrick used for lining kilns. He files one edge of a piece of K&S tubing, who's ID is slightly larger than the ID of the wick tube, with a triangular file to make teeth. Then, holding he K&S tube in his hand, he carefully twists it back and forth into the brick, cutting a plug. He then carefully sands or files the plug for a light press fit in the wick tube. The height of the wick is adjusted for optimum performance. John claims excellent performance and longer running times for his engines with these wicks.

Another material that people have experimented with is fine, stainless-steel mesh, rolled tightly and inserted into the wick tube. I have no personal experience of this but have been told that it is difficult to roll the mesh tightly enough for proper wicking.

Adjusting wicks is something of a dark art. You'll most likely have a certain amount of trial and error before you get it right. There's also some controversy about what *is* right. Jack Wheldon used to trim his wicks flat, ⅟₁₆in or ³⁄₃₂in above the wick tube. The inner blue cone of the flame should just touch the bottom of the boiler, on a pot boiler.

On the other hand, Stewart Browne, in his Archangel loco-motives, splayed the wicks out up to a half inch or more to the sides of the tubes. His engines are great runners using a small number of small-diameter wicks, but they tend to be thirsty.

You want the wick to burn cleanly and efficiently. If there's too little air or fuel, the fire will suffer and you'll most likely be able to smell it. Most commercially made engines have well-designed fuel systems, but they can still get out of

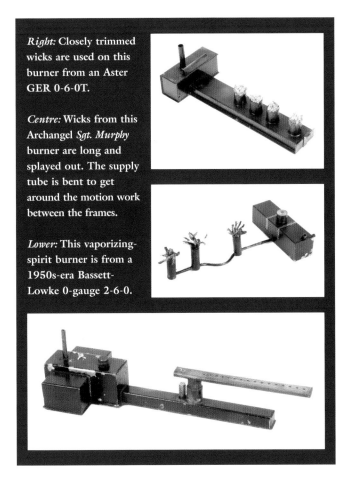

Right: Closely trimmed wicks are used on this burner from an Aster GER 0-6-0T.

Centre: Wicks from this Archangel *Sgt. Murphy* burner are long and splayed out. The supply tube is bent to get around the motion work between the frames.

Lower: This vaporizing-spirit burner is from a 1950s-era Bassett-Lowke 0-gauge 2-6-0.

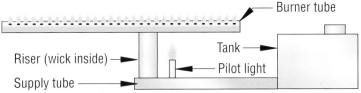

Figure 4
Vaporizing-spirit burner

Mounted to the supply tube, just behind the riser and under the burner tube, is a tiny wick, or pilot light.

Alcohol boils at a relatively low temperature (173°F; 78.3°C at sea level). When you light the little wick, the metal heats up fairly quickly. Alcohol is wicked up the large internal wick to the hot burner tube, where it vaporises. The alcohol vapor comes out the tiny holes and ignites, creating myriad tiny, hot blue flames. The system is self-sustaining until the fuel is exhausted or until the fire is blown out.

A disadvantage to this type of burner is that it is really only suited to pot boilers. The biggest disadvantage, however, is that the fire is easily blown out. Bassett-Lowke engines fitted with these burners had reputations for being excellent runners on calm days. The slightest breeze disabled them. Aster's engine, however, solved this problem by enclosing the burner in an excellent, protected firebox.

Gas burners

When we speak of gas in the context of miniature steam engines, we speak primarily of butane (or isobutane, an isomer of butane). Propane, another common and readily available gas, is not be considered for use in little steamers. The reason for this is its much higher storage pressure.

Gas is stored in tanks under pressure as a liquid. In simple terms, as the liquid is released from pressure and allowed to escape into the air, it turns into its gaseous form. As the ambient temperature rises, the pressure of the liquid gas within the tank also rises. For instance, the storage pressure of butane at 100°F (not an unreasonable temperature for a fuel tank, say, under the roof of the cab in a small engine) is 38psi. The storage pressure for propane under the same conditions is 173psi. The fuel tanks in our engines are not designed for such pressures. Charlie Mynhier uses propane to run his locomotives, but designs his tanks specifically for that gas and builds them of stainless steel.

We also run into trouble at the other end of the temperature scale, as butane will not gasify at all at around the freezing temperature of water, and is stored at very low pressures up to about 60°F. This can cause sluggish operation of engines running in cold weather. Of course, if the gas tank is in the cab or in a side tank, this isn't a problem, as heat from the boiler will keep the gas tank warm.

If, however, the gas tank is in the tender of a larger engine, you could be in for difficulties. Even on relatively warm days,

adjustment. The addition or deletion of as little as one or two strands of wick can make a great difference. You can do a certain amount on the bench, when packing wicks, but a burner outside the engine will behave differently when it's in place, as it will generally have more oxygen outside. However, if you get it burning well on the bench, you've made a good start. As a general rule, the wicks closest to the fuel tank should be packed more tightly than those farther away. This will help to even out the flames on the individual wick tubes.

With a pot boiler, one trick is to fire it up at night, when you can clearly see the flame. If you have a wild, leaping fire that jumps high above the side tanks, your wicks need to be packed more tightly.

There is one last type of alcohol burner that has faded from popularity, but that should be mentioned. This is the vaporizing-spirit burner (figure 4). These were widely used in toy engines in the early part of the 20th century. Märklin used mushroom-shaped burners in its engines (some quite large), while Bassett-Lowke used linear burners. More recently, Aster used a vaporising-spirit burner in its BR86 2-8-2T (1987).

With these burners, there is a fuel tank from which comes a supply tube. Rising from the supply tube (in a Bassett-Lowke-style burner) is a wick entirely encased in a tube. Atop this wick tube is the burner tube, which is sealed at both ends, but which is perforated with a multitude of tiny holes on its upper surface.

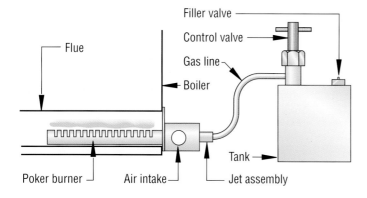

Figure 5
Gas burner

a protected tank could still fail to deliver. One of the characteristics of gas is that, as the pressure in the tank drops, so does the temperature of the tank. So, a tank relatively insulated in a tender cavity could soon have frost on it. A common solution to this problem is to mount the gas tank in a water-tight vessel, then surround it with a warm-water bath, with the gas filler valve protruding above. It will take a while for the cooling gas tank to suck all the warmth out of the surrounding water. Meantime, you're enjoying a fine run on a cool day.

I was once running a Shay on a warm afternoon. Its fuel tank was in the bunker, well away from the boiler. The engine ran fine. As the sun dipped, the ambient temperature dropped, unnoticed by us, who were wrapped up in our steamy pleasures. As the weather cooled, the Shay got cranky, not wanting to move above a crawl, even with the gas valve and throttle wide open. It took a while for the penny to drop. I finally put a finger on the gas tank. It was frigid. I filled the bunker with warm water and the engine's recovery was nothing short of miraculous.

Another solution to this problem, which has been gaining wider acceptance, is the use of what is called 'camping gas' in the US. 'Gaz' is one of the trade names for this product. This is actually a mixture of butane (80%) and propane (20%). This is sort of the best of both worlds, combining the relatively low storage pressure of butane at high temperatures (65psi at 100°F) and the flowability of propane at low temperatures (10psi@ 30°F). Isobutane is another possibility for cold-weather running. Like butane/propane mixes, it is sold for cold-weather camping.

One of the characteristics of gas of which you should be aware is that it is heavier than air. If you're running outdoors, this is generally not an issue. Indoors, it can be hazardous. In my very early days in the hobby, I was testing a newly acquired engine on my shop floor. It being summertime, I was dressed in shorts. I filled the gas tank as usual, not realizing that a little bit of the gas bleeds out when the tank is being filled. Unbeknownst to me, that gas settled around my feet. I was soon aware of the fact, though, because it ignited as soon as I lit a match, causing me the instantaneous loss of all the hair on my shins. It could have been worse.

Butane is a clean-burning fuel that has little odour. On a well-designed system it is easy to get the fire going, and a gas fire is adjustable. Once you learn your locomotive, you'll learn the best settings for the burner to get the most efficient run out of the engine. In general terms, you want the lowest gas setting you can use and still have the engine perform well. If the safety valve is constantly blowing off, the gas is probably turned up too high.

A typical gas-firing system works like this. There is a fuel tank, which is a small pressure vessel. In it is a filler valve. This valve has a spring-loaded nipple that is depressed by the fitting on the gas-supply reservoir, which opens the valve and allows gas (in liquid form) to flow from the supply into the tank. Most of the valves on commercial models are known as self-bleeding valves. These release the gas or vapour in the tank to make room for the liquid. Once the tank is full, the gas will start sputtering at the valve, and the reservoir is removed.

Also on the tank is a control valve that allows the pressurized gas to pass to the burner. It must be closed while the tank is being filled. The valve is placed at the very top of the tank so that butane gas is released by the valve instead of liquid. I've seen some tanks that are possible to overfill, at which time the liquid at the top has to be let out before the burner will work properly.

The gas travels down a gas line until just before the burner. Here it ends in a fine jet, the hole of which is often too small to be seen by the naked eye. Jets come in different sizes. The ones used in garden-size locomotives are usually #3 to #6 (the larger the number, the larger the hole). The jet squirts gas into a mixing tube outside the burner. In the sides of this tube are holes that admit air. As the gas passes through the tube, it entrains air (draws air into the mixture) to aid combustion.

The gas/air mixture then enters the burner, which is often (but not always) a tube, closed at the front end, but with slits cut in it along the top or bottom (figure 5). This is commonly known as a poker burner. The burner resides inside the boiler in a tube or flue that communicates with the smokebox.

When the fire is lit at the smokebox door or stack, it should flash back to the burner. Sometimes, though, the fire will refuse to flash back, burning in the front of the flue or in the smokebox; or it will not light at all. There are several possible causes of this. One is that the gas/air mixture is not right. Some burners are equipped with a sliding sleeve over the air holes so that the air intake can be adjusted. Another possible cause is an incorrectly sized gas jet. Yet another is a blocked or (worse) partially blocked gas line. Also, if the boiler produces an overabundance of steam, this could also be a jet problem. Try a smaller one. And sometimes, you might just have the gas turned up too high.

Gas-line blockage is sometimes difficult to diagnose. If you open the valve and nothing at all comes out, then it's pretty obvious. Sometimes, though, it isn't that easy. I was once firing up an engine where the burner lit just fine. However, I couldn't adjust the fire much above the puny level. After trying several things it occurred to me that perhaps there was something in the line. The jets are so small that it doesn't take much. I cleared the line and all was well.

There are several possible sources of grit than can block (or partially block) a jet. These can include soldering debris left

Right: Roger Marsh used
a gas burner under a the
externally fired boiler in
his *Ogwen* engines. A
similar gas 'poker' is used
in single-flue boilers.

Below: A self contained,
drop-in gas burner for
Mamod engines, made by
Roger Marsh in the 1980s.

over from gas-tank construction that can, if the engine is
turned upside down or on its side, get into the gas line. Some
cheap brands of gas can contain dirt particles, or waxes or
other additives that can clog jets.

Clearing a gas jet can be tricky. The orifice is extremely
small and fragile. Some engines come supplied with fine
pricker wires that you can use to insert into the jet from the
front. Use these only as a last resort. For one thing, even if
it works, you've only pushed the blockage back into the line,
where it can continue to bedevil you. For another thing,
depending on how these pricker wires were made, they can
have tiny, invisible burrs on them that can damage the jet.
Once, after using a pricker wire, I tried to fire the engine up
again. Gas was definitely coming out, but the burner, which
had been fine before, was acting very strangely. Fortunately,
I had another jet, which I put in, and all was well. I later
examined the faulty jet under a microscope. The tiny orifice,
which should have been round, was definitely not. The hole,
damaged by the pricker wire, caused the gas stream to
diverge at odd angles.

The best way to clear a gas jet is to remove it from the gas
line (which can be problematic on some engines) and blow
it out from the *outside* using compressed air. I've also seen
people actually use their gas-supply cans to blow it out,
which also seems to work sometimes. This way you're not

introducing a piece of metal into the delicate orifice and you
are blowing the blockage entirely clear of the system.

If your fire burns yellow or green, that's another indicator
of poor mixture. It should be bright blue. Sometimes,
because of the design of the engine, there just might not be
enough oxygen available. As you rise in altitude, the oxygen
level (and air pressure) diminishes. Both of these things can
affect the way your gas-fired engine performs. I once tested an
engine from Russia. This locomotive had worked fine at sea
level. However, where I live, a mile above sea level, nothing we
could do would get it to light. The engine had been designed
at low altitude and we just didn't have enough oxygen.

Poker burners usually reside inside a single flue. However,
with larger locomotives, like Aster's 'Big Boy' and Accucraft's
K-27, there may be multiple flues. The 'Big Boy' has one very
large flue with a single burner, which then divides into three
smaller flues. The K-27 has two separate flues, side by side,
each with its own burner. With this engine, it is possible for
one fire to go out while the other keeps burning. With
practice, you can tell by the sound what's going on.

The poker design can also be used on externally-fired boilers,
being placed underneath like an alcohol flame. Roger Marsh
used this system in his *Ogwen*, a gas-fired pot boiler. He also
offered a little gas unit as a replacement burner for Mamod
engines, which were guaranteed to burn up the boiler if the
driver was unfortunate enough to let it run dry.

Another type of gas burner uses a ceramic element.
Cheddar used this system in their engines. It is a particularly
good system for vertical boilers. This system, up to the air
intake, is the same as for a poker burner – only the burner
itself is different. The element is made from a special ceramic
and is perforated with holes. It is held in a sort of metal
frame. Beneath the burner is a plenum or space into which

Cheddar used a ceramic gas burner in its engines. This is a radiant-heat burner that glows orange when in use.

the air/gas mixture enters. When the fire is lit, it will burn for a few second atop the ceramic, which will begin to glow. The fire then burns within it, causing it to glow bright orange, providing radiant heat for the boiler.

Coal firing

Just as operating a live-steam locomotive is a thing apart from all other forms of model railroading, coal firing is a thing apart from all other forms of live steam. It's not for everyone. If you enjoy firing up your steamer, then sitting back and watching it trundle around for the next half hour or so, don't even think about coal firing.

Coal is considered by many to be the elite fuel for model locomotives. After all, that's what full-size engines burn. And there's little to beat being able to open the fire door and put coals on a roaring fire. Also, nothing beats the smell of real coal, which says 'steam locomotive' like nothing else.

A coal-fired engine must have a proper locomotive-type boiler, with either a wet or dry firebox (see the section about boilers). The bottom of the firebox is open, and in it is a removable grate. Below the grate there is usually an ashpan that, as its name suggests, catches the ashes. It can also be used to control the amount of air available to the fire.

The best coal-fired engines in our small scales have wide and deep fireboxes – the deeper the better. The fire door is placed as high as is practical to give more depth to the fire. If there is not enough volume in the firebox, it will be very difficult to sustain a fire. A 'thin' fire – one that is not deep enough – is easily burned through, creating a hole through which cold air can enter and extinguish the fire.

Full-size and large model engines often have an arch in the firebox that directs the heat back, up, and over before it goes into the flues, causing it to heat the firebox more evenly and efficiently. In full-size locomotives, this arch is made of fire brick; in smaller ones, it is usually formed from a metal sheet. In our little engines, these are seldom used.

Coal is an organic material made mostly of plants that died millions of years ago and were slowly compressed by rock and earth that moved on top of them over geologic time. The more they were compressed, the harder the resultant coal.

Because coal is organic, there is a more or less infinite range in its quality, but for all practical purposes it comes in four main flavours, as follows, from soft to hard: lignite, or brown coal; sub-bituminous; bituminous; and anthracite. The latter, anthracite, has the most calorific value of all the coals, with 85-95% carbon (as opposed to 25-35% for lignite, which also has a high water content).

For our purposes, anthracite is the only coal to be considered. It burns cleanly, leaving a powdery ash and little, if any, clinker to clog the grate (a clinker is an incombustible, vitreous mass that is often formed by burning inferior grades of coal); doesn't produce volatile gases; makes little smoke; and still gives us that nice, locomotive smell. It is commonly felt that the best coal comes from Wales, and this is known as Welsh steam coal. This is getting harder to find, particularly in the US. Some people have reported good luck with Pennsylvania anthracite, while others have had bad experiences with it. If you can get yourself a fifty-pound bag of really fine coal, it will last you a long time.

Coal firing is messy, dirty, smelly, tricky, and time consuming – in short, everything anyone could ask from a live steamer. It is the most interactive of all forms of live steam. You have to constantly watch the fire and the water, tending each as necessary. Firing up takes much longer and the unattended runs you get with coal are much shorter – coal needs to be added, generally, in five to ten minute intervals. Why would anyone want it, especially in an engine you can't even ride on?

Well, firing one of these little beasties is about as close as you can come to operating a full-size locomotive. It's not something one should do hurriedly or when under pressure. That can only lead to tears. There's a definite mindset that one must cultivate before success can be achieved in firing a miniature coal-burner. It takes on an almost Zen-like quality. It is definitely a skill that must be mastered, but the satisfaction in successfully firing a coal-fired locomotive is great indeed. A more thorough discussion of how a coal-fired engine is actually brought to life can be found in chapter 11.

Chapter 9
Boiler fittings

Boiler fittings are the things that not only add functionality to a boiler, but help to give an engine character. Nothing brings a tingle to the scalp like a boiler festooned with fittings, all of which have function and purpose. As part of learning steamcraft, it is not only good to know what all these fitting are for and how they work, but also, through that same knowledge, to learn how an engine behaves without some of them and how to get along without them.

Safety valves

The essential fitting, the one that no boiler can be without, is the safety valve. This is (usually) a spring loaded, one-way valve that is preset to release at a given pressure, called the blow-off pressure. This is always a fraction – often half – of the pressure at which the boiler was tested. On higher-end engines – some of Aster's, for instance – two safety valves are used as a failsafe.

Although the function of all safety valves is more or less the same, their design can vary widely. On the simplest, low pressure, pot-boilered toys, the valve takes the form of something like a nail protruding through a loose-fitting housing. Around the head of the nail is an 0-ring or fibre washer to make the seal. On the shank of the nail, inside the boiler, is a

When the steam pressure overcomes the spring strength, the ball lifts and relieves the pressure (amount of lift exaggerated here)

Ball
Seat
Housing
Shaft
Spring
Retainer

Figure 1
Simple ball-type safety valve

spring that is retained at the end of the shaft and that bears against housing, forcing the head of the 'nail' and the seal against the top of the housing.

Instead of the flat head making the seal with a washer, a ball can also be used (figure 1). This must be carefully 'seated' to make a steam-tight fit. When this sort of valve goes off, it lets go with a gentle hiss.

There is a similar valve, but with the spring on the outside, that represents a Salter safety valve, used on early steam

A steamy Archangel 'Taw' commences its run on a cold, wet day. This engine has Hackworth valve gear and a pot boiler.

Safety Valves

Safety valves come in all shapes, types, and sizes. Here are just a few:

1. Mamod toy-type
2. Beck toy-type
3. Twin valves on an Aster Mikado
4. Archangel

5. A scratchbuilt valve by the author
6. Wheldon 'Pooter'
7. Merlin
8. David Hick, on a Peckett 0-4-0

9. Archangel, external spring
10. Aster/LGB *Frank S.*, external spring
11. Charlie Mynhier, silicone tube
12. Safety on a John Turner *Caledonia*

locomotives. This external spring forces a ball or cone-shaped part into a seat, creating the seal.

A ball-type safety valve (figure 2) is used on more sophisticated locomotives. This type of valve has a loose ball, usually phosphor bronze or stainless steel (although I've heard of ceramic, plastic, and hard-rubber balls being used with varying degrees of success), inside a cylindrical housing. Atop the ball is a stem with a foot on it that is scooped out underneath to engage the ball. Around the stem is a spring. The inside of the cylindrical housing is threaded, and a threaded retainer is screwed into the housing. The retainer has a hole in its middle to accommodate the shaft of the stem and notches or holes cut into the perimeter to let the steam escape. The blow-off pressure can be adjusted by how much the retainer is screwed down. On commercially produced engines, this is set at the factory and shouldn't be tampered with.

The design of the inside of the housing is a fairly complex matter. The ball must sit on a 'seat' to make a steam-tight seal. There is a special relationship between the diameter of the ball, the diameter of the hole below the ball, and the diameter of the cavity in which the ball sits. Depending upon how the interior of the valve is designed and how well its construction is executed, the valve will either release with a hiss or a satisfying pop, as a full-size locomotive's.

The most desirable safety valve is a true 'pop' valve. Ideally, it will snap open, release 5-8 pounds of pressure, then smartly snap closed again, not languidly start to fizzle and hiss until it is fully open, then repeat the process in reverse to close. It's amazing how small a true pop valve can be made, with care. On a cold day, there's nothing finer than to see a high-pressure locomotive blowing off at speed, sending a thick plume of steam into the atmosphere.

Archangel safety valves (which aren't small) have a certain cachet about them. Typically, the valve is surmounted by a heavy, solid-brass dome. In certain instances, the valve has been known to release with such violence that it fires the hot, loose-fitting dome a dozen feet into the air! Another trick of the Archangel valves is their tendency to release steam in short, flatulent bursts, to the delight of onlookers.

There is one last type of safety valve that has seen little use, but that is relatively simple to make and provides good territory for experimentation. Charles Mynhier developed this valve and Larry Lindsay used it on some of his Shays. This valve consists of a brass or bronze tube, blocked at the top, that extends above the boiler. Holes are cross-drilled through this tube, and a piece of silicone tubing is fitted tightly over the brass tube. As pressure builds in the boiler (and hence the tube), the silicone tubing will begin to expand until it releases steam. The relationship between the respective diameters of the brass and silicone tubes will determine the blow-off pressure. This is essentially a Goodall valve (see below) in reverse.

The throttle or regulator

On a full-size locomotive, when the throttle valve is opened, one or more small steam ports is partially or fully uncovered, allowing steam to pass into the cylinders. On our little

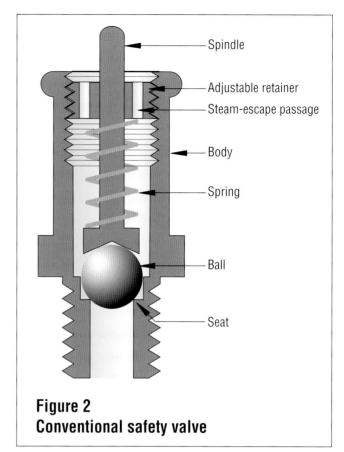

**Figure 2
Conventional safety valve**

- Spindle
- Adjustable retainer
- Steam-escape passage
- Body
- Spring
- Ball
- Seat

Above: A standard screw-type throttle or regulator, this one on an Accucraft 'Ruby'.

Right: The throttle on this Salem Steam Models engine is mounted vertically atop the boiler.

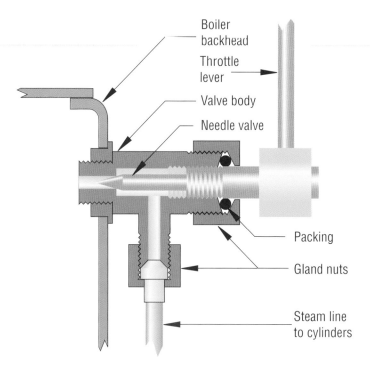

Figure 3
Common throttle valve

Boiler backhead
Throttle lever
Valve body
Needle valve
Packing
Gland nuts
Steam line to cylinders

engines, this system is largely impractical, and the simple screw throttle has been almost universally adopted in one form or another.

In its simplest form, the screw throttle is a threaded rod with a cone on the end (figure 3). This cone, when screwed home, seats in a hole, thus preventing the passage of steam. In this position, the throttle is closed. As the throttle is opened, the screw is withdrawn from the hole and steam is allowed to pass into the cylinders. As the cone emerges from the hole, the area of the opening becomes larger and larger, allowing more and more steam to pass, accelerating the locomotive.

Throttle sensitivity is governed by a number of factors. These include the sharpness of the cone and the fineness of the thread on the screw. It is possible to make a throttle so sensitive that it would take several revolutions of the handle for the engine to attain full speed. This is generally not desirable. On the other hand, I have any number of engines where it seems that between full closed to full open is a matter of only around 10 degrees of rotation. These engines are exceedingly difficult to control without hanging a heavy train on them, making for some interesting moments at the track. I try not to run these in front of a crowd.

Generally speaking, if you can get full, linear control in about 90° of valve rotation, that satisfies most requirements. It is a good number for both manually and radio controlled locomotives. For a manually controlled engine, the throttle lever can be accessed through a side door or through the back of the cab. If you know the engine well, you'll know by the position of the handle what to expect speed-wise. With radio control, a servo's useful range is 90-100°.

Some engines are supplied with knobs to control the throttle valve. These can be unsatisfactory for a couple of reasons. They can get quite hot (unless made of plastic) and they do not have the fineness of control that is offered by a lever. Retrofitting a lever to a knob-supplied locomotive is usually not a difficult task and is one that is well with the effort.

Steam is taken from near the top of the boiler, which is where the throttle is almost always mounted. In rare cases, the locomotive will have a proper steam dome, and the steam-collection pipe will extend into the dome where, theoretically anyway, the hottest, driest steam is located. From the collection pipe (if there is one) the steam goes to the throttle. On most small engines, the throttle is an external affair, with the steam pipe departing from it outside the boiler, going the to the cylinders. Naturally, this will have a cooling effect on the steam, lessening the engine's efficiency. One way

Top: This scratchbuilt, LBSC-designed locomotive has an internal throttle.

Lower: The throttle on this Archangel C&M 0-4-2T is radio controlled. The servo is in the foreground, with a linkage to the throttle lever.

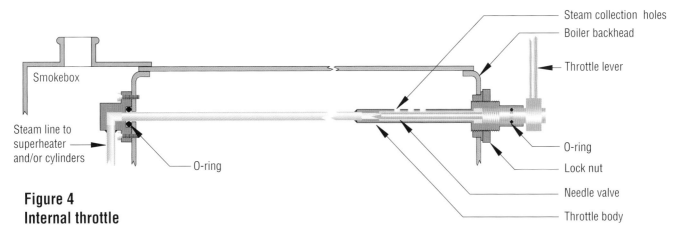

Smokebox

Steam line to superheater and/or cylinders

O-ring

Steam collection holes
Boiler backhead
Throttle lever
O-ring
Lock nut
Needle valve
Throttle body

Figure 4
Internal throttle

Right: Aster's *Frank S.* has a glass window for viewing the water level.

Lower: Mamod's water glass is actually a little plastic window in the backhead. If the boiler runs dry, the plastic melts.

around this is to pass the steam line through the fire on the way, to pick up a little superheat.

On more sophisticated boilers, the throttle is internal (figure 4). This is a more complicated system, but more efficient. While the throttle lever is in the cab, the steam exits the front of the boiler right into the smokebox. From there it most likely passes through one or more superheater flues before arriving at the cylinders. The steam line is never exposed to the outside air.

While not a boiler fitting proper, some engines are fitted with exhaust regulators in addition to the main throttle. As the name suggests, this restricts the engine's exhaust and is situated in the exhaust line. This type of regulator can only be used on locomotives that do not require the exhaust to draw the fire, such as pot boilers. While some people look down their noses at such devices, an exhaust regulator is a way of taming a lively engine. The way it goes is this. You open the primary throttle, then set the exhaust regulator until the engine's top speed is manageable. Then the primary throttle is used to control the engine's movements.

The water glass
The water glass, as the name suggests, is a device made partially of glass that will let you know how much water is in the boiler. On some engines it is a luxury – perhaps even an unnecessary one – and on some engines it is mandatory.

On low-pressure locomotives, like Beck's *Anna,* LGB's (Aster's) *Frank S,* and others, the water glass is actually a little window on the back of the boiler that lets you see the water inside.

More commonly, the water glass is a vertical glass tube that, through fittings, communicates with the boiler through

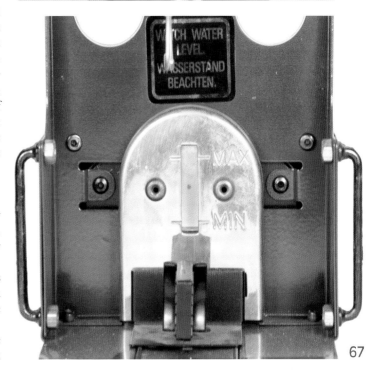

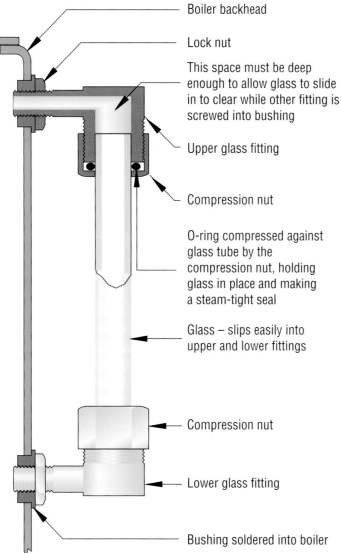

— Boiler backhead

— Lock nut

This space must be deep enough to allow glass to slide in to clear while other fitting is screwed into bushing

— Upper glass fitting

— Compression nut

O-ring compressed against glass tube by the compression nut, holding glass in place and making a steam-tight seal

Glass – slips easily into upper and lower fittings

— Compression nut

— Lower glass fitting

— Bushing soldered into boiler

Figure 5
Water glass

Note: There are many ways to fit a water glass. This is one of them

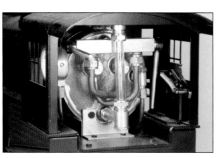

Above: Aster's USRA Mikado has a tall glass. The vertical red line on the glass, just visible, provides an aid in seeing the level.

Right: The water glass on Deryck Goodall's *Usk.* Unusually, the pressure gauge is piped into the top of the glass.

both the top and the bottom, creating a loop (figure 5). When all is well, the glass will give you an accurate reading of the water level in the boiler. However, all is sometimes not well. With small-diameter glasses particularly, it is not uncommon to get a bubble in there, which prevents an accurate reading. And if you are unwise enough to use hard water in your boiler, or unlucky enough to get oil in it, the glass can become clouded, again giving you a hard-to-see reading at best or a false one at worst. Some water glasses are equipped with a blowdown valve on the bottom. If there's a bubble in the glass, this blowdown can be opened momentarily to blow out the bubble.

The larger the glass tube, the more accurate the reading. Some people feel that ¼in is the minimum diameter for an accurate reading. However, if the glass gets too big, it becomes too out of scale and is unsightly. There must be a compromise that satisfies all requirements.

Reading a glass, especially on the fly, can be an iffy thing. One device, used on full-size water glasses, can also be used to good effect on miniature ones. A painted plate, with diagonally painted lines of contrasting colours on it, is positioned behind the glass. The refraction of light through water is radically different than that through air. Because of this characteristic, the lines will be at a distinctly different angle behind the part of the glass that is full of water.

The vertical placement of the glass is important, too, and will vary depending on the type of boiler it is attached to. You don't want the top of the glass to be too high (unless the optimum maximum level is marked on it), as the water will

begin to impinge upon the steam space. Likewise, you don't want it too low, either, as, for instance, in a single flue gas boiler. The bottom of the glass should be above the top level of the flue so that the flue is never without a protective covering of water.

With most locomotives, you can get by without a water glass. You learn to drive your engine with care, getting to know it and learning its characteristics. With experience, you will be able to tell by its behaviour that water is getting low. On a coal-fired engine, however, a water glass is an essential tool in preserving the integrity of the boiler. If the crown sheet is not covered by water, severe damage can occur, including the ruination of the boiler in extreme cases. The water glass can help prevent this catastrophe.

Pressure Gauge

A tiny, working pressure gauge is a thing of beauty. This fitting above all others says 'steam engine.' It's a handy thing to have, but not essential on all engines.

The heart of a pressure gauge is its Bourdon tube, named after Frenchman Eugene Bourdon, who patented it in 1849. This is a tube, flat or oval in cross section, made of thin metal. The flattened tube is formed into a circular shape and one end is soldered closed. The other end is connected to the pressure line. The closed end, which is unsupported, is connected to the gauge's needle through links and levers (figure 6). As the tube is pressurized, it tries to straighten, moving a little. That movement is translated to the needle via the linkages.

On lower-pressure locomotives with externally fired boilers, a pressure gauge is an attractive luxury. Yes, it will tell you when the pressure is up, but so will the safety valve. With these engines, the behaviour of the engine will tell you more about the state of the boiler than a pressure gauge. Still, they are nice to have and they certainly add to the appearance of the engine. However, if your engine has a blow-off pressure of less than about 30psi, a pressure gauge becomes superfluous, as you'll hardly get an accurate reading and most of the dial will never be used.

On sophisticated, internally fired engines, a pressure gauge is more of a necessity. When raising steam with a fan, the gauge will tell you when it is time to switch over to the engine's blower. Wild fluctuations in boiler pressure can indicate low water or a problem with the fire. A pressure gauge can be a tool in preventing serious damage to the locomotive.

Gauges should be periodically checked against a known large gauge for accuracy. To do this, both gauges must be

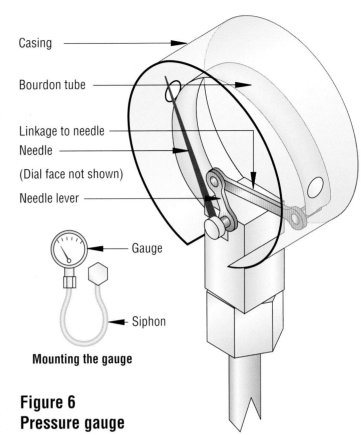

Casing
Bourdon tube
Linkage to needle
Needle
(Dial face not shown)
Needle lever
Gauge
Siphon
Mounting the gauge

**Figure 6
Pressure gauge**

Top: The pressure gauge on this Hugh Saunders *Jubilee* is the type most commonly used. Note the striped back plate on the water glass, which helps the driver see the level accurately.

Lower left: A large, toy-like (but easy to read) pressure gauge is prominent on Beck's *Anna.*

Lower right: On the *Frank S.*, the pressure gauge is in the roof of the cab, concealed by a rubber cover when not being read.

hooked up to the same system and pressure applied. There should be no more than five pounds variation. If there is, replace the little gauge.

These tiny gauges are delicate instruments that can be damaged by over-pressurization (should your safety valve fail), heat (should your boiler run dry), misuse, and old age. To protect them from heat, they are mounted to the boiler on a siphon, or loop of pipe. Water will collect in this pipe to create a sort of thermal buffer between the gauge and the boiler.

Blowdown valves and vacuum taps

A blowdown valve, as the name suggests, is used to release residual pressure from the boiler at the end of a run. The valve can be in the form of a screw-type valve or a plug valve, like a try-cock. The valve can be placed at the lower end of a water glass, towards the bottom of the boiler, or at the optimal water level when the boiler is full.

If the valve is placed lower down, when it is opened, it will not only release residual steam, but will also drain the boiler down to that level. It's a fine thing, on a cold day, to open

the blowdown, as the engine is instantly engulfed in a cloud of steam. Needless to say, this should be done at a place where no damage from the steam or water can occur.

In some engines, the blowdown just opens to the air right at the valve. This often leaves a very damp cab. In others, the steam is piped away, sometimes down through the floor of the cab, to exhaust near ground level.

Some locomotives, particularly pot boilers, have the blowdown positioned in the backhead at the upper level of the water for a full boiler. Archangel engines were often made this way. When steam is released from a boiler, it all comes out until no more pressure remains. However, there will still be a little steam in the boiler. That steam, as it condenses, creates a vacuum. If you hook a flexible line up to the blowdown pipe, and put the other end into a container of distilled water, you can use that vacuum to pull water into the boiler, thus refilling it. This is called a vacuum tap. This was a favourite technique of Jack Wheldon. It was on his Border Counties Railway that I first saw this done. Jack hooked the tube up to the engine, stuck the other end into his water source (an old teapot), and opened the valve. The steam hissed and gurgled in the water until there was no more pressure. Then, as if by magic, the water level in the teapot started to drop as water was sucked into the boiler. It's a great system, simple and sure. The disadvantage is that you have to drop the fire first.

At the end of a run, it's a good idea to leave the blowdown open and the throttle closed until the engine has fully cooled. This will prevent the vacuum from forming inside the boiler and possibly pulling in oil from the lubricator.

Filler valves

The ability to put water into the boiler while it is under pressure is a good thing. In this way, the engine can be kept in steam indefinitely. But to do this, you must use a valve that will let

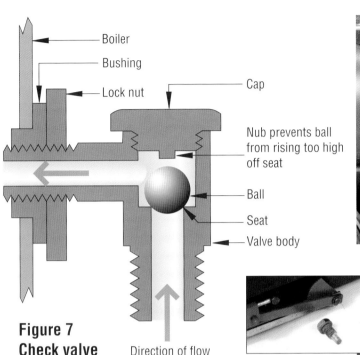

Boiler

Bushing

Lock nut

Cap

Nub prevents ball from rising too high off seat

Ball

Seat

Valve body

Figure 7
Check valve

Direction of flow

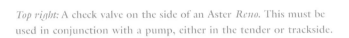

Top right: A check valve on the side of an Aster *Reno.* This must be used in conjunction with a pump, either in the tender or trackside.

Centre: A Goodall valve, just behind the dome on this Salem Steam Models 0-4-0T, can be used, in conjunction with a plastic syringe or filler tube, to inject water into a boiler under pressure.

Inset: The Goodall valve out of the engine. A silicone tube around the bottom end of the valve expands to admit water.

Lower: Graham Stowell used an Enots valve on this engine. This proprietary valve has been adapted to live-steam use.

the water pass in one direction, but not the other – a one-way valve. There are three types of one-way valve in use today on small-scale steam locomotives.

The traditional valve is called a check valve (figure 7). A check valve (sometimes two) is fitted to the boiler with a water line coming into it. It might be fitted to one or both sides of the boiler, or it might be fitted to the backhead. Inside the valve is a ball on a seat. Pressure from the boiler keeps the ball firmly on its seat, preventing any backflow. When water is pumped into the boiler, the line pressure will be higher than that of the boiler, which will force the ball off its seat, allowing water to pass into the boiler.

A check valve is a simple, reliable device. However, if hard water has been used in the locomotive, mineral deposits can build up inside the valve, interfering with its function. Also, if an engine has been left standing for months or years, the ball can get stuck to its seat and refuse to work. If you are

steaming an engine that is new to you or that has been sitting for a long time, make sure the check valve is in good order by pumping some water through it with the engine cold. If it rattles a little, chances are it's OK.

Another common valve is known as the Goodall valve, after Deryck Goodall, who developed and commercialized it. This valve is similar to the silicone-tube safety valve mentioned earlier, only inverted. It is mounted in the top of the boiler with the silicone-wrapped stem inside. Water is forced through the

The whistle on this Archangel *Jack* 0-4-2T occupies a prominent place right in the open cab. Strangely, it is controlled by a screw-type valve.

Every toy engine worth its salt must have a whistle. This one, with its nicely turned wooden handle, is atop an early Carette engine.

The long, horizontal tank under the cab on this Hugh Saunders coal-fired 2-6-2T is actually a whistle. It is actuated by a spring-loaded valve in the cab.

valve, usually with a large plastic syringe or a tube from a pump bottle that fits snugly into the valve, expanding the silicone tube and allowing water into the boiler. The pressure in the syringe must overcome the boiler pressure.

The last valve is a proprietary product called an Enots valve. This is a fitting into which a plastic tube from a pump-action water bottle can be inserted and water pumped into the boiler. The fitting holds the plastic tube securely until it is manually released.

Blower valve

The blower valve is simply the valve that controls an engine's blower (see the chapter on boilers). This is a screw-type valve, similar to common throttle valves, that lets a variable amount of steam into the blower pipe as necessary. Needless to say, if your engine has no blower, neither will it have a blower valve!

Whistles

Not a lot can be said about whistles on garden-scale engines. This is one thing that, because of the laws of physics, just can't be scaled down. If the sound of a whistle could be scaled, it would probably be out of the range of human hearing. And if we could hear it, we wouldn't like it.

In many parts of the world, full-size locomotives had high pitched, single-chime whistles, often called 'peanut whistles.' In the USA, particularly on larger, modern steam locomotives, the whistles were deep throated and multi-chimed.

Many toy and model locomotives were and are supplied with whistles. A tiny whistle that sits atop the boiler is nearly

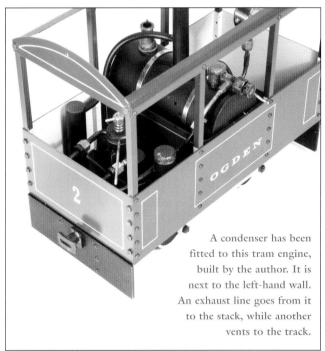

A condenser has been fitted to this tram engine, built by the author. It is next to the left-hand wall. An exhaust line goes from it to the stack, while another vents to the track.

useless. When it sounds at all, it gives a high-pitched screech that sets one's teeth on edge. Often, it just gurgles and hisses, especially if cold. When the steam hits a cold whistle it just condenses into water.

A whistle that will produce a more acceptable tone (but rarely one that sounds anything like a full-size whistle) must be considerably larger. These whistles, also single chimed, are sometimes tucked under a running board, disguised as an air tank, or hidden between the frames. These horizontal whistles should have their mouths pointing down at the track to let the

condensate escape. When they are blown, steam comes out of the most surprising places.

Having maligned most small-scale whistles, I must mention the work of Larry Bangham, of California. Larry, a professional musician, has taken on the task of researching, designing, and producing deep-toned, multi-chime whistles for garden-scale locomotives that sound fairly prototypical. He uses a resonating chamber with the whistle to deepen its tone, much like blowing across the top of a bottle. His results, when applied to large, American-style locomotives, are remarkable.

Condensers

While not a boiler fitting *per se*, a condenser is sometimes seen on little engines. After a run, your engine will probably look like it has come through a rain of oil, which, in fact, it has. Steam mixed with cylinder oil is exhausted from the stack and it usually falls upon the engine and rolling stock, leaving them an oily mess. A way to minimize this is through the use of a condenser.

Not all engines can have them fitted, as they take up space and must be plumbed into the exhaust line. Often, there simply isn't room for one or, if there is, it might do more harm than good. The *Frank S.* has one built into the smokebox. It has a cap on the top and you must use a syringe to drain it. It partially covers the flue and makes it difficult to view the fire. Many people consider this condenser to be a nuisance and they remove it.

I built a small tram engine that did not have a condenser. As with most engines, the exhaust was just piped up the stack. This engine has an enthusiastic lubricator and, at the end of the day, the engine's roof is sloppy with oil.

On a second, similar engine, I decided to add a condenser. I didn't want the hassle of having to drain it at the end of the run, so I gave it two outlets. One exhausts to the stack, while a second line simply empties to the track. In use, the oily exhaust steam enters the condenser, where the heavier oil separates and falls to the track (along with some of the steam), while the cleaner exhaust steam goes out the stack. The result was an amazingly clean engine at the end of the run, with the added bonus of visible steam coming from the track vent as well as the stack on cool days.

Above: An Aster JNR 2-6-0 with a full head of steam, owned by Rich Maul, is ready for a day of work on the author's railway.

Below: The driver stands by his early Roundhouse *Dylan* as his train pauses at Gatorbone Halt.

Chapter 10
Feedwater systems

If your boiler should run dry, any number of problems might be created. At the least, it's bad form and you'll spend a long time living it down. At the worst, serious damage to the boiler or other parts of the locomotive might be caused. This is something you really *don't* want to do. If your engine has no way of accepting water while the boiler is under pressure, you have no choice but to shut it down between runs. However, if you can add water to the working boiler, you can keep your engine in steam indefinitely.

There are a few different ways of getting water into a boiler under pressure. Some were discussed in the chapter on boiler fittings (vacuum tap, Goodall valve, Enots valve). Those that remain involve pumps.

External pumps

Some locomotives, particularly small ones, do not carry a pump onboard. However, they may be fitted with a check valve through which water can be pumped by an external pump (see the chapter on boiler fittings). If this is the case, the end of the

An Aster trackside pump, seen here ready to fill the boiler of the company's SNCF 232 tank engine. The fitting on the exterior of the engine is plumbed to a check valve near the backhead.

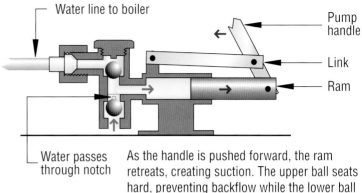

Water line to boiler · Pump handle · Link · Ram

Water passes through notch

As the handle is pushed forward, the ram retreats, creating suction. The upper ball seats hard, preventing backflow while the lower ball lifts, admitting water into the pump cavity.

Water level in tank shown low for clarity. Ordinarily, the pump would be entirely submerged.

Above: The not-very-photogenic tube on the floor of the cab of this Archangel *Rheidol* is the balance pipe between the two side tanks, allowing the pump in one tank to drain both.

Right: This hand pump is fitted in the side tank of Hugh Saunders' Alco 2-6-2T. The handle, projecting upwards, is removable.

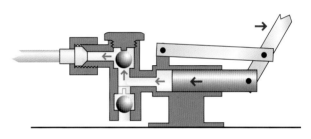

Figure 1
Tender pump
(Drawing not to scale)

When the handle is pulled back, the ram advances, creating pressure in the system. The lower ball seats, preventing backflow into the tank, while the upper ball lifts to let water into the feed line.

line opposite the check valve will have a fitting (usually threaded) to which the external pump can be attached. An external hand pump is usually permanently attached to the bottom of a receptacle, which might be nothing more than a tin can. The receptacle is filled with distilled water, the line from the pump is attached to the locomotive, and the water is pumped in. Aster used to offer a very nice external pump mounted in a brass tank. The external-pump system is both unsightly and inconvenient, but sometimes it's necessary.

Tender or tank pumps
Full-size locomotives carry additional water in tanks. On smaller (full size) engines, these tanks are part of the locomotive itself, in the form of side tanks, saddle tanks, well tanks, pannier tanks, and so forth. Larger engines have their tank in a separate car that they drag along, called a tender. More sophisticated model engines can function in the same way.

On a locomotive with working side tanks, a pump may be fitted inside one of the tanks. Since the tanks are separated from each other, for that single pump to be able to drain both tanks, the tanks must be connected somehow. This is usually done through a balance pipe – a pipe that runs

A saddle tank is not conducive to a hand pump. On this Hugh Saunders *Edward Thomas*, the pump is mounted in the cab. You can just see its green handle.

under the boiler or through the cab to connect the tanks. A hatch in the tank can be opened to reveal the pump and a detachable handle is used to pump the water into the boiler through a check valve.

Locomotives that have other types of tanks – saddle tanks, for instance – that do not allow a pump to be carried within, can have a pump mounted on the footplate or in some other convenient place, that can be plumbed into the tank.

Tender locomotives can utilize the whole of the tank part of the tender (that part that doesn't carry fuel) for water. A pump will often reside in the back of the tank, accessed through a hinged or lift-off hatch. Again, a detachable pump handle is used. Some model locomotives are built to carry the handle right on the engine.

Axle pumps
All of the above systems require you to stop the train to refill the boiler. This is time consuming and unprototypical. Full-size locomotives keep their boilers full on the fly, and so do most higher-end model locomotives. This is done with a pump mounted on a driven axle so that, as the engine runs, it is constantly pumping water.

In order that the boiler not be overfilled, an ingenious system of valves and plumbing is used. A bypass valve will be mounted somewhere on the engine, usually near the backhead or under the footplate. When the valve is fully closed, all pumped water goes into the boiler. When it is fully open, all pumped water is returned to the tank or tender. The trick is to learn your locomotive well enough to know how much to open the valve under various conditions so that the pump will keep the boiler topped up to its optimum level, while returning the excess water to the tank. This takes practice, experience, and a sound working knowledge of your engine.

All engines fitted with axle pumps will also have a hand pump. This is so that water can be added while the engine is standing or if the axle pump fails for some reason.

Injectors
Full-size locomotives use injectors to maintain the water level in their boilers. This system uses the energy from boiler steam

Above: A pump is mounted in the tender of this Aster *Reno*. Aster supplies a beautifully turned pump handle with its engines, but a piece of old brass tubing works just as well.

Below: Mike Gaskin fitted an axle pump to his 4-8-2. The eccentric driving the pump is on the second axle; the pump itself is above axles three and four.

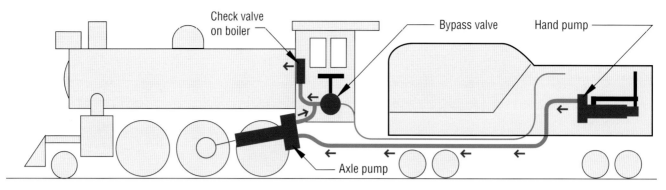

Check valve on boiler — Bypass valve — Hand pump

Axle pump

With the bypass valve closed, water from the pumps is forced into the boiler.

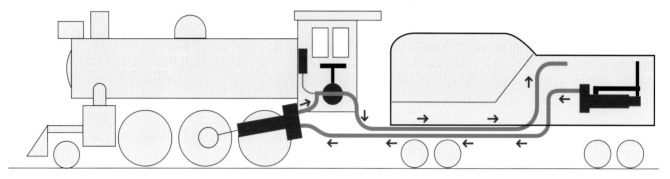

With the bypass valve open, water from the pumps is returned to the tender.

Figure 2
Axle-pump plumbing schematic

As with most things concerning little steam engines, there is more than one way to accomplish the goal. In this diagram, the hand and axle pumps are in the same hydraulic circuit, but they could be separate.

This unusual, external crosshead pump is on an Archangel coal-fired *Jack*.

to add water to the boiler in a way that almost defies belief. Although injectors small enough to work on our little engines have been built, they tend to be problematic and are rarely used on locomotives so small. Because of that, they will not be further addressed here. If you'd like to learn more about them, they have been fully covered in the older model-engineering books.

Above: An Archangel *Taw* takes its goods train past a crumbling concrete tool shed on a cold winter's day.

Below: Peregrin is a pot-boilered locomotive based on Archangel practice, built by Mike Horner.

Chapter 11
Sundries

In this final chapter of the technical section of this book, I'd like to touch on some miscellaneous topics in no particular order. These pertain to aspects of little steam engines not fully discussed elsewhere.

Running on air and running in

It is sometimes desirable to run an engine without the benefit of steam. When building a kit or even a scratchbuilt chassis, it's always good to know if the steam mechanism works before going so far beyond it that it requires a lot of effort to get back to that stage to fix any problem that might arise.

The most common way of testing an engine or chassis is by using compressed air. For this you need an air source. This can be as basic as a bicycle pump or as elaborate as an air compressor. The latter is often more convenient, but the former will give you more control over the pressure. Of course, you can't expect to run the chassis continuously with a bicycle pump.

You must have a way of attaching the engine to the air source. If you are working with a bare chassis, the steam line to the cylinders is often your best bet. A rubber hose slipped over the end of it, secured with a piece of wire, is all you may need. If the engine is complete, it's usually easiest to pressurize the boiler, then use the engine's cab controls to run the mechanism. I have made a set of fittings, one of which will fit almost any engine I come across. I can screw one of these into the boiler in place of the safety valve, sealing

Opposite page: A *Ruby* undergoing an air test on the stand.

This page:
Top: A variety of adapters, made over the years as necessary, for air testing different engines.

Centre: Locomotives can be run stationary on rollers. This set was made for a specific locomotive and is not adjustable.

Lower: An adjustable wooden test stand, made by the author. The balks are moveable and can be arranged to prop up just about any engine.

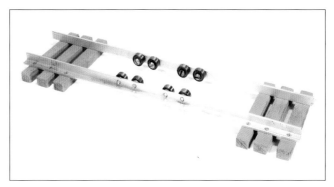

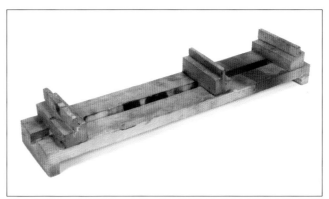

it with some Teflon tape or on O-ring. The rubber hose slips over the end.

The chassis or locomotive can be propped up so that its wheels are in the air, or it can be run on a roller stand. If the engine is sprung, it is sometimes better for its weight to be on its wheels, so that the springs can function properly. On a rigid-chassis locomotive, though, it doesn't matter too much. I made an adjustable wooden stand that can be set to fit just about any engine that comes along.

When powering a bare chassis on air, especially a new one or one that you're not familiar with, take care not to put too much air to it all at once. If you have a compressor with a regulator on it, set it at around 10psi to start with, then gradually move it up if you need to. If you put too high a pressure to an engine that may have mechanical problems (bad timing or problems with the rods, for instance), you could damage the mechanism in a heartbeat, creating untold amounts of unnecessary work and tears. If your compressor doesn't have a regulator, use a rubber tube for the air supply. Just bend it until it kinks, choking off the air. Then you can carefully and slowly unkink it, allowing a little air into the cylinders, until you know what's going to happen.

Likewise, don't run any proven engine on too much air. These little engines will run at astonishing speeds and can do themselves an injury if you're not careful.

Running on air, especially at slow speeds, has a variety of uses. You can find tight spots in the works, as the mechanism will tend to stop at the same place each revolution. You can check your valve timing by running the engine first in forward, then in reverse. If the speeds are equal, chances are the valves are set correctly. I have sometimes used a cheap tachometer from the auto-parts store to check speeds in both directions.

A new engine will often need some running in. Although not as common today, in days past, even commercial engines from the finest builders required a good break-in period. Scratchbuilt locomotives almost always need some running in. A good engine will be made to very tight tolerances and will naturally have some stiffness. I have seen locomotives that, when new, will not move themselves at all. The combined friction of the tight joints prevents them. These same engines,

after a suitable period of breaking in, become silky smooth in operation.

To run in an engine or chassis, first thoroughly lubricate it. This is one time when you can be generous with the oil. You need to be certain that every moving joint is well lubricated, and that includes the inside of the cylinders, too. If you are working with just a chassis, squirt some oil down the steam line. At this juncture, lightweight machine oil is fine – you don't need steam oil yet.

Once everything is lubricated, get the engine propped up or on rollers. Apply enough air to get the chassis running. You want it going well, but not so fast that you risk damaging it. Then just let it run for a while, checking the lubrication from time to time. Stay with it – don't let it run alone. You need to be there if something should come loose or otherwise go wrong. As the engine runs, it will gradually loosen up. The wheels should roll over easily by hand.

Once all seems well under air pressure, you can try it under steam (if the engine is complete). You'll find that the engine behaves differently under steam than under air, this being due

Above: All moving parts of the engine should be lubricated with a lightweight machine oil.

Left: A syringe is being used to remove the water from this displacement lubricator.

Opposite: Once empty, the lubricator can be filled with proper steam oil.

to the differing properties of the two media. Again, run the engine stationary. It might be pretty lumpy, but keep at it. In time it will loosen up, if all else is well.

If it seems like it will never loosen up, perhaps there is another problem. This could be misalignment of rods, a joint too tight, a hole slightly misplaced, or something similar. There comes a point in the testing when you must decide that an external problem is keeping the engine from performing up to snuff, then find and fix it.

Finally comes the track test. If the engine has been running pretty well on blocks, you might just find that it runs very well indeed on the track. When on blocks or rollers, the engine doesn't have the benefit of its own weight to smooth out the minor lumps via momentum. Most new engines continue to improve until they reach an optimum point. After that, they should be good for years until they finally begin to wear out.

General notes on care and feeding

A well-made miniature steam locomotive is a pretty tough critter. I have seen engines that were shockingly abused that still ran splendidly. However, it's just common sense that a well-cared-for engine will last a lot longer than one that isn't. Caring for a steam engine, especially a little one, is neither difficult nor onerous. A little time before and after a run is all it takes.

To get an engine ready for a run, it needs, first, to be well lubricated. 'Well' lubricated doesn't mean generously lubricated. Tiny drops of oil in the right spots are all that's required. Despite your best efforts, your engine will probably become quite oily after a while anyway, but you should try to minimize this. Oil becomes a magnet for dirt and abrasive grit, an engine's enemies.

Provide a soft surface on which to lay your engine, either on its side or (preferably) on its top. Fine models with a lot of detail on them are more difficult to handle, so you'll have to develop your own procedures to best accomplish this task. Once the underside is exposed, put a tiny drop of lightweight machine oil (3-in-One is fine; WD-40 is not) on each moving joint. I like to put a drop on the valve rods and piston rods, as well. Some people recommend that this be done before every run. I suggest common sense. You can often just look and see if a joint still has lubrication on it. Don't forget to oil

Above: If an engine has no auxiliary water storage, water is let directly into the boiler.

Left: This engine carries water in its tender. Inside the water tank is a pump for transferring water to the boiler.

Opposite: A removable pump handle is used to actuate the pump.

the moving parts in the cab, too, including valves, reversing levers, and the like.

Once the engine has been oiled, you can service the lubricator. Either drain or suck out any water and replace it with proper steam oil.

Then it's time to fill the boiler. This should be with distilled water only. Tap water in many areas contains minerals that will, at best, cloud your water glass and, at worst, clog your plumbing (I've seen it). Rainwater used to be considered acceptable, and may still be in some areas, but in areas of high pollution, I'd think twice about it, as the pollution clings to

rain droplets as they fall. Water from a de-humidifier can be used. De-ionized water is said to cause problems, so best stay away from it, too.

Boilers are commonly filled with syringes through filler plugs or safety-valve holes. If you have no water glass, fill the boiler to its top, noting how much you've put in. Then remove about a third. The next time, if you're filling from empty, you'll know how much to put in. If the boiler is already partially full, you'll know how much to remove when it's filled all the way. If your boiler has to be filled with a hand pump, you'll either be able to tell how much is in it via the

water glass or, through experience, you'll know how much water your engine takes and when to add it.

Once all else is ready, the engine can be fuelled.

Fuelling and firing an alcohol-burning engine

Care must be exercised when using alcohol. It ignites readily and can pose a danger if spilled. Also, it's not uncommon to see an over-filled burner dripping flaming meths on everything below. This can be quite exciting and has been responsible for the destruction of any amount of plastic track. Wooden ties (sleepers) fare better. On my own railway, you don't have to look far to find charred wood.

Carefully fill the fuel tank with a syringe and appropriate-size tubing, either rubber or brass. Most alcohol tanks have either an overflow pipe or a large enough filler hole that you can see the level, say in a chicken-feed system. When the tank is full, or meths starts to come out the overflow, move the engine. If alcohol has been spilled on the track, roll the engine forward, away from any spilled meths. If on the bench, put the engine on the track.

If your engine is internally fired, put a suction fan in the stack and turn it on before lighting the fire. Some people like those butane barbecue 'matches' to light their fires. I find them problematic and prefer to use an old-fashion igniter – a bit of wick material on the end of a wire. I dip the wick in meths and light it with a match. It's hard to blow out, even in a strong wind. Then I insert the igniter between the wheels, under the firebox, or wherever the engine's wicks happen to be. An old dental mirror is a handy tool to help determine if all the wicks are lit and the state of the fire in general.

On internally fired engines, when pressure comes up to around 20psi, the fan can be removed and the engine's blower turned on. Don't turn it up too high. It doesn't take much to draw the fire. Pressure should come up rapidly from that point.

If you're a complete Luddite, like I am, and you rebel at using an electrically powered fan to bring your live-steam locomotive

Opposite: The engine's fuel tank is filled with alcohol. Note the attractive blue hue. Meths should be tinted (if it isn't already) to prevent mistaking it for water.

Above: To draw the fire through a cold boiler, an electric fan in the smoke stack is used. Here, the fire is being lit with an igniter. The alcohol flame in sunlight is invisible.

Inset: A homemade igniter – a bit of wicking on a stout copper rod – is the best implement for lighting meths fires.

Centre left: The state of a meths-fired engine's burner can be checked with a dental mirror.

Centre right: The pressure-gauge's needle is off the peg. Soon the fan can be removed and the engine's blower turned on.

Lower: Burning meths can spill, so keep a sharp eye out and be prepared for grass fires.

89

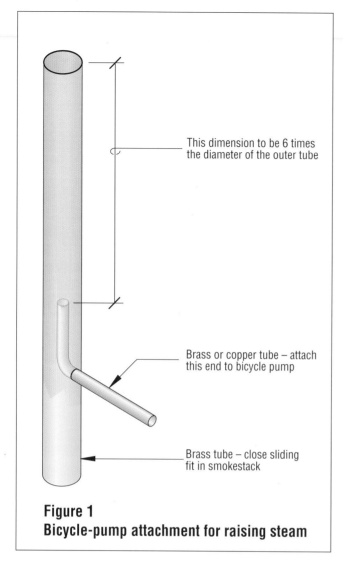

This dimension to be 6 times the diameter of the outer tube

Brass or copper tube – attach this end to bicycle pump

Brass tube – close sliding fit in smokestack

Figure 1
Bicycle-pump attachment for raising steam

make steam. This is called priming and it has ruined many a good shirt. Engines react differently. With experience, you'll know how much water is good for yours.

Finally, the engine will show signs of life. It will lurch forward a few times before finally clearing the cylinders and moving smoothly off. Be prepared for a sudden spurt of speed at this point.

Some engines, seemingly inexplicably, are much better behaved than others. When their pressure is up and the throttle is opened, they move smoothly off without a murmur.

During the run, if your engine is so equipped, you'll want to add water and fuel. Generally speaking, fuel will need to be added more often than water. When adding water, don't dump a lot of cold water into the boiler at once or you may lose pressure. When adding alcohol, do so with extreme care, and have a water bucket handy in case of fire.

Once the run has been deemed complete, let the engine cool down some on a siding. Make sure the throttle is closed so that the boiler won't draw oil from the lubricator into itself as it cools. If your engine has a blower, you can open it to equalize the pressure in the boiler. Then take the engine to the bench and give it a nice wipe down with a soft rag. When the engine is still warm, that's the best time to wipe it down, and it's a satisfying activity. Drain, siphon off, or otherwise dispose of any remaining fuel. The lubricator can be drained and refilled, or left for next time. There is some controversy as to whether water should be left in the boiler. I don't find anything wrong with leaving some water in, as long as the engine won't be exposed to freezing temperatures. Once the engine is fully cool and clean, it can be returned to its pride of place on the mantle piece.

Fuelling and firing a gas-burning engine

The care and feeding of gas-fired engines is much the same as with meths-fired locomotives, with a few differences. When fuelling up, make sure the gas-control valve is closed. Most engines today have self-venting filler valves on them. You merely place the nipple of the supply tank onto that of the filler valve (via an adapter, if necessary) and push down. Both valves will open and the gas will transfer from the higher pressure supply tank into the empty fuel tank. This takes place in liquid form (butane under pressure turns to liquid). You'll see a little gas leaking out as you fill (which is why you want to fill your engines away from any fire, including other engines in steam). This is normal. When the tank is full, a lot of gas will come sputtering out. Then you're ready to go.

Some engines don't seem to have self-venting valves (Regner, for instance). With these, it sometimes helps to open the control valve slightly to relieve pressure in the tank.

Getting the gas from its original container into the engine's gas tank can be problematic. Ronson (and other) lighter refills often come with a variety of plastic nipples, one of which will probably fit your engine's inlet valve. However, this is an expensive way to buy gas. Larger put-ups from camping-supply stores or Asian groceries (where they are used for table-top braziers) are a better way to go. But to use these, you'll need an adapter. If you are

to life, you can do as they did in the old days, and use a bicycle pump with a special attachment that fits in the stack (figure 1). I have done this and it works surprisingly well. You have to have patience and be willing to spend the time. The plunger is slowly depressed – again, it doesn't take a lot to draw the fire. When you hit the bottom, you rapidly raise it and repeat the process, keeping a steady flow of air going. In this way you bring the engine to life by your own hand, which I find gratifying.

Once steam is up, you're ready to go. With most engines, when you open the throttle, the steam rushes into the cold cylinders and immediately condenses into water. The cylinders must be cleared and warmed before the engine will perform properly. To do this, gently roll the engine backward and forward, shutting the throttle and adjusting the reverse lever (if your engine has one) with each direction change. If your engine seems to lock up (more common on piston-valve engines), it's best not to force it. Try just opening the throttle a little and moving the reverse lever back and forth. Full-size locomotives have drain cocks on the cylinders to help alleviate this problem. Some of our little engines do, too, but most do not.

If you've over-filled the boiler, all you'll get is a jet of water out the stack until the level drops enough for the engine to

Right: Butane comes in a variety of different cans. To transfer the liquid gas to the locomotive, an adapter like the one shown here is necessary.

Far right: To transfer the gas, all that's necessary is to invert the gas can, mate the adapter tip to the filler valve, and press.

Lower: When the gas tank is full, liquid gas will spurt out around the valve.

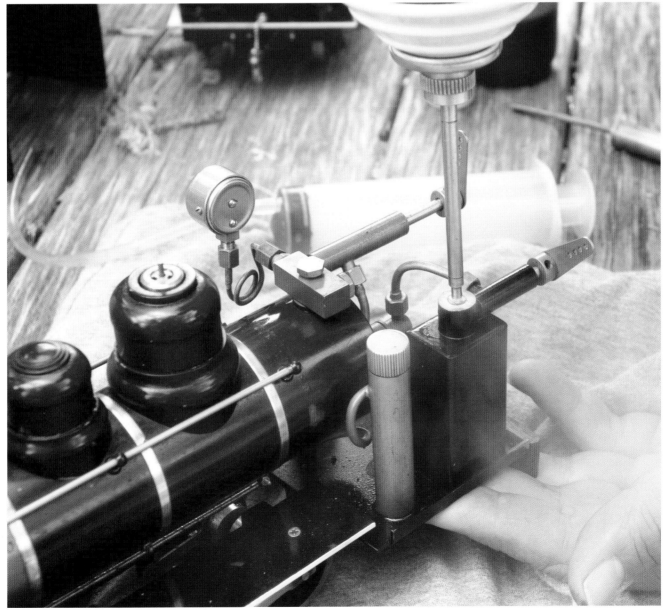

Above: Gas-fired burners are often lit at the smokebox door or the top of the stack.

Left: A properly burning fire will be above (or below) the burner at the back of the flue.

handy with a lathe, you can probably make your own. Otherwise, the trade can usually supply you with something that will work.

Also, the supply tank must be warmer than the receiving tank. If you've been running on a cold day and your supply tank has been left out, while the engine's tank has heated nicely next to the boiler, you'll have a great deal of difficulty getting the gas to transfer.

Some gas-fired locomotives are lit by opening the smokebox door. This is good because you can actually look inside and see the fire burning to make sure that it is burning atop (or below, as the case may be) the burner, and not in front of

it. Other engines, though, are lit at the stack or under the smokebox. Read the manual.

To light your engine, slowly open the gas valve until you can hear the gas flowing at the stack. These valves are often very touchy, so this may take a little practice. Put a lit match near the ignition point. The gas usually ignites with a pop, then, if all is well, it will flash back into the burner tube, where it burns with a low roar. If you are new at this, ask someone with experience to stand by to make sure the burner is behaving as it should.

If the gas is turned up too high, the fire may not ignite; may not flash back, burning at the stack; or may only partially

Top right: The smokebox and flues must be cleaned at the beginning or end of each run.

Lower right: In the jar is charcoal nuggets soaking in kerosene (paraffin), which is used to get the fire going. In front is the actual anthracite grains.

Below: A special set of tools is required for coal firing. From to to bottom, these are a flue brush for cleaning the flues; a rake to agitate the fire and clear any clinker; a poker, also to encourage the fire; and a shovel.

flash back, burning in the smokebox or ahead of the burner in the flue. The latter poses the greatest hazard to the locomotive, especially with inexperienced drivers, as the fire will seemed to have flashed back when it hasn't. I've actually seen steam raised in engines with the fire burning in the smokebox, before the smokebox door finally melted. At best, your paint will become blistered or discoloured. With experience, you'll know when the fire is where it should be.

With gas-fired locomotives, fuel cannot be safely added without shutting off the fire, so don't try. While running, keep a close eye (and ear) on the fire. If the engine runs out of water first, be aware of it and shut off the fire immediately. In an alcohol-fired engine, you risk ruining the paint if the boiler runs dry. With a gas-fired engine, you risk ruining the boiler, which is considered by most to be bad form.

When refilling a gas-fired locomotive, take it well away from any open flame. Several times at the Diamondhead steamup I've watched while fellows refilled their engines on the track. As soon as another train passed on the adjoining track, all of the gas that leaked out and settled ignited, with predictable results. Some people never learn.

Shutting down a gas-fired engine is much the same as a meths engine. For safety's sake, you should probably release any gas left in the tank, as many of these little tanks are not 100% gas tight and gas could leak out in small quantities, causing a potential hazard.

Fuelling and firing a coal-burning engine
Surprisingly, coal doesn't burn easily. You can hold a match to a lump of coal all day and never set it alight.

You can't just fill the firebox with coal, light a match, and expect results.

To get a coal fire going, you must first build a fire of charcoal. Put some chunks of charcoal between some sheets of newspaper and beat it with a hammer until it has degenerated into pea-size pieces. To avoid the mess of crushing your own charcoal, you might find charcoal already crushed at your local garden centre, for use in growing African violets. Soak these nuggets at least overnight in kerosene or lamp oil and you're ready to go. This will ignite readily.

Some people prefer to soak their charcoal in meths. I don't like this, as the meths always seems to go everywhere and a

Left: With the fire going well, coal can be gradually added to it.

Lower: Although the smoke looks great, this is just the kerosene burning off. Anthracite produces little smoke, but a wonderful smell.

Opposite: A steaming bay with an open space under the rails is a handy place to service locomotives. This one is on David Pinniger's Ambledown Valley Railway. The engine in the bay, *Princess Hester*, is a Jack Wheldon rebuild.

D.B. Pinniger

meths fire is invisible in sunlight. Cab fires are common with this, and its easy to transfer the fire, via an invisibly burning shovel, to your container of meths-soaked charcoal. Also, the meths tends to burn off much more quickly, giving the charcoal less chance to ignite. Kerosene will give you more grime in your flues and smokebox, but I still prefer it.

Filling the firebox is always tricky. Ideally, you should have a round-back shovel. A square back tends to snag when you are trying to remove it from the firebox. Fill the firebox full with charcoal, right up to the bottom of the firehole. Before you stick the last shovelful in, put the fan in the stack, turn it on, and set the last shovelful of kerosene-soaked charcoal alight. It will then ignite everything in the firebox nicely.

Close the firebox door and wait for things to happen, adding charcoal from time to time, if necessary. Keep the fire door closed as much as possible between shovels of charcoal or coal, and especially when you are trying to get the coal to ignite from the charcoal. This will prevent cold air from coming in and destroying the draft and, hence, the fire. Once pressure comes up to 20psi or so, you can turn on the engine's blower and remove the fan. Pressure will continue to rise. Charcoal burns quickly, so keep your eye on the fire.

Once you've got a good, red fire going, add a few lumps of coal. If you add too much, you can smother the fire at this point. If you don't add enough, the charcoal will burn away and you'll have to start over. As you gradually change over from charcoal to coal, the atmosphere will begin to take on a pleasant, railroady aroma, one that cannot be duplicated by any other means.

As more coal is added to the fire, make sure it is evenly spread in the firebox. Holes in the fire let in cold air. Add one shovel full to the middle of the fire, one to the left, and one to the right. Make this a habit of good firing. By now, the

safety valve may have blown (several times!). To keep boiler pressure more manageable, add water to the boiler with the hand pump from time to time, which will cool things down and maintain a reasonable water level. Also, you might turn the blower down a bit to lessen the intensity of the fire.

Finally, the boiler will be running entirely on coal. Add a last scoop or so, topping up the fire to the bottom of the fire hole, check the water, and off you go. Most little coal burners will run for five to ten minutes or so unattended, though some will run longer. You must keep a constant eye on the water. A locomotive-type boiler has less water space because of all those flues and the large firebox. Keep an eye on the fire, too, and add coal as necessary. 'Little and often' is a good rule of thumb. If pressure drops while the engine is in motion, open the blower a little. Once you get the hang of it, you can keep your engine in steam all day long. Fantastic!

At the end of the run are a few tasks, as well. You can drop the fire, literally dropping the grate onto the track, or you can just turn off the blower and open the fire door, which will kill the fire fairly quickly. Blow down the boiler with its blowdown valve. When the engine is cool, remove the ashpan and grate to clean the ashes and clinkers out of the firebox. Sweep out the flues, the smokebox, and the firebox. You might also spray the running gear with WD-40 to remove any grit, then wipe it down and re-oil it with proper machine oil. Give the whole engine a good wipe-down and you're ready for the next session.

The steaming bay

A handy thing to have for steaming up is a proper steaming bay. As one who does not have one, I can attest to its usefulness! The steaming bay is nothing more than an elevated siding in which the rails float free in the air, so to speak, being supported

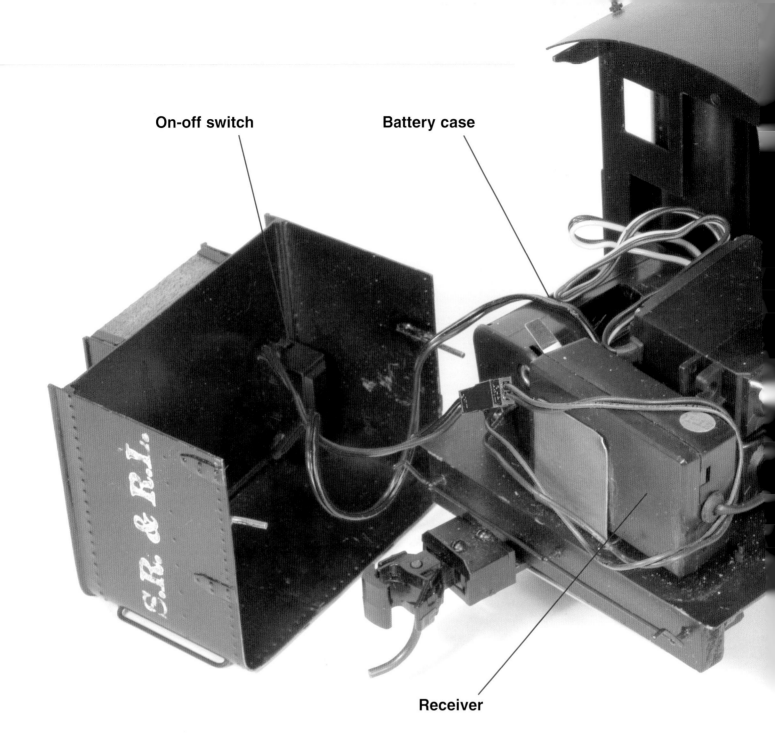

On-off switch

Battery case

Receiver

only on their ends. Regular rail is too flimsy for this task, so small angle iron is often used in place of the rails here.

The bay itself is a sort of three-sided pit over which the rails cross. With no ties or sleepers to act as obstructions, free access to the underside of the locomotive is provided, making it much easier to service the engine, light its fire, check on its status, and so forth. If you have no steaming bay, you can tend your engine like I do, on tables or blocks, then inelegantly carry it to the track when it is ready to light up.

Learning your engine
Every steam locomotive is different from every other. Even engines from the same mass-produced batch will have slightly different characteristics from their siblings. Given this fact, to get the most out of your engine and become skilled at running it, you must get to know it intimately, including all of its faults and virtues. Once you succeed in doing this, you and your locomotive become a smooth-acting team. What follows are just a few of the things you'll need to learn.

The optimum water level in the boiler is not a thing that should be left to chance. If there's too much in there, your engine will cough and spit; if too little, you risk using it up before the fuel is gone. Once you get to know your engine, you'll be able to tell how much water is left by the way the engine acts. A loco that is extremely lively, only to suddenly lose all enthusiasm, but then quickly revive again

Servos

The radio gear is carried in the bunker. Some engines lend themselves well to R/C while others cannot be radio controlled at all.

is surely low on water – perhaps very low. On the other hand, I have engines that, if the water level is too high, even though all else seems well, will not raise steam above 20psi. Once the level drops some, the pressure will come up nicely.

On internally alcohol-fired engines, the state of the boiler and the fire are intimately intertwined. Some engines, if running light, need the blower to be cracked open to keep the fire strong. Once a train has been attached, the blower can be closed when under way. Through practice, you'll learn how to get the best performance.

On single flue, gas-fired engines, you'll want to learn the optimum level of the fire. It's always best to run with the

smallest fire possible. All too often I see people running their engines with raging fires and the safety valve blowing off all the time. This is wasteful of fuel and steam and you can even damage the smokebox with the excessive heat, not to say the boiler itself if you are so unlucky as to let the water run out. This is completely unnecessary, and a skilled driver will run his engine at maximum pressure just under blow-off, with the minimum amount of fire required to achieve that pressure.

Once steam is up, you'll need to know how your engine behaves with cold cylinders, and the best way to get them warmed up. You'll have to figure out the best combination of pushing, reversing, and fiddling.

Some engines are equipped with hand pumps, but no water glass, so there's no external way of knowing how much water is in the boiler. However, once you get to know your engine, it will tell you how much is there just by how it acts.

Watching an engineer and engine who have worked together for a long time is a joy. The engineer's actions are smooth, fluid, and minimal in nature. He knows just what to do to get the best from the engine. The engine performs flawlessly, with never a false move or irritable disposition. It's something to strive for.

Managing speed

Controlling an engine's speed can be done in different ways. Some engines are built for speed and are happiest when running flat out. Others, like narrow-gauge models, we like to see just creeping along. Shays and other geared engines run slowly naturally, but others do not.

The most obvious way to control speed is via the **engine's throttle or regulator**. However, on many engines, this is quite touchy and difficult to manage. The next best way is to tie a train onto the engine. After all, that's what it's intended for, right? I've seen the most spirited locomotives tamed by trains.

Some people have devised **special braking cars**. Some of these have adjustable, centrifugal braking devices inside that allow a top speed to be set. Others have rigged **devices that automatically adjust the throttle lever** as the train speeds up. I once read of a fellow who had an Archangel locomotive with a throttle lever that protruded through the back of the cab wall. He extended the lever handle upwards until it stuck up above the cab roof an inch or so. He had a hilly railway. To control the speed of the engine, he constructed gantries under which the engine ran. Special guides in the gantries would grab the extended throttle lever and open or close it a little, as dictated by the terrain. It seemed to work.

An **inertia car** is another possibility. This will have a large flywheel concealed in it, geared to the wheels via a high gear ratio. This creates drag when the engine is first starting, provides a load while the engine is running, and helps the engine to stop more gradually and prototypically.

Gauge-1 pioneer Victor Harrison devised a speed controller that used a small **air pump** connected to an axle in a piece of

This Argyle 0-4-4T Forney was supplied from the factory with radio control of the throttle and the reversing lever.

rolling stock. Air pressure produced by the pump, via linkages, opened and closed the throttle as needed.

And of course, there's **radio control.** Some people love it, some disdain it. I'm no great fan of it, although I confess to owning a few radio-controlled locomotives. I think that radio control is a legacy from our electric-train days, where it was a wonderful, magical thing to be able to control the train without touching it. For me, though, live steam is a different hobby altogether. It is interactive and hands on. I want to be there running the engine, with my finger on the throttle. A radio separates the driver and his engine. I know this attitude will be cause for disagreement and there is admittedly argument in favour of radio. Jack Verducci operates his railroad just like a full-size line, with all live-steam locomotives. All his locomotives are radio controlled, and it is unlikely that he could do what he does with manually controlled engines.

Radio-controlled locomotives generally use just two servos – one for the throttle/regulator and one for the reverser – although more can be added for other functions, such as blower and whistle. These servos are powered by batteries. Between the servos and the batteries is the receiver. Space must be found for all this equipment, preferably far enough from the heat that it won't be damaged. Servos are usually (but not always) mounted in the cab. Linkages must be

devised (if your engine was not supplied with them) to the locomotive's controls.

A transmitter is required, to talk to the receiver. This is a box, usually with a couple of handles and an antenna. Radio sets come in different frequencies, which is a good thing. You need to be operating on a different frequency from your neighbour so that his engine doesn't receive your commands. At large steam ups, there is a 'frequency board,' with all the frequencies listed and a clothes pin for each. You take the clothes pin for your frequency and clip it to your antenna. If you go to the board and find no clothes pin for your frequency, that means it's in use and you'll have to wait.

On sophisticated engines, particularly those intended for high speed, you can actually 'notch up' the engine while it is running. This means to increase the cut-off (and the engine's efficiency) by moving the reversing lever towards the centre. Most people don't do this, though.

One of the big bugaboos associated with radio control, at least in the past, is 'glitching.' This is radio interference that causes erratic servo (and engine) behaviour. It is thought to come from the wheels contacting the rails, which creates radio noise. It can also be caused by nearby chain-link fences, metal buildings, other locomotives, and a host of other mysterious sources.

However, in recent times, new generations of radios have come onto the market that solve all of these problems. They have little computers in both the transmitters and receivers, so that they talk to each other. You can dial in whatever frequency you want to use (or is not being used by others). Glitching has become almost a thing of the past because the receiver is smart enough to know if what it has received is an actual command from its twinned transmitter or just some random evil signal.

Steam logs

The older I get the more I realize the importance of history. It has been said that you can't know where you're going if you don't know where you've been. The grand, and even not-so-grand, histories of the world have been pretty well documented, but what about our own trivial, personal histories? They are important to us, at least, and are worth keeping track of, one way or another. One of my favourite ways, as pertains to the more steamy aspects of our lives, is the steam log.

A steam log is used by few people. I've kept one for only around eight years, as this is being written, and have already found it to be invaluable as well as interesting. It works like this: On our Ogden Botanical Railway, every run or attempted run is logged in a book I made. This has been done since the loop was closed on the current OBR. The following entries are made for each run: The date; the driver's name; the engine being run; and comments about the run. In the margins I note which runs were made during special events or get-togethers. I am diligent to the point of obnoxiousness in getting drivers to sign the book. To date there are approximately 650 entries. Hence, I can go back and see that on October 5, 2002, Larry Herget ran a scratchbuilt 2-2-0, which had trouble with a switch and fell over, setting the foliage alight; or that, on May 26, 2003, Joe Crea got a fine run out of his Lindsay Shay after a hiatus of six years. So, not only is the log an historical account of the goings-on on the railway, it also makes great reading.

As I mentioned, few people seem to keep logs. One other I know who does is David Pinniger. However, his log takes a different form. He logs the different locomotives that have run on his line, not each run. David's log entries include the date, locomotive name, type, wheel arrangement, fuel, builder, and owner.

A steam log could also be a good way of recording a locomotive's performance as well as experimentation. Modifications can be made to the engine and the results noted for future reference.

You might give this some thought. It's probably not for everyone, but it is one more fun way to enjoy the hobby.

Shipping an engine

Having received a goodly number of miniature steam locomotives from around the world, and posted no small number, too, I have learned a few things about shipping them, especially from unfortunate experience. I never cease to be amazed at the faith some people put in the loving-kindness of the world's various postal authorities, evidently believing with heart and soul that if 'Handle with Care' is written on a box, that it will, in fact, be handled with care. I harbour the notion that, in the eyes of postal workers, 'Handle with Care' actually translates to 'See How Much Damage You Can Do Without Getting Caught.' At least, that is what is suggested by some of the packages I have received over the years. All is not lost, however, if you follow a few precautions and assume that all postal workers are lower life forms.

Preparing the engine. Much damage can be avoided just by preparing the engine properly for shipment. Most of this damage is a result of water left in the engine. I've received any number of locomotives with rusted rods and wheels or pitted paint from being trapped in wet plastic for days or weeks.

An obvious precaution is to empty the boiler. However, this is usually not enough. Even if all valves are tightly closed, any residual water will find a way out. What I do now, and what I ask those who ship engines me to do, is to remove the safety valve and light a fire in the engine after removing as much water from the boiler as possible. If you have a gas-fired engine, turn the fire down as low as it will go. I know this sounds like heresy, but it works. Keep a close eye on the boiler. As it heats up, residual water will boil off and come out the safety-valve hole as steam. As soon as the steam stops coming out, extinguish the fire and allow the engine to cool before replacing the valve. This will usually dry up any water left in the system.

If there has been water in the tender, drain it completely, work the pump back and forth to get as much water as possible out of the lines, and let the tender stand open for a few days. Cap off all water lines with plastic wrap and rubber bands as a precaution.

With meths-fired engines, all fuel must be drained from the tank. It's best to remove the wicks from their tubes, sealing them in a plastic sandwich bag for later re-insertion. Let the burner and tank sit open for a few days so all the alcohol can evaporate.

Remove as much oil from the lubricator as possible (as well as any residual water). Give the engine a good wipe down to remove any blobs of oil on the underside. A little loose oil generally won't hurt anything, but removing it makes for less cleanup at the other end of the trip. The engine should now be ready for shipping.

Packing. If your engine is a commercial model and you still have all of the packing and shipping materials it came with, you should be fairly safe in reusing them if they are still in good shape. With smaller engines, it's always a good idea to place the fully packed engine in a second box, surrounded on all sides with plastic peanuts. I have found this system capable of defeating the worst the post office can offer.

If you don't have the original packing material, which is often the case, here is a procedure that I like.

• Remove all the loose, small, fragile, or otherwise easily damaged pieces and pack them separately. These could include domes, lamps, cab roofs, pump handles, safety-valve covers, lubricator covers, etc., and may also include things that need to be unscrewed, like pilots on American engines. Wrap these bits tightly in plastic bubble wrap so that they are not in contact with each other and set them aside.

- Always wrap the loco and tender separately. If they are large, it might even be a good idea to pack them in separate boxes and ship them separately. Yes, the postage will be expensive, but compare that to your investment in the engine.
- Wrap the engine (and tender) in two or three layers of tissue paper. This is to prevent them from coming into contact with plastic. I have more than one locomotive that has a nice, symmetrical pattern of plastic bubbles permanently etched into its paintwork, evidently as the result of a chemical reaction between the paint and the plastic.
- Look at the 'skyline' of the top of the engine – stack, domes, sand boxes, etc. If there are gaps, fill them with small rolls of bubble wrap. If you want to do this before wrapping with tissue, wrap the bubble rolls in tissue, too. This evens out the shape of the engine.
- Wrap the engine tightly in *many* layers of bubble wrap. If using small bubbles, you'll want to increase the engine's dimensions by one-to-two inches all around. The loco should be inside a cocoon. If using large bubbles, go even bigger.
- Find a box that is several inches bigger all around than the coccooned loco. Put the engine in it on a bed of plastic peanuts and surround the engine with peanuts on all sides by at least two inches. Make sure that it is packed tightly. The odd bits that you packed earlier can be tucked into a corner. When closing the box, tape all exposed edges. Make sure everything is *tightly* packed. You should be able to shake the box and feel and hear nothing at all moving around inside.

If you follow this procedure, when the post office drops your box off the loading dock or kicks it into a truck, you'll have the last laugh.

Miniature Steam Locomotives as Investments

If you are considering the purchase of a little live-steam locomotive as an investment, you should abandon that notion immediately. While it is true that some locomotives have significantly appreciated in value over time – some startlingly so – most do not. You'll be lucky to keep up with inflation. This is especially true with the mass produced, workaday engines that were intended for actual use in the garden. If you want to invest money, see an investment counsellor. If you want to enjoy life in the garden, buy a live-steam locomotive.

Safety

Although this section is the last in this book, it is certainly one of the most important. Most safety precautions are just common sense, but it's surprising how often we seem to leave that behind.

Always be careful when dealing with fuels. Gas is heavier than air and will settle around your engine or around your feet. It can be ignited in an instant by a passing engine or someone else firing up. Always be conscious of what you and the people around you are doing, and always use gas properly in a ventilated space.

An alcohol fire is invisible in sunlight, so be careful around your engine, especially on hot days when the tank may have a tendency to bubble up or spill over. It's not unusual to encounter an invisible cab fire.

Always have a fire extinguisher or even a bucket of water handy, not only for engine fires, but for lineside fires caused by your engine. You never know when a patch of your garden might go up in flames.

Always give the safety valve a tweak before a run by grabbing the spindle with some thin-nose pliers and pulling it up. This is especially true with engines that have been sitting for a while, as the valves might stick.

Never run a used engine for the first time without having some assurance that the safety valve is set properly and that the boiler is sound. This assurance can often come from the previous owner. However, if your engine came from an unknown source (an auction, for instance), you owe it to yourself to do some tests before running it for the first time.

When operating your engine, consider wearing gloves to prevent burns. If you prefer not to wear gloves, at least keep a rag in your pocket that you can put between you and your hot engine when the need arises.

Never look down the stack of an engine that is in steam.

When stepping across the track, never do so when a train is passing.

Always start your exhaust fan before allowing alcohol into the burner and lighting it. This helps prevent overflows.

Never attempt to remove the safety valve while the boiler has any pressure in it at all.

If you follow these simple precautions, you will get into good habits and will safely enjoy this wonderful hobby of ours for many years to come.

Chapter 12

A sampling of steamers

As obscure as the question "Why does one love railways?" is another: "Why does one collect?" As a dyed-in-the-wool collector for much of my life, I have no good answer to that one either. I just accept it as part of my lot in life and get on with the next acquisition.

My interest in railways in general and small-scale steam locomotives in particular made little engines a natural subject for a collection. However, I didn't approach it scientifically, concentrating on a single scale, gauge, manufacturer, or type; I just picked up whatever appealed to me.

After a while, I realized that what appealed to me was diversity. I was amazed by the ingenuity that went into the design of little steam engines, and all the tricks and dodges that could be employed in them that would have no place on a full-size locomotive.

Also, as I began to acquire more engines hand made by individuals, I came to realize that any given engine was, in a certain way, a reflection of the personality of its maker. I have no doubt that, if enough engines could be gathered together and studied, the personality traits of the builders could be discerned in them in much the same way that handwriting can be analyzed.

Not all of the engines shown in the following pages are in pristine, showroom condition. Most have seen at least some use, while some have seen decades of it, and sometimes hard use at that. No attempt has been made to make the engine pretty for the pictures, except to clean them up. All the dents, dings, scratches, rust, worn paint, corrosion, and evidence of collision or other catastrophe are

Kevin Strong's 2-6-0, built on a Roundhouse chassis, crosses a temporary trestle made of privet logs.

completely authentic. After all, this is what these locomotives were meant for.

The collection has been gathered from a wide variety of sources over a period of about three decades. Some of the previous owners cherished their engines and treated them with wonderful care, while others rode their iron horses hard and put them away wet. I never intentionally bought a clapped-out locomotive, but one or two slipped through. Even those, though, had stories to tell and lessons to teach.

So, what follows is a sampling of some of the work that has been done in this fascinating field. In trying to determine how best to organize them here, many ideas were tried on: boiler type, cylinder type, wheel arrangement, scale, and gauge were just a few. After a lot of cogitation, I finally decided just to present them chronologically by date of construction. This seemed to make as much sense as anything.

These engines are all from my own collection. The entire collection is not included for lack of space. I tried to choose carefully to convey an impression of the amazing variety that exists. These locomotives represent only a tiny fraction of what is out there in the world. This presentation is not intended in any way to be definitive or exhaustive. Indeed, there are some serious gaps present.

What is here, though, is diversity – that same diversity that attracts me, and thousands like me, to steam locomotives in the garden scales. I hope that you enjoy them as much as I have.

John Bateman's *Thunderer*

This old brass engine has a certain majesty about it. The massive boiler atop the spindly looking wheels is characteristic of the era, when models of this nature were made by instrument makers.

This locomotive came to me via the grandson of the original owner, who had played with it as a child and brought it with him from England when he emigrated to America. It's an impressive beast, made entirely of brass. The wheels are fine brass castings that have the thin, lacy spokes typical of its era. No doubt, the entire engine was highly polished when new. There is some paint on it, but not much. The cylinders, the inset panel of the splashers over the drivers, and the spokes of the wheels are a deep, dull red. On one side of the boiler is a cast-brass nameplate: *Thunderer*. There is no indication that there ever was a plate on the other side.

I originally did not know the maker of this engine. Aside from the nameplate, there was no obvious marking. Upon close examination, though, I found what appeared to be a maker's symbol or logo hand-scratched (I would hesitate to call it engraved) into the backplate on the open cab. It looked like 'JB & Co.,' with the 'J' and the 'B' formed back-to-back as a single character. In checking my reference books, the only reasonable match was John Bateman & Company of High Holborn in London. (Bassett-Lowke, years later, would also have a High Holborn address.)

As it happened, I had a reproduction of a John Bateman catalogue. I hoped to be able to identify the engine as Bateman by comparing details of this locomotive with those of engines that appeared in the catalogue. However, while thumbing through the catalogue, I came upon the very engine itself. Eureka!

The gauge of this locomotive is 3¼in, which seems odd today, but was a standard gauge of the time. While not a scale model of any specific engine, this locomotive is more than a toy and it captures the lines and essence of early British locomotives. It was intended to be run on the floor or on track. Engines that were intended solely for floor use often had their axles angled inward, aimed at the centre point of an imaginary circle, so that the engine would travel in a circle when operating on a flat surface. This engine's axles are parallel to one another.

There is a throttle lever in the cab, on either side of which are pegs that act as stops. On the right side of the boiler are a pair of petcocks, one above the other. These take the place of the sight glass. When filling the boiler, the top one is opened. When water comes out, the boiler is filled to the proper level. While operating, the bottom cock is periodically opened for a second. If water comes out, there's still ample in the boiler. If steam comes out, it's time to shut down and refill.

Water can be added to the boiler by unscrewing the rear dome cover. This cover also houses the safety valve. Ahead of it is a working peanut whistle and ahead of that is a dummy steam dome.

The backhead has a throttle and a pair of petcocks. The latter can be used to help determine water level.

The burner on this example is gone, alas. It would not be difficult, though, to build a reasonable facsimile of the original, which was nothing more than a large tank that was hung under the footplate behind the rear wheel, with a feed tube extending forward to three or four wicks. The original burner tank was soldered to the backplate of the cab.

The outside cylinders are brass castings. Piston rods are fitted with crossheads, crosshead guides, and gland nuts. Front cylinder covers appear to be soldered in place, while the rear ones are screwed on. The valves are inside the frames and are controlled by slip eccentrics on the driven axle. Valve stems are also fitted with gland nuts (one is missing, but could be remade). Originally there was an exhaust pipe from each cylinder that ran up the stack. One of those is also missing on this engine, as are a pair of buffers on the front beam.

With all of the little things wrong, this engine is a non-runner, needless to say. However, it is a good candidate for restoration, the only significant missing part being the burner.

Specifications

Builder: John Bateman & Co. (UK)
Date built: Circa 1885
Gauge: 3¼in
Scale: 1:17 (nominal)
Boiler: Pot
Fittings: Safety valve, whistle, throttle, two petcocks
Fuel: Alcohol
Blow-off pressure: 10-15psi
Cylinders: Two, double-acting D-valve
Reversing gear: Slip eccentrics
Lubricator: None
Weight: 5lbs 10oz
Dimensions: Length, 11¾in over frame; width, 3¾in; height, 7¼in

Carette's 'Storkleg'

Possessing a simple elegance, this Carette
storkleg is still in running condition after 100 years.
Note the coach behind – 0 gauge on a 1-gauge chassis.

The firm of George Carette & Cie. has an interesting history. Georges Carette, a Frenchman, moved to Germany as a youth or young man. In Nürnberg he opened a toy company in 1886, backed by his German foster father. (Georges was then, and would always be, a French citizen.) The firm did well and made toys of all different types, including railways. It competed with the likes of Bing, Märklin, and other large toymakers of the time.

Because of his nationality and politics, Georges fell afoul of the German authorities upon the outbreak of WWI and had to flee Germany, through Switzerland, back to France, where he spent the rest of his life. The toy company in Germany was run by a partner until 1917, when it closed.

Carette, like the other toymakers of the time, produced a wide variety of railway equipment in several different gauges. The 'storkleg' locomotive was typical of its time and similar ones were made by different companies. They were given this appellation because of the very long drive rods powering a single large wheel on each side. When in motion, this gave them the ungainly look of a stork walking. Storkleg engines were commonly available in gauges 0 and 1. Carette even made them in gauge 3. Storklegs could have either oscillating or fixed cylinders.

Specifications

Builder: George Carette & Cie.(Germany)
Date built: Circa 1903
Gauge: 1 (45mm)
Scale: None, really
Boiler: Pot
Fittings: Safety valve, whistle
Fuel: Alcohol
Blow-off pressure: 10psi
Cylinders: Two, single-acting oscillators
Reversing gear: Rotary valve
Lubricator: None
Weight: 2lbs 11oz (with tender)
Dimensions: Length with tender, 14⅛in; width, 2⅞in; height, 5¼in

The model

My example of this locomotive shows signs of its age. The paint is blistered, the cab roof has been bent and straightened, and the cowcatcher is gone. The fact that it even had a cowcatcher indicates that it was made for the American market. That, though, was the engine's only concession to American railroad tradition. Aside from that, it is purely German.

The locomotive has the usual low-pressure pot boiler. Boiler fittings include a safety valve and a whistle. Every toy engine *must* have a whistle. The boiler is fired by an alcohol burner with three flat wicks. A large tank is clipped in place beneath the cab.

The long piston rod and large driver gave the type of engine its name. Reversing is via the lever in the cab.

Two, single-acting oscillating cylinders power the engine. These are reversed by a rotary valve between them, controlled from the cab by a long rod on the right side of the boiler that actuates a rocker arm that takes the motion inside, between the frames to the valve.

The tinplate tender has no practical function and is just there for looks. It has a formed-metal coal load. There is an apron on the engine that folds down to cover the gap between the loco and tender when they are coupled, which is a nice feature.

A trio of 0-gauge-size coaches, mounted to gauge-1 chassis, came with the engine. This practice was not unusual with the old toy makers. It lowered the cost of an already cheap set, and kids never seemed to notice the difference. It does make for an odd-looking train, though.

Storkleg engines were made in the thousands. Many were destroyed by young hands, but a few survive. Of those, most languish in private collections, spending their time on shelves. However, a few enlightened souls, like Murray Wilson, continue to play with these trains. Every year at the fabled Diamondhead steam meet in Mississippi, Murray shows up with a handful of ancient engines and makes them live again. It's magic!

Bassett-Lowke's gauge-3 *Experiment*

The locomotive after which this model is patterned was designed by George Whale and ran on the London & North Western Railway. It was introduced in 1905 and was the successor to the smaller, but highly successful, 'Precursor' class of 4-4-0s, which had been introduced the previous year. *Experiment* was intended for passenger work, but it spawned the 'Experiment' class of 19in (cylinder diameter) goods engines. The only difference between these and the original *Experiment* was that the goods engines had smaller drivers.

The model

In Bassett-Lowke's earlier days, the company commissioned a lot of its products from other manufacturers. One of the primary suppliers of 2½in-gauge locomotives prior to 1913 was Carson & Co. (James Carson). In 1913, Bassett-Lowke acquired all of Carson's tooling and continued to make at least some of the Carson range for some time afterwards.

Experiment is one of Carson's better-known engines and it reflects the high level of commercial model building in Britain at the time. This is truly a scale model of a specific locomotive, not a toy representation of something it little resembles.

This is a beautiful model. It has a cast-iron cab, footplate, and other parts, while the tender has a cast-iron frame and end beams. The boiler is of the Smithies variety, fired by a

Above: The pipe with the cap, just inside the smokebox door, is a lubricator line to the cylinders

Left: The backhead of the Smithies boiler is fully configured. At the left side of the cab is the reversing lever. Below the footplate is the sump, fed by the tender tank.

massive six-wick alcohol burner with a sump below the cab. Fuel is carried in the tender, which is simply a large tank. A feed tube departs the bottom of the tank and goes to a valve mounted to the left-hand frame. From there, the tube leads to the sump on the engine. The idea is to adjust the valve on the tender to supply the engine's needs – no more and no less.

The engine has no pumps, neither hand or axle, so must be shut down between the runs. There is a check valve on the backhead, but it is not plumbed into anything.

Two inside cylinders drive the leading axle, which can be removed from the frames. The other two axles are trapped in place. The chassis is unsprung. Like the prototype, the model has Joy valve gear, controlled from the cab. Construction is robust – the engine was designed for operation. Backhead fittings include a throttle, blower, water glass with blowdown valve, and a pressure gauge.

The smokebox door snaps open. Inside are the usual things, including blower and exhaust pipes. There is also a cylinder-lubricator line with a cap on it. I could find no evidence of an actual lubricator reservoir. I surmise that this is a direct line into the cylinders.

When I received the engine, the safety-valve shell was there, but it had no innards. I sent the shell to Rafe Shirley, who kindly made and installed the missing pieces. Aside from that, this old engine is complete and in excellent mechanical condition. It certainly shows signs of use and has the patina of age on it, all of which adds immensely to its character. As of this writing, I've not run it on steam. It runs beautifully on compressed air, the throttle giving fine control. I hope, one day, to run it on steam, but must give it a proper boiler test first.

Top: This magnificent model of an impressive prototype is a fine example of the state of commercial model building in the early 20th century.

Above: Like the prototype, the model has Joy valve gear and inside cylinders. These drive the leading axle.

Specifications

Builder: Carson & Co. for Bassett-Lowke (UK)
Date built: Circa 1910
Gauge: 3 (2½in)
Scale: 1:24
Boiler: Smithies
Fittings: Safety valve, throttle, blower, water glass with blowdown, pressure gauge, check valve
Fuel: Alcohol
Blow-off pressure: 60psi
Cylinders: Two, double-acting D-valve
Reversing gear: Joy valve gear
Lubricator: Direct feed
Weight: 18lbs 14oz (loco and tender)
Dimensions: Length (loco and tender), 27¾in; width, 4¼in; height, 6¾in

LBSC's *Small Bass*

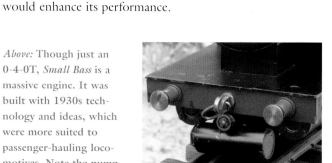

L BSC were the initials of Britain's London, Brighton & South Coast Railway. LBSC was also the pseudonym of one of the most famous and idiosyncratic of all miniature-steam-locomotive designers. LBSC – Curly, to his friends – was born around 1882 and christened Lillian Lawrence. Why he was given a girl's name is unclear, as are whatever reasons there might have been for him not changing it later.

Curly loved steam locomotives from the time he was a child and spent several years in the employ of the LBSC Railway, from which he later adopted his pen name. He began writing construction articles for the various British model-engineering magazines around the mid-1920s, continuing through most of the 1960s. During this time, designs for well over one hundred and fifty different locomotives, from gauge 0 up to 5in gauge, were offered in a variety of publications.

It was LBSC's contention that any person with enough desire could build a working steam locomotive. Many of his designs were based on actual engines, though they were often simplified for the home builder. All were robust in nature and good performers. His notes on various aspects of locomotive construction were compiled into a book called *Shop, Shed, and Road*, still considered to be a standard reference for the model engineer.

Curly Lawrence, through his entertaining and readable 'words and music,' introduced thousands of people to the joys of machine work and miniature steam locomotives. There are countless locomotives built to his plans still operating on tracks around the world. He passed away in 1967.

The model

Small Bass is one of LBSC's lesser-known designs and almost the only one that could be construed as a narrow-gauge engine. It was published in *English Mechanics* magazine in 1930, evidently for both gauge 0 and 1. My example (builder unknown) is gauge 1, and is a truly unusual engine. It is to an indeterminate scale and is oddly proportioned. In ⅞in scale (or larger) it could almost be considered a model of a miniature engine.

The back sheet is removable, revealing a well-supplied backhead. There is a throttle lever, a blower valve, a blowdown valve, and a water glass, all neatly laid out. A pressure gauge was evidently added at a later date and this, too, was neatly done. The engine sports working side tanks; there's a hand pump in the left one, with a balance pipe between the two to keep the water level even.

A Smithies boiler with three water tubes in the fire space supplies the steam. The outer shell is a whopping 3in in diameter and the inner boiler is relatively large, too. The smokebox door is removable (though it is not hinged) and the exhaust and blower pipes can be seen inside. A displacement lubricator rides below the front deck and the engine must be turned on its side to fill it.

Traditional, fixed, D-valve cylinders power the engine. These have their valves inside the frames and are controlled by slip eccentrics. A copious fuel tank is slung beneath the footplate in the cab, feeding a three-wick burner in the firebox. This engine has an unusual and pleasing feature for a boiler of this type – a firedoor in the backhead through which the fire can be lit. The burner can be instantly dropped by removing a retaining pin in the cab. All in all, the workmanship on this locomotive is to a pretty high, workmanlike standard.

Running light, this is a difficult engine to control. It can run slowly, with the regulator just cracked, but a heavy train would enhance its performance.

Above: Though just an 0-4-0T, *Small Bass* is a massive engine. It was built with 1930s technology and ideas, which were more suited to passenger-hauling locomotives. Note the pump handle sticking up from the side tank.

Centre: An oversize displacement lubricator sits under the pilot beam.

Lower: With the back sheet removed, the neatly made backhead is visible. The patina of age gives this locomotive a lot of character.

Specifications

Designer: LBSC (UK)
Builder: Unknown
Date built: Unknown (1930 design)
Gauge: 1 (45mm)
Scale: Indeterminate
Boiler: Smithies
Fittings: Safety valve, throttle, blower, pressure gauge, water glass, blowdown, hand pump
Fuel: Alcohol
Blow-off pressure: 50psi
Cylinders: Two, double-acting D-valve
Reversing gear: Slip eccentrics
Lubricator: Displacement
Weight: 11lbs 9oz
Dimensions: Length over buffers, 13in; width, 4⅛in; height over stack, 6½in

Bowman's 4-4-0

This Bowman 4-4-0, the top of the company's line, has seen better days. Despite a long, hard life, it's still a strong runner.

Bowman Models, begun in 1923 by Geoffrey Bowman Jenkins, produced a variety of steam toys and models in the mid 1920s and 1930s. These included stationary engines for driving Meccano models, boats of different varieties, and locomotives.

The engine pictured here is Bowman's 234, 4-4-0 'Express' engine, the star of the company's railway line. This engine is as simple as an engine can be, even more so than the Mamod engines that arrived half a century later. It has a pair of single-acting oscillating cylinders that drive the rear axle. The front axle is unpowered (sort of making it a 4-2-2-0, or something). The tender is entirely ornamental. There is a steam pipe leading from the boiler to each of the cylinders. Atop the boiler is a safety valve and at the front is an overflow plug. That's it. There's no throttle, reversing gear, or even lubricator. The engines were originally fitted with felt-like

material on the piston rods, behind the brass pistons. These were to be soaked with oil and probably did a pretty good job of lubricating the cylinders, at least for a while. Unfortunately, on my example, these felts are long gone.

The locomotive is supplied with a capacious alcohol tank that feeds half a dozen wicks spaced out under the pot boiler. The top of the fuel tank is actually a small tray that houses a lead weight, no doubt intended to add a little traction and balance. There's a screw-on filler cap and a screw-type over-flow plug on the side of the tank.

The engine is robustly made of heavy-gauge metal. Although it runs on gauge-0 track, it is closer to N° 1 scale in size and proportion. Bowman also supplied lithographed-tin coaches to go with this engine. The engines were offered in a variety of different liveries. This is the green LNER version. These engines were obviously made to last, and last they did. Bowman engines, despite being three-quarters of a century old, are one of the most commonly found vintage steam locomotives today.

As you can no doubt see from the pictures, this example has been through the wars. There is a missing buffer and the boiler is blackened by many fires. Paint is chipped off the cylinders and elsewhere, and the cab roof has a distinct crease in it. The engine just oozes character. Despite being as old as it is, it still runs well. It travels at a reasonable speed and will perk along for half an hour or so, with the occasional refilling of the fuel tank.

The backhead of this engine is as bare as can be. The only actual boiler fitting is a safety valve. The pipes emanating from the backhead are the steam lines to each cylinder.

Specifications

Builder: Bowman Models (UK)
Date built: 1930
Gauge: 0 (32mm)
Scale: Nothing definite
Boiler: Pot
Fittings: Safety valve
Fuel: Alcohol
Blow-off pressure: 10-15psi
Cylinders: Two, single-acting oscillators
Reversing gear: None
Lubricator: None
Weight: 4lbs 2oz (loco and tender)
Dimensions: Length (loco and tender), 18½in; width, 2¾in; height over stack, 4⅜in

This 0-4-4T is a work-a-day locomotive designed by LBSC and serialized in a British magazine in the 1930s. This example was built by an unknown builder.

T he prototype, in this instance, is of little importance. It was just an excuse to build an engine, really. The model is patterned after a Southern Railways 'Brighton' 0-4-4T but, as is often the case with LBSC's locomotives, liberties were taken, this time for the sake of simplicity.

The model

This locomotive was designed by Lillian Lawrence, better known as LBSC or Curly. As with most of his engines, it was serialized in a magazine as a construction series: this one in *English Mechanics* in June and July, 1936.

The engine came about as a result of readers requesting a largish-but-simple locomotive following the publication of an 0-6-0 in 0 gauge, then a similar one in 2½in gauge, both of which proved quite popular. This engine, like the 0-6-0, has a Smithies boiler, the usual backhead fittings (but no water glass), and a pump that could be used to pump water into the boiler from an external source (the side tanks are dummies). The boiler is fired by a huge, four-wick alcohol burner, fed by a monstrous (to someone mostly used to smaller-gauge engines) tank under the footplate.

There is a single, large cylinder between the frames, with a slip eccentric controlling a D-valve. The drivers on this engine are sprung (although LBSC said in the series that you could just run the axles through holes in the frames, if you wished). A displacement lubricator lives under a removable plate just below the smokebox and there is a whistle concealed under the right-hand side tank. The cab roof is removable, and so, surprisingly, is the whole cab, making everything inside very accessible. Castings were made available at the time, although they weren't necessary for the cylinder.

The model in question was made by an unknown builder. Whoever made the engine did a workmanlike job and the paint finish (chipping in several places) is all that could be wished for in a working locomotive. LBSC's engines were designed for use, not show. It was his goal to put the skills for the making of steam locomotives into the hands of anyone who desired them. He succeeded admirably.

The name on the side of the engine is *Doris*, not the name LBSC gave to the design. The engine has one final appealing attribute – the builder glued a St. Christopher's medal (patron saint of travellers) under the footplate, presumably to protect the engine on its journeys.

When I first ran this engine on blocks, it performed poorly. There was quite a bit of knocking in the system, suggesting wear, especially in the main rod's big end. Steam leaked from every connection and there seemed to be a lot of blow by past the piston. The whistle valve was problematic so, since the whistle was a bit of a farce anyway, I removed the whole thing, which eliminated some of the leaks. I tightened or otherwise attended to all of the other fittings as well.

I then tackled the cylinder. Once the piston was out, I could see that the packing was shot. I repacked it and the rod glands and made new springs for the suspension, since everything was apart. I also took apart the big end and eliminated most of the slop there. Once everything was back together I tried it on air. All seemed good. I later took it to Jim Hadden's gauge-3 track and tried it again under steam. It was transformed into a fine, strong engine that was a pleasure to run.

Both the cab roof and the cab itself are removable. For running, only the roof need come off. An ineffective whistle has been removed. The pump on the left side is for filling the boiler from an external source.

A single, large cylinder, reversed by a slip eccentric, powers the engine. A St. Christopher's medal can be seen in the lower right corner.

Specifications

Designer: LBSC (UK)
Builder: Unknown
Date built: 1952? (1936 design)
Gauge: 3 (2½in)
Scale: 1:24
Boiler: Smithies
Fittings: Safety valve, throttle, blower, pressure gauge, blowdown, whistle (removed)
Fuel: Alcohol
Blow-off pressure: 60psi
Cylinders: One, double-acting D-valve
Reversing gear: Slip eccentric
Lubricator: Displacement
Weight: 14lbs
Dimensions: Length over end beams, 17¼in; width, 4⅝in; height, 7in

Bassett-Lowke's 'Super Enterprise' 4-6-0

For what is really just a better class of toy engine, the 'Super Enterprise' has excellent proportions. This one shows the scorching typical on a well-loved engine.

Bassett-Lowke is arguably the best-know model-railway manufacturer in the world. Wenman J. Bassett-Lowke produced his first catalogue in 1900. The company imported and produced models into the 1960s. Today the name is owned by Corgi, who acquired it in 1996. Bassett-Lowke offered trains in all gauges up to 15in and in all modes of power (clockwork, steam, and electric). They were also well known for their ship models, some of which graced the board rooms of the largest steamship companies of the time.

The Bassett-Lowke 'Super Enterprise' is the very first live-steam locomotive I ever acquired, around 1977. My example is green and is lettered for the LNER (London & North Eastern Railway). It was produced (according to the book *The Bassett-Lowke Story* by Roland Fuller) in 1937. Also in this year were produced engines painted and lettered for the LMS, SR, and BR. The book indicates that the 'Super Enterprise' was made from the early 1930s into the 1950s.

The engine is mechanically similar in most respects to the company's 2-6-0, but is not nearly as common. It features a simple pot boiler fired by a vaporizing-spirit burner held in place with a clip. In the cab is a throttle, a level plug that can be used to fill the boiler to the proper level, and a whistle of little value beyond that of ornamentation. There's a toy-type safety valve atop the boiler. This was originally concealed beneath a steam dome, which was a simple brass pressing with a hole in the middle through which projected the stem of the safety valve. This is commonly missing.

The engine has two, double-acting cylinders with inside piston valves controlled by slip eccentrics (the Mogul is controlled by a rotary reversing valve). A displacement lubricator is located in the smokebox. A filler plug for the lubricator is just in front of the stack and a drain plug is located in the middle of the smokebox front. The tender is purely ornamental, doing nothing but looking pretty and following along behind.

The burner is interesting. This type was commonly used in Bassett-Lowke's lower-end models. Alcohol is held in a tank beneath the cab. A tube brings the fuel forward to a riser, inside of which is a wick to draw the meths up. Just behind the riser is a pilot wick whose job it is to preheat the burner tube. The horizontal burner tube is attached to the riser and is perforated with a row of little holes. When the pilot wick is lit, it begins heating the burner tube. As the alcohol inside heats, it begins to vaporise and come out the row of holes. As soon as this happens, the vapour ignites, producing a series of tiny but very hot flames atop the burner tube. It is these that heat the boiler. The burners in these engines are not well shielded, which makes them susceptible to the slightest breeze. Unlike wick fires, this one is easily blown out.

My example is typical of any well-used model of this type. The sides of the boiler are scorched and the paint is coming off the splashers and frames. The last time I ran it, it slowly gained speed until it was running wide open, which was not at all fast. It clattered around the railway lap after lap, the hollow tinplate tender rattling along behind. Nothing can match the sound of a tinplate box on wheels. It was great – a bit of living history, recreating the same sights, sounds, and smells experienced by garden railroaders more than a half century ago.

Specifications

Builder: Bassett-Lowke Ltd. (UK)
Date built: 1937
Gauge: 0 (32mm)
Scale: 7mm
Boiler: Pot
Fittings: Safety valve, throttle, whistle
Fuel: Alcohol
Blow-off pressure: 15psi
Cylinders: Two, double-acting piston-valve
Reversing gear: Slip eccentrics
Lubricator: Displacement
Weight: 3lbs 2oz (loco and tender)
Dimensions: Length (including tender), 16⅝in over the end beams; width, 2½in; height, 4in

On the backhead is a throttle lever, a whistle, and a level plug. The fuel tank is held beneath the footplate by a clip.

LBSC's 'Chingford Express'

Specifications

Builder: Unknown (Built to LBSC's 'Chingford Express' design)
Date built: Unknown (1944 design)
Gauge: 1 (45mm)
Scale: 1:32
Boiler: Smithies
Fittings: Safety valve, throttle, blower, filler plug
Fuel: Alcohol
Blow-off pressure: 50psi
Cylinders: One, double-acting D-valve
Reversing gear: Slip eccentric
Lubricator: None
Weight: 4lbs 4oz
Dimensions: Length, 9½in; width, 3¼in; height, 5in

Despite its plain appearance and relatively crude body work, this engine has certain charm and presence. It's a work-a-day locomotive and a good runner.

This is a model of a British, standard-gauge 0-6-0T, evidently patterned after a Lancashire & Yorkshire Railway class 23. The prototype was introduced in 1877, originally as a tender engine, but was later rebuilt as a saddle tanker. One of these locomotives has been preserved.

The model

As a model, this is a most interesting specimen. It was scratchbuilt by an unknown builder. Its age is also unknown. It appears to be based on an LBSC design, the 'Chingford Express,' as published in *Model Engineer* in 1944. This was intended to be a 'quickie' project. However, the 'Chingford Express,' as published in the magazine series, was a side-tank engine based on a Great Eastern Railway 0-6-0T, while this one has been modified into a saddle-tanker. Other details adhere closely to the Chingford Express drawings, though.

The mechanical parts of the engine are fairly well made. It has a single cylinder between the frames, controlled by a D-valve.

A single cylinder ahead of the leading axle powers the engine. The steam line passes directly from the boiler to the cylinder without the benefit of a lubricator.

Reversing is via a slip eccentric on the middle, crank axle. An interesting feature is the lack of a cylinder lubricator of any sort. The steam line passes directly from the regulator to the valve chest.

The boiler is a Smithies with water tubes, fired by a four-wick burner fed by a fuel tank under the footplate. The burner/fuel tank can be quickly removed by extracting a pin that passes through the frames and the tank, thus securing it. A filler port for fuel can be found on the footplate in the cab.

Boiler fittings include a safety valve, a filler plug, a regulator valve, and a blower. There is no pressure gauge or water glass. To raise steam, a fan is required.

The sheet-metal work – tank and cab – are somewhat less well made than the mechanical bits. They are made of thin sheet metal and are rather crudely formed. A lift-off dome that conceals the filler plug adorns the saddle tank. The entire engine was hand painted gloss black with a broad brush. The numeral '5' and 'L.Y' appear on the cab sides, surrounded by red lining. There is little detail aside from the non-functional smokebox door and unsprung buffers.

When I first tried to run this locomotive I found that the timing was out and it ran poorly. I adjusted the eccentric-driver angle, which transformed the engine into a strong, smooth, lively runner. With a train of half a dozen wagons, it was easy to control and a pleasure to run.

Controls consist of only the essentials – a throttle (left) and a blower. Reversing is via a slip eccentric.

Bassett-Lowke's gauge-0 Mogul

This was one of Bassett-Lowke's most popular live-steam locomotives in 0 scale. It was simply constructed and easy to run, yet had a scale appearance.

One of the most popular and successful locomotives ever produced by Bassett-Lowke was its 2-6-0 for gauge-0 track. Introduced in 1925, the engine was produced for around three decades, and it was briefly reissued in 1968, when a batch of one hundred were made. This locomotive was offered, over the years, in a wide variety of liveries and railway names, with appropriate cosmetic detail differences. It was offered in clockwork, electric, and live-steam versions, but the steam ones are the most common. It was, for a while, even offered in kit form. Corgi, who now owns the Bassett-Lowke name, even issued a made-in-China exact replica of the Mogul in steam.

The version shown here is black, lettered for the London & North Eastern Railway. Construction is generally tinplate, painted and nicely lined and lettered. The brass boiler is a pot-type of the low-pressure variety. It is fired by one of Bassett-Lowke's effective vaporising-spirit burners, held in place by a simple clip under the cab.

Atop the boiler is a simple safety valve. Over this sits an ornamental steam dome. As this small, light piece relies on gravity to keep it in place, it is frequently lost. On the backhead

Specifications

Builder: Bassett-Lowke Ltd. (UK)
Date built: Late 1940s (?)
Gauge: 0 (32mm)
Scale: 7mm
Boiler: Pot
Fittings: Safety valve, whistle
Fuel: Alcohol
Blow-off pressure: 10psi
Cylinders: Two, double-acting piston valves
Reversing gear: Rotary valve
Lubricator: Displacement
Weight: 3lbs 1oz (loco and tender)
Dimensions: Length over end beams (loco and tender), 16¾in; width, 2½in; height, 3¾in

is mounted a tiny whistle with a lever. The whistle protrudes through the cab roof.

Spoked wheels are all cast and all of the rods are stampings. The nicely proportioned tender serves no functional purpose, but simply trails along behind. It has a drawbar with a pin on it that engages a loop on the locomotive, close-coupling one to the other. There is the added attractive feature of an apron

that folds down over the drawbar, resting on the footplate of the cab.

Cylinders are fixed, controlled by piston valves. Reversing is via a rotary valve, controlled by a lever in the cab. This lever also protrudes through the cab roof through a slot that is notched to lock the lever in the central, neutral position, presumably as a safety measure.

The smokebox pulls off to reveal a large displacement lubricator with a pair of filler plugs. You remove both plugs and fill the lubricator with oil until it comes out the other plug.

This engine required some work before it would run. The valve timing was off and the engine was a non-starter. All the linkages are fixed, as far as any adjustments that might be made. The only thing that can be changed is the angle of the eccentric (return) crank. The crank has a square hole in it that registers on the square end of the crankpin, a screw holding it in place. The only way to change the setting is to rotate the crankpin.

The crankpin is screwed into the driver and a lock nut retains it. By loosening the lock nut, the crankpin can be moved to a new position, when the lock nut is then retightened. By a process of trial and error I arrived at valve settings that worked. Once that was accomplished, the engine could run on steam.

In operation, the vaporising spirit burner makes a very soft hissing sound. After five or six minutes on a warm, still day, steam comes up. When the control lever is pushed forward or back and the engine is pushed a couple of yards to clear the cylinders, it moves off by itself, smoothly and quietly.

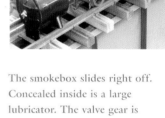

The smokebox slides right off. Concealed inside is a large lubricator. The valve gear is suggestive of full-size practice without actually adhering to it.

Aster's 'Schools' Class 4-4-0

The Southern Railways 'Schools' class 4-4-0 was introduced in 1930 as a passenger-hauling locomotive for the Hastings line, a route with severe gradients, lots of curves, and clearance restrictions. The 4-6-0 'King Arthur' class engines were favoured at the time but were too large and heavy for the line. REL Maunsell, the Southern Railway's locomotive designer, came up with the 'Schools' 4-4-0, based on both the 'Lord Nelson' and 'King Arthur' 4-6-0s.

The new 'Schools' proved to be up to the task. It had three cylinders and was the largest 4-4-0 ever built in Britain or, some say, in Europe. It was developed quickly and cheaply and proved a popular and efficient engine, eventually replacing the 'King Arthurs' on the Bournemouth route. Around 40 of them were produced in all.

The model

I've always considered Aster's 'Schools' to be an historic model. After all, it was the first engine Aster ever produced (made simultaneously with the company's JNR 2-6-0). There were 3,000 of them made, mostly in kit form. This was a bold new step in the live-steam hobby – kits for fully functional, scale steam locomotives that needed no machine work, drilling and tapping, paint, or finishing. Even most of the tools required for assembly were included with the kit. As with all subsequent Aster kits, instructions came in two parts: written and pictorial. In these early days, not all of the holes always aligned properly, and a set of needle files was almost a prerequisite for successful construction. The kit was a wonderful way to get to know your engine intimately.

Like many of Aster's earlier engines, this one is, to me, a quintessential British, gauge-1 locomotive, not because it is a model of a British engine, but because it was designed using early 20th century, British gauge-1 technology.

While the prototype was a three-cylindered locomotive, Aster's model has but two. It is alcohol fired, using a chicken-feed system carried in the tender, feeding a three-wick

(asbestos yarn) burner in the firebox. It has an internally fired boiler of the simplest kind, a Smithies. This design offers large heating surface at the expense of water capacity.

Fittings are basic, consisting of a pair of safety valves, a throttle, and a blower. There is also an extra plug in the

Above: Aster's seminal 4-4-0, the 'Schools' held much portent of things to come. It almost single-handedly gave the live-steam hobby a huge boost.

Left: The kit-built engine is robust and colourful. Valves are controlled by slip return cranks.

backhead, to which could be fitted a check valve for filling the boiler with an external pump, or a pressure gauge. I chose the latter.

Reversing is via slip return cranks. A Roscoe displacement lubricator sits on the pilot deck. No drain is provided.

Aster's locomotive bears the name *Winchester* (all of this class were named after schools, hence the class designation). It is a pretty good model of the prototype – not too many compromises were made. It certainly captures the feeling of the full-size engine. It looks great, with its malachite-green paint and elephant ears. These well known and much-liked models have been repainted and modified in many different ways over the years. Some have even been fitted with coal-fired boilers. Ironically, in 1979 Aster developed its 'King Arthur' 4-6-0 based on leftover 'Schools' parts. Only 300 of these were made.

This is a fun engine to run. With a load of a few Aster coaches, the engine really comes into its own. Its sharp, deep exhaust beats are loud and distinct. All the sounds you hear from an alcohol-fired engine are made by steam and machine. There's no roar, hiss, or whistle from a pressurized fuel system. With the engine pulling a train, you need only open the throttle and step back. The train slowly accelerates in a wonderfully prototypical manner until it is running at speed. From there it just goes and goes, the exhaust audible from any point on the line.

Throttle and blower adorn the backhead. The pressure gauge is an add-on. The valve on the tender releases meths to the chicken-feed system.

Specifications

Builder: Aster Hobby Company (Japan)
Date built: 1975
Gauge: 1 (45mm)
Scale: 1:32
Boiler: Smithies
Fittings: Throttle, blower, pressure gauge (not standard), safety valves (2)
Fuel: Alcohol
Blow-off pressure: 45psi
Cylinders: Two, double-acting D-valve
Reversing gear: Slip return cranks
Lubricator: Displacement
Weight: 8lbs (with tender)
Dimensions: Length over end beams (with tender), 20¾in; width, 3¼in; height, 5in

Archangel's *The Princess*

The *Princess* (later just *Princess*) was one of four locomotives supplied to the Ffestiniog Railway in Wales in 1863-64. It was designed by C.M. Holland and built by George England & Co. in 1863. When first built, it weighed 7.5tons. It was rebuilt two or three times, ending up with a large saddle tank. It finally left service in 1946.

The model

Archangel's model of *The Princess* is almost a parody of the full-size engine. The prototype was a tiny thing, with a wheelbase of 4ft 6in. This model has a wheelbase of 6ft 4in in 16mm scale. While the prototype was small and delicate in appearance, the model at hand is a sort of large and hulking caricature of the original.

I acquired the engine as a disreputable box of bits from a friend, and went through the enjoyable process of repairing and reassembling the locomotive. It is relatively early Archangel, having been made in 1976. It has cast-iron wheels that were evidently intended for an 0 scale, standard-gauge engine.

Mechanically, this is an interesting locomotive. It is Archangel's common single-cylinder job. However, because of the forward placement of the front axle, there was not room for the cylinder between the frames. Instead of occupying its usual place, the cylinder was reversed and placed between the two axles towards the rear, driving the first axle by means of an amazingly short rod. Reversing is by slip eccentric.

In the open cab is a throttle, the lever of which conveniently extends past the back plate. There is also a pressure gauge, a blow-

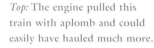

Top: The engine pulled this train with aplomb and could easily have hauled much more.

Above: The cab is a mess of plumbing and fittings. The throttle lever extends beyond the backplate, making it easy to reach and tweak while the engine is in motion. Below it in the picture is the blowdown valve. The whistle valve and whistle are merely suspended from their respective plumbing.

Left: Archangel's *The Princess* is nearly a spoof of the engine it purports to portray. It's chunky proportions do not convey the delicacy of the prototype. Note the 0-scale drivers.

down/vacuum tap, and a whistle, the latter of which is actuated by Archangel's nearly impossible whistle valve. The whistle isn't mounted to anything – it just sort of hangs off its own steam line. The lubricator is fitted with a drain screw and a huge, unsightly filler screw (which I've been assured is original equipment!). The lubricator, as well, is not attached to anything but the steam line – it just floats in the air a few millimeters above the deck.

The Princess is an alcohol burner, the tank being carried between the frames at the rear. A three-wick burner heats the boiler, with the wicks contorted around the engine's mechanics. The long asbestos wicks are splayed out at the top. The high-pressure engine is easy to control and docile in manner, pulling its train with nary a complaint.

A three-wick burner powers the boiler. Wicks are fitted wherever they will go. The single cylinder points forward, driving the first axle by an extremely short (and oddly bent) connecting rod.

Specifications

Builder: Archangel models (UK)
Date built: 1976
Gauge: 0 (32mm)
Scale: 16mm
Boiler: Pot
Fittings: Safety valve, throttle, blowdown valve, whistle
Fuel: Alcohol
Blow-off pressure: 75psi
Cylinders: One, double-acting D-valve
Reversing gear: Slip eccentric
Lubricator: Displacement
Weight: 5lbs 8oz
Dimensions: Length over end beams, 10⅞in; width, 4⅛in; height over stack, 6in

115

Bassett-Lowke's 'Birmingham Dribbler'

Although its proportions are less than elegant, this chunky toy does exude a certain charm. It could be considered the Basic Steam Locomotive, having just enough in the way of appurtenances to qualify as one.

old ceased making model trains in 1953, when W.J. Bassett-Lowke died. In the late 1960s, a new company was formed by Ivan Rutherford Scott, Allen Levy, and Roland Fuller. This company was called Bassett Lowke (Railways) and it took over the old Bassett-Lowke logo. The company had a wonderful store, called The Steam Age, on Cadogan Street in London. Here, they sold new and second-hand steam models of all types, but mostly railway related. I had the pleasure of visiting a couple of times and the store was spectacular in its displays. Sadly it did not survive past the 1980s.

The dribbler shown here was marketed by Bassett-Lowke (Railways) as their own, but it was probably made by Maxwell Hemmens, who marketed a nearly identical engine later.

Back in the earliest days of steam, in the mid to late 1800s, the idea of the railway captured the public's imagination like nothing had before. Toy makers soon were making replicas of greater or lesser fidelity to the prototypes for children of all ages to play with. It wasn't long before primitive steam toys came into being, as well.

The earliest of these toys, made by any number of German and British manufacturers, had oscillating cylinders that tended to leak, leaving a wet trail wherever they went. These became generally known as 'dribblers' and more specifically in Britain as 'Birmingham dribblers,' since that's where many were made.

The example at hand is of more recent manufacture. It's not a replica of a specific model, though it incorporates features of many. It is constructed entirely of brass and has a pair of single-acting oscillating cylinders set at 180° for continuous running. It has the added amenity of a throttle (which many dribblers lacked), and a whistle that would produce a high-pitched peep. These were commonly called 'peanut whistles.' An ornate safety valve sits atop the boiler.

The locomotive has cast wheels and a cast frame. All other parts are turnings or bar stock. A wooden buffer beam is featured at the front. No coupler is provided, as it is doubtful that an engine like this would have had the power to pull much anyway. It was considered something of a minor miracle that it would go at all. While the unit could run on rails, it was also designed as a floor toy. The front axle can be turned so that the engine would travel in a circle. The drivers have knurled flanges, too, to prevent the engine from slipping on slick kitchen floors.

The burner on this little monster is nothing but a chunk of cotton wadding held in place beneath the boiler by a steel clip. The idea was that you fill the boiler halfway with water, soak the cotton in alcohol and set it alight. I've never run this engine – I'm not that adventurous.

This engine was marketed in the mid 1970s as a product of Bassett-Lowke (Railways). The Bassett-Lowke company of

The engine has a crude throttle and whistle. On the backhead, below the throttle, is a level plug for checking the water level when filling the boiler.

When used as a floor toy (which was more likely than track operation) the front axle could be turned so that the engine would travel in a circle.

Specifications

Builder: Bassett-Lowke (Railways) (nominally)
Date built: Mid 1970s
Gauge: 2⅜in
Scale: None
Boiler: Pot
Fittings: Safety valve, throttle, whistle, level plug
Fuel: Alcohol
Blow-off pressure: 10psi (?)
Cylinders: Two, single-acting oscillators
Reversing gear: None
Lubricator: None
Weight: 2lbs 2oz
Dimensions: Length over end beams, 6¾in; width, 4in; height, 5⅛in

Colin Binnie's Tram, *Victoria*

Above: Victoria is a geared engine. The hole in the side of the boiler at the bottom is the gas-inlet port. The gas jet can just be seen next to the left-hand axle. Gas is simply squirted across the intervening space, entraining air as it goes.

Left: An unusual locomotive, to say the least, *Victoria* is a boxy thing with a vertical boiler. The chimney exits through the side of the boiler and penetrates the roof in front of it.

Victoria was the first locomotive owned by the Plynlimon & Hafan Tramway. It was one of two built to a similar design. The Plynlimon & Hafan was a little known railway in the Leri Valley of Wales. The seven plus mile long, 2ft 3in gauge line was opened in 1897 and closed just two years later, when the lead mining business didn't pan out (although it did become lucrative some years later).

Victoria, an 0-4-0T, was an unusual locomotive, to say the least, with its oddly shaped body and vertical boiler. Unfortunately, it did not survive and little is known about it.

The model
This model was constructed by the well-known British builder, Colin Binnie. Mr. Binnie says: "I built the engine around 1976 for Doug Jones, as a simple but reliable steamer of externally scale appearance. It was the first loco I built with an enclosed ceramic gas burner. The burner consists of a pan with the mixture tube extended across the diameter. The tube is cut away adjacent to the bottom of the pan to act as a diffuser. The top of the pan was fitted with a piece of ceramic from a commercial space heater. Needless to say, I would not do it quite that way today."

Victoria is a basic locomotive. There is the gas-fired vertical boiler of the above-mentioned unusual design, with the chimney exiting the side of the boiler near the top. A safety valve (the boiler's only amenity) is located in the middle of the top plate and doubles as a filler valve.

The locomotive has one of Mr. Binnie's oscillating motors mounted vertically next to the boiler, geared to the driving axle. The steam motor is controlled by a rotary valve built into it, which also serves as a throttle. There is a dead-leg lubricator with a drain, to keep the cylinders oiled. The lubricator hides behind a wall and is all but inaccessible.

The jet squirts gas into an orifice in the side of the ceramic burner from a distance of about half an inch. The burner is entirely enclosed. The boiler is a shell within a shell, the outer one forming a sort of all-around firebox. The gas tank is filled through the roof and the gas-control valve requires an allen key to operate it. Body work is plain and neat, and the engine is fitted with unsprung buffers.

The engine is a prodigious steamer and an excellent runner. There is audible gear noise, which, to my mind, adds to the quirky charm of this locomotive. I normally don't like to see the reversing valve used as a throttle, but on this engine it works pretty well. Slow, smooth running is not a problem.

The steam motor can just be seen in front of the boiler. It is controlled by the lever at the side of the boiler, which operates the rotary valve mounted on the steam motor.

Specifications

Builder: Colin Binnie (UK)
Date built: 1976
Gauge: 0 (32mm)
Scale: 16mm
Boiler: Vertical
Fittings: Safety valve
Fuel: Butane
Blow-off pressure: 20psi (estimated)
Cylinders: Two, double-acting oscillators
Reversing gear: Rotary valve
Lubricator: Displacement
Weight: 3lbs 13oz
Dimensions: Length, 8¼in over end beams; width, 4⅛in; height, 6¼in

Fred Freeman's Hunslet

Top: Fred Freeman's Hunslet had a reputation for setting the landscape alight. The external cylinders are merely for show.

Lower left: The firebox for the Smithies boiler straddles the rear axle. The sump is at the rear. The single cylinder runs a jackshaft, which is geared to the forward axle in a 2:1 ratio. Note the secondary frame with the jogged members that supports the steam motor inside the outer frame that carries the drivers.

Lower right: Cab fittings are neatly arranged. Behind the pressure gauge, sloping up to the left, is the whistle. The whistle-control handle is the little one to the left and down from the pressure gauge. The larger handle on the left side of the cab is the blower. Below the whistle handle, and mostly obscured in this picture, is the throttle lever.

The Hunslet Engine Company was founded in Leeds in 1864 and still exists today. Amongst modellers, it is probably most famous for its small industrial tank engines, especially those that worked the Welsh slate quarries. However, the company produced industrial engines in many gauges and exported them to thirty countries. Among their more unusual products were the 0-3-0 engines produced for the Listowell & Ballybunnion monorailway in Ireland. Although the name on the engine shown here is, I believe, fictitious, the engine bears a strong resemblance to *Lilla*, one of the larger quarry Hunslets, now working on the Ffestiniog Railway in Wales.

The model
This interesting model, built by Fred Freeman, is equipped with a Smithies boiler (internally fired). The saddle tank is functional, carrying water with which the boiler is fed through a hand pump on the right running board. A plastic balance pipe connects the legs of the tank under the boiler. The backhead is fully equipped, with throttle, blower, pressure gauge, and a (nearly useless) whistle tucked up under the cab roof. Lamentably lacking is a water glass, so, when pumping up, you have to sort of go by feel. Little and often is the byword.

The engine is alcohol fired via a two-wick burner in the firebox. Two alcohol tanks reside in the cab, one on either side. A fuel-control valve, disguised as a brake screw, releases the fuel to a sump under the footplate.

Perhaps the engine's most interesting feature is its drive. The visible cylinders on either side are dummies. The engine is, in fact, powered by a single, double acting, D-valve cylinder between the frames. This is geared 2:1 to the axle, not only pro-

viding the correct number of exhaust beats per revolution of the drivers, but also making the engine much more controllable. The cylinder and gears are supported by a second frame system contained within the engine's overall frame. Even though the engine is not highly detailed, the workmanship is to a high standard.

This engine has a tender that is not original equipment. It was built after the fact by Frank Warren, the engine's owner at the time, as a sort of accessory wagon. The front half holds the suction fan required to get the engine started, while the rear holds odd bits, including the detachable pump handle. It is nicely painted to match the engine.

The engine came with a reputation for setting the railway alight as it passed, by spilling flaming meths everywhere. In operation, this proved true. Closing the fuel valve temporarily solved that problem. In examining the engine and thinking about the fire problem, it occurred to me that this was not, as it appeared, a standard chicken-feed fuel system, but just a drip system. When the valve was opened, alcohol simply flowed into the sump. You had to close the valve to stop the flow – it wasn't self regulating. By opening the fuel valve often, but just for a few seconds the fire problem was largely solved.

The engine is a sweet runner and easy to control. With its hand pump, it can be kept in steam indefinitely.

Specifications

Builder: Fred Freeman (UK)
Date built: 1976
Gauge: 0 (32mm)
Scale: 16mm
Boiler: Smithies
Fittings: Safety valve, throttle, pressure gauge, blower, whistle, check valve
Fuel: Alcohol
Blow-off pressure: 60psi
Cylinders: One, double-acting D-valve
Reversing gear: Slip eccentric
Lubricator: Displacement
Weight: 6lbs 12oz (without tender)
Dimensions: Length without tender, 10¾in; width, 4in; height over stack, 5⅝in

Archangel's *Sgt. Murphy*

In 1968, small-scale steam in the garden didn't enjoy much by way of commercial suppliers. But in that year, Stewart Browne of Archangel Models (then of High Wycombe, England), began producing his line of engines. His first was a 16mm-scale model of a Vale of Rheidol Railway 2-4-0.

Stewart Browne went on to develop an engine that was to embody the steam locomotive at its most basic. This locomotive, known as *Brick* (it was loosely modelled after a brickworks engine) featured a pot boiler, one double-acting cylinder between the frames, a throttle (regulator), and little else by way of amenities. But *Brick* had one sterling quality. It ran exceedingly well, being both controllable and powerful. It was simple to operate and could be turned loose in the garden without fear of mishap. It became, to my mind anyway, the quintessential garden-railway steam locomotive.

Archangel's engines ran well, but success was doubly assured when people like Jack Wheldon and DG Rowlands took notice and began to write about the company's remarkable locomotives in the mainstream British model press.

Over the years, Stewart Browne, working mostly alone, produced both an astonishing variety and quantity of engines. Each was essentially handmade and it is difficult to find two that are exactly alike. He made engines that ran on alcohol, gas, and coal. Not all of them are easy to run and a few are downright dogs. However, each has its own character and personality, which contributes to its charm and the fun of getting to know it.

The model

Sgt. Murphy was introduced in the late 1970s. It is modelled after an industrial 0-6-0T, to which it bears a faint resemblance (Stewart Brown freely took liberties with proportions and details). It went on to become a staple at the low end of Archangel's lineup of locomotives.

Mechanically, it is similar to *Brick*, with a single, double acting, slide-valve cylinder between the frames. It is a pot boiler, running on a three-wick alcohol burner. The fuel tank resides under the footplate of the cab. Side tanks are simply solid slabs of aluminium. The 2in-diameter boiler is 8in long and its entire interior space is devoted to water, giving the engine extraordinary duration. I've heard tales of some of these engines running for as long as an hour before requiring a refill of water (though the fuel needs to be topped up periodically, a matter of a few seconds).

Sgt. Murphy came in different colours, but green was common. They were always hand lined by the maker. In later years they were offered in different variations, including gas firing; twin, working outside cylinders; and sometimes even Hackworth valve gear. Whistles could also be had, if required.

The engine in the photos is not a standard *Sgt. Murphy*. It belonged to DG Rowlands and ran on his (then) well-known Alderbrook Valley Railway. He renamed the engine *Empress of Blandings* after a famous character from PG Wodehouse. At his request, the locomotive was modified by David Pinniger, who, among other things, reduced the height of the cab and removed sections from the lower front of the tanks to make the engine more Hunslet-like. The engine was then painted by the same company that was, at the time, painting all of the Mamod locomotives. The final colour was a much paler shade of green than what was expected!

Specifications

Builder: Archangel Models (UK)
Date built: 1977
Gauge: 0 (32mm)
Scale: 16mm
Boiler: Pot
Fittings: Safety valve, blowdown
Fuel: Alcohol
Blow-off pressure: 75psi
Cylinders: One, double-acting D-valve
Reversing gear: Slip eccentric
Lubricator: Displacement
Weight: 6lbs 12oz
Dimensions: Length over end beams, 10⅞in; width, 3⅜in; height, 6⅜in over stack

Running light, this engine can be quite lively. With a reasonable train, it calms right down, running with a nice, audible chuff.

T he Vale of Rheidol Railway (VoR) is a 1ft 11½in line that runs between Aberystwyth and Devil's Bridge in Wales, a distance of over eleven miles. It was begun in 1901, intended to haul ore from the lead mines in the Rheidol Valley, as well as timber and passengers. It was the last steam line to be operated as part of the nationalized British Railways network. The line had a chequered history, passing through many hands, until it became a private tourist line in 1989, as it is today.

The prototype of the locomotive shown here was originally built to 2ft 6in gauge for a foreign railway by Bagnall, and named *Trezio de Mai*. It was never delivered and was subsequently regauged a to 2ft 3in for the Plynlimon & Hafan, who named it *Talybont*. When the P&H closed, the engine and a number of wagons were again regauged, this time to two feet. They were purchased by Pethicks, the contractors who were building the Vale of Rheidol. When the railway was completed, the 2-4-0 was kept, as it was the only engine that could work the harbour branch, the railway's larger 2-6-2Ts being too heavy. It was named *Rheidol* and became the railway's N° 3. The engine was withdrawn from service in 1924.

The model

This is one of Archangel's earlier models, and a popular one at that, appearing in many variations over the years. It is a simple engine in some ways, but with several sophisticated features.

The loco is alcohol fired, with the meths being carried in the large tank (the dummy coal bunker) behind the cab. It uses a chicken-feed system, with an odd control valve in the form of a screw in the rear buffer beam that can be opened with a screwdriver to allow meths to flow into the sump, then

to the two-wick burner. The engine is internally fired, with a Smithies boiler. A superheater line passes between the inner boiler and outer shell to the engine's single cylinder between the frames. The two outside cylinders are dummies. Reversing is via a slip eccentric.

Backhead fittings include the usual throttle and blower valves, along with a pressure gauge and a whistle valve. The whistle is tucked up under the roof of the cab. Cylinder lubrication is provided by the displacement lubricator in the cab, suspended from the steam line. A large safety valve sits on the boiler ahead of the cab.

The cab, with the dummy bunker removed. The thing that looks like a plunger is the whistle valve. The throttle lever is sticking up next to it.

The side tanks on this engine are functional. They can be filled from either side, as there is a balance pipe between them. A hand pump resides in the left-hand tank. Since there's no water glass, the rule for filling the boiler is 'little and often.' When you become familiar with an engine's habits, you can usually tell when it's low on water. The actual inner boiler is pretty small, so one must pay attention to it. On my locomotive, the paint is flaking off the boiler, but is sound on the rest of the engine.

Stewart Browne's locomotives, as a rule, are unusual, nonconformist, and quirky, and this one is no exception. It's because of these qualities that they endear themselves to people. *Rheidol* is high on my list of favorites.

Specifications

Builder: Archangel Models (UK)
Date built: 1977
Gauge: 0 (32mm)
Scale: 16mm
Boiler: Smithies
Fittings: Safety valve, throttle, blower, whistle, pressure gauge, clack valve from hand pump
Fuel: Alcohol
Blow-off pressure: 60psi
Cylinders: One, double-acting D-valve
Reversing gear: Slip eccentric
Lubricator: Displacement
Weight: 5lbs 6oz
Dimensions: Length over end beams, 11in; width, 4in; height, 5⅝in

The underside clearly shows the single cylinder with the valve on one side, as well as the strange pilot wheels, mounted behind the (dummy) outside cylinders.

Archangel's *Snowdon Ranger*

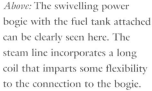

Above: The swivelling power bogie with the fuel tank attached can be clearly seen here. The steam line incorporates a long coil that imparts some flexibility to the connection to the bogie.

Left: Archangel's *Snowdon Ranger* is actually a pretty plain locomotive. Detail is minimal, as is the sheet-metal work. There is no rivet detail and the boiler fittings are the fewest possible to provide a functioning engine. The unsightly pipe that curves up in front of the smokebox is the fuel filler.

A s articulated locomotives go, I find Fairlies to be among the most interesting. Perhaps the best known of this type are the double Fairlies, developed by Robert Fairlie in the late 1860s and still running today on the Ffestiniog Railway in Wales. These are double-ended locomotives with a cab in the middle and a smokestack at either end. Beneath each boiler (actually, a single, extended boiler with a central firebox) is a swivelling steam bogie that allows this relatively long locomotive to negotiate sharp curves.

Less well known are the single Fairlies, which, as the name implies, are basically half a double Fairlie. These engines had a single, swivelling steam bogie and a non-powered trailing truck. They were the predecessors of the American Mason Bogie locomotives, built by William Mason. When you start digging, you find that, at one time, there were an astonishing number of both Fairlies and Masons, singles and doubles, in use all over the world.

Snowdon Ranger and a sister engine, *Moel Tryfan*, were 0-6-4 single Fairlies, built in Britain by the Vulcan Foundry Ltd. in 1875. These were designed by CE Spooner under Fairlie's patent and were commissioned by the North Wales Narrow Gauge Railways. After much use, the two engines were combined into one in 1917 to form a single, good locomotive. The resulting engine retained the name *Moel Tryfan*. It was finally scrapped by the Ffestiniog Railway (who had acquired it in the early 1920s) in 1954.

The model

Archangel's models often exhibit freely interpreted proportions and details, and this one is no exception. However, it does capture the feeling of the prototype. It is fitted with two, double acting, slide-valve cylinders. Valves are inside the frames and are driven by slip-eccentrics. The boiler is a simple pot, alcohol fired. Fuel is carried in a tank behind – and attached to – the swivelling steam truck. There is a long filler tube that extends to the front of the engine. While this is unsightly, it does get the filler away from the fire to some extent.

The prototype went through various alterations. Photos show it with a slanting cab rear. Archangel's model is without a back plate on the cab. Side tanks are dummies and serve as flame shields. The drivers are pierced with holes, as opposed to having spokes.

The boiler is fitted with the bare minimum; a throttle, a blow-down valve, and a safety valve under the removable steam dome. A displacement lubricator resides in the cab. Details are also minimal, and include a dummy whistle, some handrails, boiler bands, and a coal load.

The steam bogie is pivoted between the first and second drivers. The steam line contains no special articulation (i.e., no steam-tight ball joints or other arcana), just a long, looping coil that takes up the motion in its length. This loop also passes through the fire and serves as a superheater.

My *Snowdon Ranger* belonged to Peter Dobson and, I believe, appears on page two of his 1980 book, *16mm Scale Live Steam Model Locomotives, Vol. 1* (there never was a Vol. 2, alas). Another example of the same engine appears on page 7. One of the wonderful and charming things about Stewart Browne's locomotives is that there are rarely two just alike.

Specifications

Builder: Archangel Models (UK)
Date built: 1977
Gauge: 0 (32mm)
Scale: 16mm
Boiler: Pot
Fittings: Throttle, blowdown, safety valve
Fuel: Alcohol
Blow-off pressure: 75psi
Cylinders: Two, double-acting D-valve
Reversing gear: Slip eccentric
Lubricator: Displacement
Weight: 6lbs 6oz
Dimensions: Length, 12¾in; width, 4in; height, 6in

Aster's SNCF 232TC 4-6-4T

While this is a handsome model, many of its design features date from the 1930s or earlier. Reversing is via Walschaerts valve gear, controlled from the cab.

The prototype for this locomotive was one of a class of engines built from 1912 through 1923. Similar engines were built for both the Prussian Railways and the Alsace-Loraine System, when Alsace was still part of the German Empire. A total of 491 of this class was constructed – 464 for Germany and 27 for Alsace. They were popular locomotives with their drivers, easier to operate and mechanically simpler than their predecessors, and they remained in use through the late 1960s.

The model

This engine was produced by Aster in 1978, early in Aster's production. Both the French (green) and German (black) versions, which were mechanically similar, were produced. The French version is described here. The models featured full, working Walschaerts valve gear, a Smithies boiler, and alcohol firing. The locomotive was offered in both kit and built-up forms, as are most Aster locomotives. Total production was 800 of these units, equally divided between the French version and the German.

This engine is a favorite of mine. I built it from a kit. Despite its being a Japanese model of a French locomotive, it is quintessential 1930s, British gauge-1 technology.

The Smithies boiler, first designed by Fred Smithies, has been a mainstay for decades and is, perhaps, the simplest internally fired boiler to build. It is reliable, as well, though not as efficient as other types.

The firebox is at the rear of the boiler. There are three large wicks within, fed by an alcohol tank carried in the bunker behind the cab and utilising the chicken-feed system. The engine requires an auxiliary fan to draw the combustion gases forward and out the stack until enough pressure – about 20psi – is raised to turn on the locomotive's own blower.

This engine can be kept in steam indefinitely through the use of a trackside pump, which must be attached to a fitting beneath the cab when the water runs low. Otherwise, the fire must be dropped and the loco refilled through one of the safety-valve holes. The fuel tank can be refilled while the engine is under steam, too.

In action, this is a wonderful locomotive. It is easily controllable, powerful, and it has a clearly audible but somewhat muffled exhaust beat. The engine looks terrific loping around wide-radius curves. It can be left alone and will not run away.

With the roof off, controls are accessible. The throttle is in the middle, with the blower valve above it. The pressure gauge, pointing up, cannot be read with the roof in place.

Specifications

Builder: Aster Hobby Company (Japan)
Date built: 1978
Gauge: 1 (45mm)
Scale: 1:32
Boiler: Smithies
Fittings: Safety valves (2), displacement lubricator, throttle, blower, water glass, pressure gauge
Fuel: Alcohol
Blow-off pressure: 45psi
Cylinders: Two, double-acting D-valve
Reversing gear: Walschaerts
Lubricator: Displacement
Weight: 9lbs
Dimensions: Length over end beams, 16¾in; width, 4in; height, 5½in

Beck's *Anna*

The Beck *Anna* is more of a well-proportioned toy than a model locomotive. The black knob on the side tank controls the gas flow to the burner, while the one on the steam dome controls steam to the cylinders.

In 1979, there wasn't much going on in the commercial world of small-scale live steam, especially in narrow gauge. Stewart Browne was producing 32mm gauge, 16mm-scale locomotives under the name of Archangel. And, aside from Aster in Japan and a small number of custom builders, that was about it. The hobby as we know it today was in its infancy. LGB's large, attractive, electric trains from Germany had been around a decade or so – long enough to have been noticed by the market.

Chr. Beck & Söhne was an old German company making optical instruments in the city of Kassel. In 1979, the company introduced its first live-steam locomotive, *Anna*. Why it made the decision to branch out into steam engines is unknown but, in doing so, they followed a century-old tradition of optical-instrument makers who also produced steam engines. *Anna*, an 0-4-0T modelled after a series 99 Maffei locomotive, was available in the green you see here, and black. It was later followed by *Helene*, an 0-6-2T patterned after the Zillertal engines that LGB had made famous.

In fact, both *Anna* and *Helene* were intended for use with LGB track and rolling stock. They were built to the same scale as LGB trains (1:22.5) and came equipped with LGB-style loop couplers. They did not, however, have insulated wheels, and so could not be operated simultaneously with electrically powered trains. A third engine, *Bertha*, was proposed, but never produced by Beck. This was to be a non-articulated 0-4-4-0T. A few of these were later produced by Tom Cooper (see below), but were not very successful. Beck also produced a couple of high-end models of early German locomotives in very limited numbers.

Beck's engines were little more than elaborate toys. They were more-or-less well proportioned, but had little in the way of detail. They were significant, however, in establishing what has almost become standard technology for gas-fired locomotives. Theirs were the very first, commercially produced, single flue, gas-fired boilers. They were heated with what is now known as the 'poker' burner. Today, most companies producing gas-fired engines use the single flue, poker-burner technology pioneered by Beck.

Early in 1981, the company went out of business. The remaining inventory of parts and locomotives was eventually procured by Tom Cooper in Britain, who founded Merlin Locomotive Works. Merlin's engines were the first to capitalise on Beck's technology. The last of the parts eventually passed from Cooper to Roger Loxley of Roundhouse Engineering, who produced the very last batch of *Annas* in 1990, these with Roundhouse cylinders, which were much superior to the Beck/Merlin cylinders. These Roundhouse/Beck *Annas* are very scarce today.

The model

As mentioned above, *Anna* is little more than a toy, albeit a pretty good one. It carries its fuel in the right-hand side tank. A filler valve is accessible through the top of the tank, while a large control valve protrudes through the front. These engines were designed to be easy to use by people who had absolutely no familiarity with steam.

The only control is the throttle, which is a large knob sticking out of the right side of the steam dome. The backhead is fitted with a Wilesco-style water glass (window) and an oversize pressure gauge; the safety valve is of the toy variety. A cylinder lubricator also resides in the steam dome. It is just a small reservoir, accessed by unscrewing the silver dome top. In practice, most of the oil is dumped into the cylinders as soon as the throttle is open.

A large, metric-reading pressure gauge fills the right side of the cab, while a water window resides in the left side.

Dummy headlamps and a caricature of a steam pump adorn the running boards. Cylinders are of the piston-valve type, controlled by unusual, external slip eccentrics that sort of resemble outside Stephenson's or Allan valve gear. Each piston comprises a pair of Teflon cups, mounted back-to-back on the piston rod. The engine is heavily and robustly built, with extensive use of pop rivets to hold cab and frame together.

Specifications

Builder: Chr. Beck & Söhne (Germany)
Date built: 1979
Gauge: 1 (45mm)
Scale: 1:22.5
Boiler: Single flue
Fittings: Safety valve, pressure gauge, water glass, throttle
Fuel: Butane
Blow-off pressure: 30psi
Cylinders: Two, double-acting piston-valve
Reversing gear: Slip eccentric
Lubricator: Displacement
Weight: 6lbs
Dimensions: Length over end beams, 9in; width, 4¼in, height, 6½in

Maurice Cross's deWinton

Specifications

Builder: Maurice Cross to Jim Wild's design (UK)
Date built: Circa 1979
Gauge: 0 (32mm)
Scale: 16mm
Boiler: Vertical, single flue
Fittings: Safety valve
Fuel: Alcohol
Blow-off pressure: 25psi
Cylinders: One, single-acting oscillator
Reversing gear: Rotary valve
Lubricator: None
Weight: 1lb 11oz
Dimensions: Length over body, 6½in; width, 2¼in; height, 5¼in

Left: A tiny model of a diminutive prototype, this deWinton is simplicity itself. Speed and direction are both controlled by a rotary valve, actuated by the nicely crafted reversing lever.

Above: One, single-acting oscillator runs the engine. The dummy safety valve on the side of the boiler is one of few cosmetic details.

DeWinton was a builder of industrial locomotives and quarry equipment in Great Britain, starting around 1868. The company's engines were widely used in the Welsh quarries and some may even have been exported to the US. Though tiny, they were powerful. The prototype locomotive had a two-cylinder steam motor attached vertically to the boiler and geared to one axle. The engine was small enough to be easily managed by one man. At least one, *Chaloner*, has been preserved in operating condition.

The model

This is sort of a stand-off scale model, as the prototype had several distinctive features not included on the model. The most obvious, of course, is that the model is powered by one, single-acting oscillator.

This little engine (one of the tiniest 16mm locomotives I know of) was designed by Jim Wild of England around 1979 or so. He built a few of them, then turned production over to Maurice Cross, who, as I understand it, was not so much a hobbyist as a contractor. This engine is from one of his batches. I don't know how many were made in total, but it couldn't have been a lot.

The locomotive is neatly made, mostly of brass. The boiler has a single, vertical flue with one alcohol burner beneath it. It requires a suction fan to get it going, after which the exhaust from the cylinder takes over. In this respect, it's kind of a funny engine – it has the most primitive steam motor (an oscillator) driven by a fairly sophisticated boiler. The only fitting on the boiler itself is a low-pressure safety valve.

Speed (what little there is) and direction are controlled by a diminutive rotary valve mounted on the side of the port block. This is actuated by a prototypical-looking lever on a quadrant near the boiler. The cylinder powers a shaft that carries a flywheel and pulley. Around the pulley is a spring belt that drives a second shaft below the first. At the other end of this shaft is a largish pinion that drives a crown gear on one axle. The other axle is driven conventionally via side rods.

The locomotive is painted black, with rods, reversing lever, and other bits picked out in red. Altogether it's quite attractive.

In operation, the engine runs *very* slowly – perhaps a prototypical eight to ten miles per hour. Steam can be raised quickly and, when running, the engine is quite audible. It will run for a quarter of an hour, with one or two stops for fuel along the way.

A single wick fires the vertical, single-flue boiler. A combination of drive belts and gears, coupled with a flywheel, makes the engine a smooth runner that is powerful for its size.

Aster's GER 0-6-0T

Above: The steam-motor assembly sits above the leading axle. The piston drives a shaft on which there is a flywheel and a pinion. The pinion drives the large gear on the driven axle. The rotary valve can be seen to the right of the larger gear.

Left: Aster's GER 0-6-0T is a good looking but quirky engine. Once the problems had been solved, it proved to be a good runner.

This engine is loosely based on an 0-6-0T built in the early part of the 20th century by Holden & Company for England's Great Eastern Railway (GER). These engines were used mostly for suburban commuter work around London. Similar locomotives were built by Messrs. Fives-Lille for the French Western Railway Company (Ouest) in 1889 and were later transferred to the Etat region.

The model

Aster produced models of all three versions of the engine (one British and two French). They were mechanically identical and differed only in paint and external details. The blue GER version is the one that seems to be the most common.

These are interesting locomotives. They were intended to be low-cost models and, when new in 1980, sold for around £300 in kit form. The design is based on John van Reimsdijk's work with single-cylindered pot boilers. There is one, single-acting cylinder between the frames, geared 4:1 to the front axle and thus giving the proper four exhaust beats per revolution. The boiler is fitted with a water glass and safety valve, but no pressure gauge, throttle, or anything else. Reversing and a little speed control is accomplished by a lever in the cab that actuates, through a linkage, a rotary reversing valve built into the steam motor at the front of the engine. A small displacement lubricator (sans drain) resides just to the left of the smokebox.

This locomotive is full of quirks, which, I suppose, is part of the reason I like it. The shielding around the pot boiler extends into the cab and there are some spaces that actually let heat into the cab, which gets blistering hot – hot enough to melt the soft solder that at one time held a little handle onto the reversing lever. The alcohol burner, which can be quickly dropped by removing a pin, employs a box-section feed tube. This increases the fuel capacity but also tends to diffuse heat into the storage tank. The result is that the stored alcohol heats up and vaporizes at the filler and overflow tubes, which often catch fire. I was able to mitigate this problem somewhat by extending the filler tube up and away from the fire.

A steam line exits the bottom of the boiler, passing through the fire (which supplies a little superheat to the line), and then to the steam motor. As supplied, the connection between the steam motor and the steam line was a silicone tube. On one of my first runs with this engine, this tube burst with a resounding *pop* and the engine came to an abrupt halt. Once the offending silicone was replaced with a proper copper line (after unsuccessful experiments with other plastics) this particular problem was solved.

Then there were the zinc-alloy wheels. Nothing wrong there except that they seemed to expand more than their axles when hot. Thus, they would loosen and slip on the axles, causing the rods to get crossed (another abrupt halt). So, all the wheels had to be pinned to the axles to prevent this unfortunate occurrence.

Once this litany of faults had been remedied, the locomotive turned into a good, reliable runner, even though control remained difficult at best. It would pull half a dozen four-wheel cars at prototypical speed for the better part of half an hour, with the occasional top up of fuel.

Specifications

Builder: Aster Hobby Company (Japan)
Date built: 1980
Gauge: 1 (45mm)
Scale: 1:32
Boiler: Pot
Fittings: Safety valve, water glass
Fuel: Alcohol
Blow-off pressure: 30psi
Cylinders: One, single-acting oscillator
Reversing gear: Rotary valve
Lubricator: Displacement
Weight: 3lbs 12oz
Dimensions: Length over frames, 10⅛in; width, 3⅜in; height, 5¼in

In 1935, Geoffrey Malins started a manufacturing company called GM Patents Company. Under this name he made ball-race turntables (like lazy susans) and, later, toy steam engines that were sold to a company called Hobbies. These engines were commissioned by Hobbies to take the place of Bowman engines when Bowman ceased production.

Mr. Malins' engines were simple and well made. They were mostly stationary engines and marine plants. In 1939, Geoffrey Malins decided to market the engines on his own. The company name was changed to Mamod, a name coined by his wife Clarrie.

The name is properly pronounced 'May-mod', a contraction of Malins Models. Over the years the company expanded its line of stationary engines and added steam-powered vehicles as well. It was not until 1980, though, that the company's railway system first appeared. This happened during the time when the Mamod Company passed from the Malins family into other hands, after forty-four years. This is a sad story that need not be recounted here.

The Mamod Steam Railway

When it appeared in 1980, the railway system was fully formed. It was first offered as a set containing a locomotive, a log car a gondola car, and a loop of track. Other sets were added later. These initial sets were only offered in gauge 0. It would be some time before gauge-1 trains were offered,

Above: A gaggle of Mamods. Rear, left to right: A special gauge-1 engine in red, sans diamond stack, produced for G1MRA; a black, kit-built Mamod. Front: A special, limited-edition number in an odd colour to celebrate the company's Golden Jubilee Year in 1989; the standard SL1 in green, 0-gauge – the first engine to be issued; the standard SL3 in maroon with the awful diamond stack. Missing is the powder-blue SL2, along with a host of special-issue engines.

Left: Although the Mamod locomotive was, in a way, an aggregation of old ideas, it was new and innovative in that it portrayed a plausible, narrow-gauge locomotive, was a strong, reliable runner, and could pull a reasonable train. It hit the market just at the right time.

With the back off, the cab is plain, with just a little water window and the whistle pull for ornamentation. The pellet burner slides right out.

although the Gauge 1 Model Railway Association commissioned a small batch of gauge-1 locomotives from the company before they were put into standard production.

Mamod produced its own track. This was a strange product, die-cast in a zinc alloy. The pieces fitted together with interlocking tabs that were easily broken off. One radius of curve, one length of straight, and right- and left-hand points were offered. Once the tabs had been broken off, the track was useless unless it was screwed securely to boards.

The model

The locomotive, designed for Mamod by Barry Hares in 1978, was, in my opinion, a brilliant design. One might say, "It's just an insignificant little oscillator." While that may be true on the surface of it, when taken in the context of its times and the impact it subsequently had on our hobby, it becomes far more than that.

The design drew a lot from the toy engines of the 1920s and 30s, but it had some more modern innovations as well. For one thing, it replicated the proportions of a narrow-gauge locomotive, which made it the first narrow-gauge live steamer in mass production (aside from the Beck *Anna*, which was only made in limited numbers). It had a shielded firebox and double-acting cylinders, making it a self-starter. Control – both speed and direction – was provided by a single lever that operated a valve between the cylinders.

Steam, at a working pressure of about 10psi, was taken from an actual steam dome. The boiler even had a water window in the backhead. As supplied, it came with a solid-fuel burner (stinking, white pellets variously described as camel dung or worse) that barely did the job. On a good day, you might get eight to ten minutes out of the loco.

The ready-to-run engine was offered in three colours: hunter green, maroon, and, strangely, powder blue. The latter two had odd-looking diamond stacks. Later, the locomotive was offered in kit form, in black.

Mamod's locomotive has been much maligned over the years. When it came out, however, it was embraced with open arms by live steamers around the world. While marketed as a toy engine, it quickly found favour in the 16mm, narrow-gauge modeling groups. Due to its simple design, it was easily kit-bashed into a vast variety of different models.

Despite its faults, it was a decent runner, especially when fitted with some of the plethora of after-market accessories. Alcohol burners were made by a variety of different makers and there was even a drop-in gas burner available for a while. Other improvements included lubricators, proper throttles, better cylinders, better boilers, and more. In fact, if you incorporated all of the improvements, you'd be left with little original besides the frames and bodywork. The engine could even be effectively radio

controlled. The concept of the Mamod was so good that it spawned a number of knock-offs, most of which were better engines.

On the down side, as supplied, the tiny engine was under-powered, tended to leak steam around the cylinders, was difficult to control with its single lever, and tended to run away when running light. Wheels sometimes came loose on the axles and crankpins came loose in the wheels. If you had the misfortune of letting yours run dry, the water window would surely melt, as it was only made of plastic. All these problems, though, were fixable. In later years, quality control at the factory suffered greatly. This problem probably contributed more to the engine's ill-deserved poor reputation than anything else.

The Mamod locomotive, despite its shortcomings, introduced thousands of people to small-scale live steam, provided a platform for countless examples of creative work, and gave employment to the legions who provided improvements for it. Over 18,000 of these engines were made before production of the original locomotive ceased in 1989. The company changed hands several times and the engine is currently being produced by MSS (Mamod Sales & Service).

The heart of the matter. Two, double-acting oscillators, controlled by a rotary valve with a lever in front of the smokebox.

Specifications

Builder: Mamod (UK)
Date built: 1980
Gauge: 0 (32mm) and 1 (45mm) – not regaugeable
Scale: 16mm (nominal)
Boiler: Pot
Fittings: Water window, safety valve, whistle
Fuel: Solid pellets (as supplied)
Blow-off pressure: 10psi
Cylinders: Two, double-acting oscillators
Reversing gear: Rotary valve
Lubricator: None
Weight: 2lbs 3oz
Dimensions: Length, 7¼in; width, 3¼in; height, 5¼in

Maxwell Hemmens' Porter

Specifications

Builder: Maxwell Hemmens (UK)
Date built: Early 1980s
Gauge: 1 (45mm)
Scale: 1:22.5 (nominal)
Boiler: Single flue with cross tubes
Fittings: Safety valve, throttle, water glass with blowdown
Fuel: Butane
Blow-off pressure: 60psi
Cylinders: Two, double-acting piston valve
Reversing gear: Piston valve
Lubricator: Displacement
Weight: 7lbs
Dimensions: Length, including tender, 16⅝in; width, 4⅜in; height, 6⅛in

The H.K. Porter Company, established in 1866 as Smith & Porter, was one of the world's largest manufacturers of industrial locomotives. The company is perhaps best known (to modellers, anyway) for its 0-4-0 saddle-tank engines, which have been reproduced in every scale by the thousands. The prototypes, too, were produced by the thousands in different sizes and in several different gauges, from standard on down.

Over the years, Porter produced locomotives not only for US customers, but for those in forty other countries as well. The company used standardized parts and often built locomotives on speculation, to have in stock for quick delivery when orders came in. Porter ceased locomotive production in 1950 but is still in business today as a manufacturer of tools.

The model

Maxwell Hemmens' model of the Porter is, at best, an approximation of the prototype. The proportions seem odd and the detail level is low. However, it is a well-made model locomotive and a good runner.

The boiler is gas fired. It has a single flue with cross tubes. The backhead is equipped with a pressure gauge, a water glass, and a throttle. The throttle valve has no handle and must be actuated by a special tool, which is awkward to say the least. The steam line passes through a standard displacement lubricator (with drain), then runs forward through the flue pipe, which provides some superheat. Reversing is accomplished via a piston reversing valve between the cylinders, controlled by a handle in the cab.

A safety valve sits atop the boiler, inside the wooden cab, exhausting through a tube through the roof. This tube can be unscrewed and the roof slid off for cab access. The smokebox door opens – a nice feature. Cylinders are controlled by piston valves. The wheels are not spoked, as were the prototype's, but have curved slots in them instead.

The engine is provided with a large, unprototypical, wooden tender that houses the gas tank. This tank has the usual control valve and an unusual safety valve, accessed by the removal of the wood load. The filler valve is unusual, too. To get to it, you have to unscrew and remove the control valve. Underneath is

While the furniture-maker's cab and tender, along with other details, fail to capture the workaday essence of a full-size industrial Porter, this is nevertheless an attractive locomotive. The tender is fanciful in the extreme.

a standard filler valve. When the control valve is screwed back in place, it releases gas through the filler valve. Gas is fed to the burner via a silicon tube. The workmanship on the tender, as on the locomotive, is to a high standard.

In operation, this engine is fairly quiet for a single-flue engine. Perhaps this is because the cross tubes act as sound baffles – you don't get the impedance matching that you do with an unobstructed tube. The Porter is a smooth, quiet runner, that will run unattended for twenty-five minutes or so, until the gas is exhausted. It's a lively engine, though, and adjusting the throttle on the fly is impossible. You have to stop the engine manually and use that infernal tool to adjust its speed – not a good system.

Right: Valves are operated by eccentrics on the rear axle. The front axle is sprung. The long rod is the reversing rod, extending from the lever in the cab to the piston-valve reverser between the cylinders.

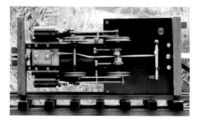

Lower: The interior of the cab is complete and neatly laid out. The throttle is immediately below the safety valve. A special tool is required to operate it. The reversing lever is on the right side. The burner sports cooling fins!

Einco/Lindale's *Sam* 0-4-0T

Sam is a plain, utilitarian locomotive. The 'sand box' on the footplate is actually the lubricator. The knob on the front of the smokebox is the exhaust throttle.

Lindale Models began business in 1981 or thereabouts. In addition to *Sam*, the company produced *Caledonia*, an 0-6-0T, as well as machined parts for a 3½in-gauge locomotive, *Rob Roy*, designed by Martin Evans. Aside from wheel arrangement and the fact that *Caledonia* had two working cylinders while *Sam* had only one, the engines were quite similar and used about 80% of the same parts. These engines were designed by John Turner, a competent and meticulous engine designer, while the company was run by his brother-in-law, Kevan Winward.

Jack Wheldon wrote a review of the then new Lindale engines in the British press. It was this review that called them to my attention. I contacted the company and became the US importer in 1981. The locomotives were available in both gauge 0 and gauge 1, but only as kits. The kits were simple to assemble (instructions were entirely pictorial), requiring only basic tools. No soldering, drilling, or machine work was necessary. Wheels, originally nickel silver, were later replaced with cast-iron, as the nickel-silver ones tended to turn on the axles.

There seemed to be a fair amount of turnover in the company. I perused my old files in preparing these notes and found that I corresponded with at least three people in the organization over a two-year period. Our relationship ended in 1982 and the company sank without trace shortly thereafter, having produced only the two different models.

The model

Sam is a big, chunky 0-4-0. Mine is one of the earlier ones, with cast nickel-silver wheels. It is nominally 16mm scale, but, for an 0-4-0T, is really oversize. However, I find its proportions pleasing and it has quite an industrial look about it.

The original locomotives, both *Sams* and *Caledonias*, were fitted with zinc-alloy side rods. These were fine for a few years, but soon the zinc began to do all the nasty things that zinc does, and the side rods fell to pieces. Most of these engines running today, including mine, have replacement side rods.

Sam is unusual in that it has only one working cylinder. That's not the unusual part – lots of engines have just one cylinder. However, on most of them, the cylinder is placed between the wheels so it can drive the engine symmetrically. *Sam's* is outside, on the right-hand side. The cylinder on the lef side is similar in appearance, but is a dummy. The only other commercially made engine like this that I can think of was Aster's first offering, the JNR 2-6-0, though there may well be others.

Another unusual feature of this locomotive is the fact that it has two throttles. There is a conventional, needle-valve throttle in the cab and a secondary throttle that chokes the exhaust as it leaves the cylinder. When used in combination, the pair make for an easily controlled locomotive. A rubber O-ring around the throttle knob in the cab is intended to keep it cool enough to comfortably handle (it doesn't!).

A massive fuel tank is carried beneath the open cab. Three wicks heat the boiler, which is shielded only by the sheet-metal dummy side tanks. A boxy displacement lubricator sits on the right-hand footplate, replicating a sand box. All steam connections are of the banjo variety, simple and reliable.

Aside from the wheels, the engine uses no castings. It is made entirely of sheet metal and machined parts. The smokebox is simply a sheet-brass wrapper projecting from the front of the boiler. The knob on the front is the exhaust regulator. Reversing is via a slip eccentric, the eccentric being between the rear driver and the frame. *Sam* has absolutely no insulation and, consequently, gets very hot in steam. Reversing the loco is best accomplished with a stick.

In operation, the engine has a peculiar gait, shifting from side to side as it travels the rails (this phenomenon is known as 'boxing'). The single cylinder on one side exaggerates the uneven forces that act on the engine, which contributes to this effect. *Sam* will run unattended for forty-five minutes on a good day. And, as darkness falls and the alcohol fire becomes visible, you can see flames spurting from between the frames, under the tank, and into the cab in a most spectacular and satisfying way.

The underside is straightforward. The huge fuel tank is on the left. You can see that only one cylinder is plumbed.

Specifications

Builder: Lindale Models (also called Model & Miniature Railways) (UK)
Date built: 1981
Gauge: 0 (32mm)
Scale: 16mm (nominal)
Boiler: Pot
Fittings: Safety valve, throttle, exhaust throttle
Fuel: Alcohol
Blow-off pressure: 40psi
Cylinders: One, double-acting D-valve
Reversing gear: Slip eccentric
Lubricator: Displacement
Weight: 3lbs 5oz
Dimensions: Length over end beams, 9in; width, 4⅛in; height, 6⅝in

Archangel's *Hercules*

Archangel locomotives range from crude to sublime. Generally speaking, the lower-end production models run toward the former and the upper end and one-offs lean more toward the latter. Stewart Browne, the company's owner, produced an astonishing number of engines over the years. No one knows how many – including Stewart.

The model

Hercules is a boxy 0-6-0T that, in many ways, resembles the company's *Sgt. Murphy* engines. The primary cosmetic difference is the windows, which on the *Sgt. Murphys* are round and on *Hercules* are rectangular with rounded corners and arched tops.

The primary mechanical difference, which is significant, is that *Hercules* has two D-valve cylinders outside the frames, whereas *Sgt. Murphy* has but one, inside. Thus, *Hercules* is a more fully realized locomotive and has the attraction of being self starting. Reversing is via Archangel's usual slip eccentrics on the rear axle. Motion is brought to the outside valves atop the cylinders by rocker arms set into the frames.

The boiler is a pot type, fired by a three-wick burner. The fuel tank resides beneath the cab floor. There's a filler pipe and overflow on the left side of the tank.

Boiler fittings include a safety valve under the steam dome; a throttle valve, the handle of which projects through the cab's back sheet for easy access; a pressure gauge and a whistle (both attached to the same steam line from the boiler); and a blowdown valve. The whistle, unsupported except for the steam line to which it's attached, has a screw-type valve of dubious utility.

Side tanks are Archangel's usual solid chunks of aluminium. The locomotive is finished in gloss black paint neatly lined in white. The engine has seen some use and paint is flaking off in places, particularly from the cab floor. Buffers are Archangel's

Above: Hercules takes a train of heavily loaded Accucraft ballast wagons across the temporary bridge on the OBR. The trestle was made of privet, harvested from a nearby hedge

Left: Hercules is a sort of refined *Sgt. Murphy*, with two, double-acting cylinders outside the frames. It's an attractive engine in its gloss-black paint, neatly lined out in white. The displacement lubricator can be seen in the cab door.

Top Right: The underside of the engine is straightforward. The three-wick burner is separated from the fuel tank by a long feed tube, but that doesn't prevent the tank from heating up and catching fire on hot days. The tank sits very low to the track, as is evidenced by the multitude of scrapes in the paint.

Lower: Looking into the left-hand cab door, the most prominent feature is the whistle, which is supported only by the steam line to which it is attached. Coming off the same steam line is the lead to the pressure gauge. The knob below and to the left of the whistle is the blowdown valve. A short length of silicone tubing has been stuck on the fuel filler pipe to extend it away from the cab a little in case of fire. The overflow pipe is just to the right of it.

standard nylon turnings (so you can pick up a hot engine) and, typically, one of them shows signs of a fuel-tank fire.

The locomotive is a fine runner, though a little thirsty, requiring fairly frequent stops for fuel. I suspect that the wicks could be packed a little tighter, which might ease this problem. If a close eye is not kept on the fuel level, the fire tends to go out.

With two, double-acting cylinders, the engine is self starting. When hauling a heavy load, which it is fully capable of doing, the exhaust beats are clearly audible. This one's safety valve, while not making the rude noise typical of Archangel valves, will sometimes release with enough force to blow the heavy dome right off the boiler.

Specifications

Builder: Archangel Models (UK)
Date built: 1981
Gauge: 0 (32mm)
Scale: 16mm
Boiler: Pot
Fittings: Safety valve, pressure gauge, throttle, whistle, blowdown valve
Fuel: Alcohol
Blow-off pressure: 50psi
Cylinders: Two, double-acting D-valve
Reversing gear: Slip eccentrics
Lubricator: Displacement
Weight: 6lbs
Dimensions: Length, 11⅛in; width, 4in; height, 6⅛in

Hugh Saunders' *Edward Thomas*

Specifications

Builder: Hugh Saunders (UK)
Date built: Early 1980s
Gauge: 0 (32mm)
Scale: 16mm
Boiler: Wrighton
Fittings: Safety valve, throttle, blower, water glass, pressure gauge, check valve
Fuel: Alcohol
Blow-off pressure: 45psi
Cylinders: Two, double-acting D-valve
Reversing gear: Hackworth
Lubricator: Displacement
Weight: 5lbs 14oz
Dimensions: Length over end beams, 9½in; width, 3½in; height, 5⅝in

Edward Thomas is an attractive, well-made model of a well-known prototype. It features Hackworth valve gear and an internally, meths-fired boiler.

Edward Thomas was built by Kerr-Stuart for the Corris Railway in Wales in 1921. In 1951, the engine went to the 2ft 3in-gauge Talyllyn Railway, a slate hauler that opened in 1866 and later became Great Britain's first preserved railway. The 0-4-2T entered service there in 1952 after some repairs had been made, and has been there ever since. For a while it was painted red and bore the name *Peter Sam*, after the Reverend Awdrey's creation in the *Thomas the Tank Engine* series. *Peter Sam*, in the story, was, in fact, modelled on *Edward Thomas*. Today, *Edward Thomas* runs under its own name and is painted bronze and black, with yellow lining – standard Talyllyn colors.

The model

Edward Thomas, the model, was constructed by Hugh Saunders, a private builder in the UK. Mr. Saunders sometimes made engines in small batches for sale. This is one of those, and was also the first model he offered commercially. Like his other models, this one is sophisticated and built to a high, workmanlike standard. The detail level is relatively low and all working parts are robust and precisely made.

The locomotive features a Wrighton-style, single flue, alcohol-fired boiler. There are water cross tubes in the large flue and additional water tubes in the top of the

firebox to increase the heating area. The burner is unusual. It is basically an open-top box, stuffed with asbestos wicking. There are eight tubes coming up through it that admit air from under the burner to the fire.

Because access is so tight, the fire must be lit through the firebox door, found in the usual place. There is a hole in the back sheet for access to the firebox. The fuel tank is forward of the burner, between the frames. Fuel can be introduced through one of two hatches, one on either side of the engine, beneath the saddle tank.

For access to the backhead, the top of the cab's back sheet comes off. The boiler has the usual fittings. A hand pump is mounted to the footplate on the right side of the cab, next to the boiler, concealed by the forward coal-bunker extension to the cab. Water is taken from the working saddle tank by a hand pump next to the boiler, but only from one side. There is no balance pipe.

Hackworth gear, reversed from the cab, controls the valves. Each of the motion parts is beautifully made. The trailing truck just clips into place. It can be removed in a second, but is held securely in position when the locomotive is on the track.

With the back sheet removed, cab controls are accessible. The engine has all the amenities, including an internal throttle. The green lever to the right of the boiler is for the hand pump. The hole in the lower back sheet is for lighting and checking on the fire.

With the trailing truck removed, the box-style burner can be seen. The meths tank is ahead of the burner, between the frames on this engine.

Archangel's *Taw*

Specifications

Builder: Archangel Models (UK)
Date built: 1982
Gauge: 0 (32mm)
Scale: 16mm
Boiler: Pot
Fittings: Safety valve, throttle, pressure gauge, whistle, blowdown
Fuel: Alcohol
Blow-off pressure: 75psi
Cylinders: Two, double-acting D-valve
Reversing gear: Hackworth
Lubricator: Displacement
Weight: 7lbs 4oz
Dimensions: Length over buffers, 16in; width, 4¼in; height, 6in

A handsome engine, *Taw* evokes a bygone era. While there are some differences between the model and the prototype, the model still captures the flavour of the original.

Taw ran on the Lynton & Barnstaple Railway in Devon, in southern England. The L&B existed from 1898 to 1935. It was purchased by the Southern Railway in 1923, which ran it until it closed.

Taw was one of three similar engines (the other two were *Exe* and *Yeo*, all named after rivers) supplied to the railway by Manning, Wardle & Company of Leeds. The L&B had high standards as far as its equipment was concerned, especially for a narrow-gauge line. The company's rolling stock included a large assortment of beautiful coaches, since it was primarily a passenger-hauling line. The Lynton & Barnstaple has been compared to the Denver & Rio Grande, as regards the high degree of interest it generated among enthusiasts and the intense loyalty of its followers.

The model

This engine, which was made during a period that might be considered Archangel's peak, follows the company's typical practice. It is robust and well made. While nicely proportioned, its proportions do not necessarily closely match those of the prototype. Detail is minimal, but the important bits are there – a large brass dome, sand boxes,

A roomy cab makes access to the controls easy. The engine was originally fitted with R/C. Servo brackets are still in place on the floor.

and the safety valve in the oversize cab. Under the dome is a removable plug for filling the boiler.

Reversing is accomplished via Hackworth valve gear, controlled from the cab, whereas the prototype had Joy gear. On the left side is a whistle, tucked under the cab and operated by a screw valve. On the other side is a blowdown valve. A displacement lubricator is mounted under the broad pilot deck, with the nylon filler cap protruding through the deck plate.

The boiler is a large pot boiler, fired by a two-wick alcohol burner. Fuel is carried in a tank in front of the rear buffer beam. It is interesting that so large a boiler could be fired by only two wicks. The burner, at fist glance, appears inadequate for such a larger boiler, but it is not.

When I received this engine, it was fitted with a radio-control system. Not being a great fan of R/C, I removed the radio gear and replaced it with manual controls, including a throttle lever and a reversing quadrant, each of which could be accessed through a cab door or from above, with the roof off.

In performance, the engine is smooth and quiet. It is a powerful runner, but easily controllable, making it a delight to operate.

A new reversing quadrant, still waiting for paint, was fitted in lieu of the original servo.

Gosling's *The Prince*

Above: A four-wick burner fires the Smithies boiler. The engine has inside valves and outside cylinders, giving it a very clean external appearance. All wheels are sprung.

Left: The Prince is a beautifully crafted model. It is very close to scale in everything except boiler fittings. The tiny tender carries both fuel and water.

The Pince (latter just *Prince*) was the third of four locomotives supplied to the famous Ffestiniog Railway in Wales, in 1863 and '64 (the others were *Mountaineer, Princess*, and *Lord Palmerston*). These were the first steam locomotives to be used by the railway, which had opened in 1836. The locomotives were constructed by George England (who is also credited with the invention of the screw jack, used to replace derailed locomotives on the track). These engines were delivered a couple of years before the railway began hauling passengers.

George England was to build two more locomotives for the Ffestiniog before his locomotive works was passed to his son-in-law, Robert Fairlie, who renamed the works the Fairlie Engine and Steam Carriage Company. He acquired a patent for the well known, unusual, double-ended locomotive, but that's a different story.

The *Prince* that is running today on the Ffestiniog is the same *Prince* delivered by George England in 1863, and is one of the oldest, if not *the* oldest, steam locomotive still in operating condition. *Prince* was originally built with side tanks, like the model. Its current saddle tank and cab were later added to the prototype at the Ffestiniog's Boston Lodge Works.

The model

Robin Gosling, the builder of *Prince*, is one of the more enigmatic and little known of the British builders. He was busy during the 1970s and early 80s, but has since dropped out of sight. He is known to have produced only three different locomotives commercially – *Prince*; a Glyn Valley Tramway loco with an oscillating cylinder (both in 16mm scale for gauge-0 track); and an 0-scale model of an LBSC 4-4-2T. None were produced in great numbers (the engine shown here is works number 110).

Robin Gosling was a craftsman of a high order. Both his machine work and his finish work are superb, as can be seen in the photos. Prince has two, small, D-valve cylinders with inside valves and slip-eccentric reversing. All wheels on the engine are sprung. The boiler is a Smithies with a wet-leg backhead, fired by a four-wick alcohol burner. Fuel is carried in the tender and uses the chicken-feed system of supply. Water can also be carried in the tender and there's a hand pump in the water cavity to supply the boiler.

Boiler fittings include a water glass with blowdown, pressure gauge, safety valve, throttle, and blower valve. Since the boiler is internally fired, steam must be raised through the use of a suction fan in the stack. *Prince* is a tiny locomotive, fine and delicate. Seeing it standing next to a larger engine of the same scale gives you a feeling for how diminutive the prototype is.

The open cab makes everything easily accessible. Despite its small size, the locomotive is fitted with all important appliances.

To say that this is a lively engine is an understatement. In fact, it is *exceedingly* lively. All the control you'd ever want is in the first few degrees of rotation of the throttle lever. Once adjusted, though, *Prince* is perfectly controllable, even running light. It will throttle down to a walking pace (with the blower cracked) and amble around all afternoon. Because the boiler capacity is so small, frequent topping-up with the tender pump is required. On the other hand, with the addition of fuel and water to the tender, the engine could be kept in steam all day

Specifications

Builder: Gosling Locomotives (UK)
Date built: Early 1980s
Gauge: 0 (32mm)
Scale: 16mm
Boiler: Smithies
Fittings: Safety valve, throttle, blower, pressure gauge, water glass, blowdown
Fuel: Alcohol
Blow-off pressure: 60psi
Cylinders: Two, double-acting D-valve
Reversing gear: Slip eccentric
Lubricator: Displacement
Weight: 5lbs (with tender)
Dimensions: Length over end beams (including tender), 13½in; width, 3⅛in; height, 4¾in

Merlin/Beck 0-4-4-0T

In 1978 or 79, Beck, an old German manufacturer of nautical instruments, came out with its first live-steam offering. *Anna* was an 0-4-0T, designed specifically to be used with LGB rolling stock. It is described elsewhere in these pages. Later, an 0-6-2T, *Helene*, similar to LGB's Zillertal locomotive, was offered. In the planning stages was *Bertha*, an 0-4-4-0T. Sadly, the company went into bankruptcy early in 1981 and its assets (as regards model-locomotive production) were acquired by Tom Cooper of Great Britain, who had recently started Merlin Locomotive Works.

One of the first engines produced by Mr. Cooper after the acquisition was his rendition of Beck's proposed *Bertha*, released in 1982 and called *Matador*. This proved to be an unpopular engine and few were ultimately made.

The model

The locomotive is an odd mix of German ingenuity and Tom Cooper's cavalier approach to engine making. Surprisingly, this is not an articulated engine. Its frame is a (very) rough iron casting. The axles pass through it without benefit of bushings. There is nearly ¼in of lateral play in all the axles, and it is this slop that allows the locomotive to negotiate curves as tight as LGB's smallest.

The engine employs the same technology that *Anna* and *Helene* used – piston-valve cylinders controlled by unusual,

The fireman's side of the engine. This side tank houses the large gas tank. The filler valve is just in front of the cab.

outside slip eccentrics. The boiler is the single-flue gas type, with a poker burner. This type of boiler/burner arrangement was originally engineered by Beck.

There is a minimalist lubricator in the steam dome. The silver dome cap is unscrewed and a few drops of steam oil are placed in the tiny reservoir. When the throttle, which is right beneath the lubricator in the steam dome, is opened, all of the oil is sucked immediately into the steam line. In fact, it is only the piston valves that require internal lubrication, as the pistons are each comprised of a pair of Teflon cups, placed back to back and mounted on the piston rod.

The throttle is simply a knob on the right side of the steam dome that releases steam to two lines, one to either side of the engine. All admission lines are copper, fastened to the cylinders via banjo fittings. Exhaust lines are made of various types of rubber. There is a massive gas tank that nearly fills the left-hand dummy water tank. Gas is controlled by a valve that protrudes through the back wall of the cab.

Top left: Not much in the cab – just the oversize pressure gauge and the water window.

Lower: The rigid frame on this large, non-articulated locomotive is a single, massive casting. Each axle has excessive lateral play that allows it to negotiate unprototypically tight curves.

Specifications

Builder: Merlin (UK), from old Beck (Germany) parts
Date built: 1982
Gauge: 1 (45mm)
Scale: 1:22.5
Boiler: Single flue
Fittings: Safety valve, throttle, pressure gauge, water window
Fuel: Butane
Blow-off pressure: 30psi
Cylinders: Four, double-acting piston-valve
Reversing gear: Outside slip eccentrics
Lubricator: Displacement
Weight: 8lbs 14oz
Dimensions: Length over buffer beams, 12⅛in; width, 4¼in; height over stack, 6¼in

Roger Marsh's *Ogwen*

Any number of small, relatively nondescript industrial engines were built by a variety of British companies for use in stone and slate quarries, gravel pits, and other unglamorous venues. Many are preserved today in far more glory than they ever experienced in their working lives, often hauling passengers on preserved railways, but never, today, doing the work for which they were intended.

Ogwen is one such engine. It, and a sister engine, *Marchlyn*, were built in 1933 for the Durham County Water Board. In 1936 they were both purchased by the Penrhyn Quarries in Wales, which owned many little engines of this nature. *Ogwen* worked there until 1965, when the quarry was closed. Later that same year it was prepared for shipment and was packed off to the USA for preservation, where it exists today, reputedly stored in Terre Haute, Indiana.

The model

Roger Marsh and his company Minimum Gauge Railways is perhaps best known for batch-produced seven and a quarter inch gauge models of various narrow-gauge locomotives. His 'Tinkerbell' class is one that the driver actually sits inside.

Ogwen was Mr. Marsh's only entry in the commercial, small-scale-live-steam field, although he initially had hopes of a whole range of engines, including mammoth K-class D&RGW locomotives. *Ogwen* was first introduced in 1982, to considerable acclaim. I became the US distributor for this engine in 1983. Unfortunately, Mr. Marsh fell on hard times and the last of the *Ogwen* was

delivered in 1984, after a brief year in the sun. These last ones, alas, had evidently been assembled with little care, as there were several problems with them, not the least being valves that were solid in the cylinders and had to be removed with a mallet to be lapped.

The design was eventually acquired by Maxwell Hemmens, who was making a version of the Porter 0-4-0 at the time. *Ogwen* emerged from Hemmens' shops as a much-changed beast.

The original Marsh *Ogwen* is a pretty little engine. It features a pot boiler, lagged with a layer of ceramic paper, with an external, gas-fired burner. In the back of the boiler is a water window; a pressure gauge is also fitted. Control is via a single lever in the cab, which operates a rotary valve under the steam block between the cylinders to control both speed and direction. A fitting is included beneath the boiler for filling it via an outside source. A displacement lubricator with a drain is carried in the left-hand (dummy) water tank and there is an odd filler plug on the left side of the boiler, so as not to foul the dummy throttle rod that travels from the cab front sheet to the steam dome. Other cosmetic details include dummy steam pipes, made of threaded rod to simulate lagging.

The two fixed cylinders are controlled by piston valves. Dummy Walschaerts valve gear adorns the running gear. The front axle is sprung, a nice touch.

Ogwen was offered in a variety of colors, including red (most common, I believe), green, blue, and black. It is a simple, well-made engine, attractively finished.

The engine likes to run fast and is hard to get to run slowly without a load. The control lever is difficult to use, being almost inaccessible in the full-forward position. Control comes as much from the burner setting as from the throttle. There is a nice bark to the stack when running, and the burner, being external, is nearly silent.

Specifications

Builder: Roger Marsh & Co. (UK)
Date built: 1982
Gauge: 0 (32mm)
Scale: 16mm
Boiler: Pot
Fittings: Safety valve, water glass, pressure gauge, filler plug, check valve
Fuel: Butane
Blow-off pressure: 30psi
Cylinders: Two, double-acting piston-valve
Reversing gear: Rotary valve
Lubricator: Displacement
Weight: 4lbs
Dimensions: Length over end beams, 8¼in; width, 3¼in; height, 5½in

Mac Muckley's Beyer-Garratt

Left: Countless Mamod locomotives have metamorphosed into something else. Mac Muckley's Garratt is one of the more imaginative Mamod-bashes. It has a new, gas-fired boiler.

Below: The rear power bogie. Note the lever and linkage to the otherwise-inaccessible reverser. Rubber and plastic tubing makes flexible steam and exhaust lines.

The Beyer-Garratt locomotive is one of the more unusual articulated engines. It was widely used in many parts of the world. It has no detachable tender, but is articulated in two places. The first section incorporates a steam power truck, or bogie. Atop this sits a water tank. The third section is a similar bogie, though reversed in wheel arrangement. Above this is another water tank and a fuel bunker. Slung between these two bogies, and pivoted to them, is the boiler. The cylinders are usually (but not always) situated at the outside ends of the bogies.

There were many advantages to this type of engine. Since there were no obstructions (wheels, motion, etc.) under the boiler, the boiler could be designed for maximum efficiency without concern for bumping into anything beneath it. These locomotives were exceedingly flexible, able to negotiate relatively rough track and very tight curves, despite being long and heavy. Also, as the engine went around a curve, its centre of gravity moved toward the centre of the curve (because of the placement of the boiler), making it extremely stable.

The Beyer-Garratt engine was the brainchild of Herman William Garratt, a British locomotive inspector, engineer, and inventor. He was granted a patent for it in 1907. Within months he had convinced Beyer, Peacock, a well-established British locomotive-building firm, of the merits of his design. The first Beyer-Garratt engines, a pair of tiny, 2ft-gauge 0-4-0+0-4-0s, were delivered to the Tasmanian Government in 1909. From there, the design took off and many locomotives were built to this plan over the years in a variety of sizes, gauges, and wheel arrangements. They were used in Africa, Australia, South America, India, Great Britain, and other places, but never in North America.

The model

I purchased this engine second-hand from the builder at a show in Britain in 1985. It is a freelance design, but incorporates all of the usual Garratt characteristics. It is built on two Mamod 0-4-0 chassis. The oscillating cylinders are hidden behind cylinder covers. A Mamod engine is reversed by a rotary valve, located at the front between the frames, that exchanges admission and exhaust steam. These valves were kept on this engine and linkages were added at each end of the locomotive so that the valves, which are pretty well hidden, could be accessed from one side of the engine. However, each engine must be manually reversed separately. If you're not careful, one engine will be travelling forward while the other wants to go back.

This locomotive has a variety of unusual goodies on it. Neither bogie exhausts up the stack. Exhaust steam from both is expelled into condensing pans. One is hidden under the front power bogie and the other, for the benefit of the rear bogie, is disguised as the firebox. On cool days, lots of steam pours from beneath the engine – an interesting effect.

The boiler is a traditional, single flue, gas-fired unit with a poker-style burner. Gas is stored in a tank above the rear bogie. The boiler is fitted with a safety valve, a pressure gauge, and a water glass. The throttle is actually under the steam dome and is actuated by a small lever on it. A vacuum tap is also fitted, which draws water from the front tank. This isn't as useful as being able to fill the loco while it's under steam, but it saves removing the safety valve to fill the boiler and it's fun to watch.

Specifications

Builder: Mac Muckley (UK)
Date built: Circa 1982
Gauge: 0 (32mm)
Scale: 16mm
Boiler: Single flue
Fittings: Safety valve, throttle, pressure gauge, water glass, vacuum tap
Fuel: Butane
Blow-off pressure: 40psi
Cylinders: Four, double-acting oscillators
Reversing gear: Rotary valve
Lubricator: Displacement
Weight: 8lbs
Dimensions: Length over pilots, 22⅞in; width, 4in; height over stack, 5¼in

Jack Wheldon's *Hecla*

Perhaps one of the oddest engines to be offered commercially, Jack Wheldon's 'Hecla' class was designed to prove that even a small, single-acting piston could drive a powerful locomotive that would run at prototypical speeds.

In the June, 1986, issue of the British magazine, *Model Railway Constructor*, Jack Wheldon wrote a seminal article called 'Tramming by Steam.' In it he described the dilemma of many small-scale steam locomotives of the time – the fact that most would not run at scale speeds and haul prototypical loads, especially engines that had pot boilers (which did not respond to things like increased load) and small cylinders. He went on to say that a locomotive with a sufficiently geared-down transmission could be run at prototypical speeds and still have plenty of power, even if run by a 'toy' cylinder like those found on Mamod stationary engines. The rest of the article described his experiments with gearing, transverse boilers, and small, oscillating cylinders. The end result of Jack's research was the 'Hecla' class of locomotive, which he offered commercially in 1981 and 1982. The price then was £200 and a total of only six were built, all named after volcanos.

The model

This is a chunky engine. The boiler, mounted sideways across the frames, is 2¼in in diameter by 3⅜in long. Behind it is the works – one single-acting Mamod cylinder driving a shaft, upon which is a large flywheel from a Mamod stationary engine. From this shaft, a pinion drives a large spur gear, giving a reduction of around 10:1. Motion is transmitted to the driving axle via sprockets and ladder chain (1:1) and to the other axle via conventional side rods.

Behind the mechanical bits is a water tank that carries a pipe from the boiler. When the fire is dropped, the steam from the boiler can be exhausted into this water-filled tank. Then, as a vacuum forms inside the cooling boiler, water is drawn into it from the tank, thus refilling the boiler. This is called a vacuum tap. Behind the water tank and under the footplate, is the alcohol reservoir, well away from the boiler. It feeds a linear-wick burner under the boiler in one of Jack's high-efficiency fireboxes.

I acquired my model from its original owner, Eric Lloyd. The engine had been well cared for and not run a great deal. As supplied to Eric, it had a wooden tram body that completely enclosed the works. Some of Jack's engines were left open and supplied with end plates that gave the unit both definition and character. I asked David Pinniger, who acquired a lot of Jack's drawings after he passed on, if he had a drawing for the end plates, as I wanted to make some to replace the body. He did better than that, and supplied me with an original plate, which I replicated for my engine. The name plates came off the original tram body.

When first I ran the engine, I was disappointed. It did not perform well at all and I was hard pressed to figure out why, as everything seemed in order. I mentioned this to Mr. Pinniger, who asked if the piston had an O-ring. It did. The problem was that the piston had been relieved a bit so that only the O-ring would contact the cylinder wall. This is fine where the piston rod is supported by a cylinder cover or gland but, on the single-acting oscillator, the O-ring acted as a pivot, causing the piston to wobble inside the cylinder. This affected the oscillating travel of the cylinder, which, in turn, affected the valve events for the worse. I removed the old piston and made a new one without an O-ring, but with as much bearing surface against the cylinder walls as possible. That did the trick, and the engine performed as advertised.

The single-acting Mamod cylinder drives the axles via a variety of chains and gears giving a 10:1 reduction between the cylinder and the axle. The flywheel is from a Mamod stationary engine.

A transversely mounted pot boiler is fired by alcohol. The pipe going from the boiler to the water tank is the vacuum tap/blowdown.

Specifications

Builder: Jack Wheldon (UK)
Date built: 1982
Gauge: 0 (32mm)
Scale: 16mm
Boiler: Pot
Fittings: Safety valve, throttle, pressure gauge, blowdown/vacuum tap
Fuel: Alcohol
Blow-off pressure: 50psi
Cylinders: One, single-acting oscillator
Reversing gear: Rotary valve
Lubricator: Displacement
Weight: 5lbs
Dimensions: Length, 10¼in; width, 4½in; height, 6⅞in

Archangel's Vale of Rheidol 2-6-2T

Specifications

Builder: Archangel Models (UK)
Date built: 1983
Gauge: 0 (32mm)
Scale: 16mm
Boiler: Internally fired, multi-flue
Fittings: Safety valve, water glass, pressure gauge, throttle, blower, hand pump in tank, crosshead pump, bypass system, blowdown
Fuel: Alcohol
Blow-off pressure: 75psi
Cylinders: Two, double-acting D-valves
Reversing gear: Slip eccentrics
Lubricator: Displacement
Weight: 8lbs 8oz
Dimensions: Length, 14⅛in over end beams; width, 4⅛in; height, 5¾in

Although slab-sided and massive, this locomotive has a certain quiet dignity about it. It was modelled by Archangel as originally supplied to the Vale of Rheidol.

In 1902, Davies & Metcalf (Manchester) produced a pair of 2-6-2T locomotives for the Vale of Rheidol Railway when it first opened. The 1ft 11¾in-gauge line was originally built to serve the lead mines in the Rheidol Valley of Wales. Both the engines and the railway underwent significant changes throughout the years. The railway is in existence today, running much modified engines over its nearly twelve mile length.

The model
Like most Archangel models, this locomotive was offered in several variations. The one presented here has the more sophisticated internally fired, multi-flue boiler. A simpler pot boiler was also offered. Because of the type of boiler fitted to this engine, it has more amenities than the pot-boilered version. These include all the usual boiler fittings (safety valve, water glass, pressure gauge, blowdown valve) plus a blower to create draft, working side tanks, and two pumps – a hand pump in the left side tank and a rather unsightly crosshead pump, also on the left side.

The crosshead pump is tied into a bypass system, with water being controlled by a valve in the cab. A displacement lubricator also sits in the cab, as does a large alcohol tank with a drip-feed system to a sump below the footplate. Fuel flow is controlled by a screw on the rear end beam.

Given the complexity and sophistication of the boiler, the valve gear is remarkably simple. D-valves are controlled by slip eccentrics on the middle driven axle. Rocker arms bring the motion outside the frames.

Although the detail level of the model is relatively low,

The crosshead pump. While easier to construct and fit than an axle pump, it does mar the fine lines of the engine.

it is a reasonable rendition of the prototype in its early years. The proportions are accurate and the model conveys the massiveness of this large narrow-gauge locomotive. The engine is named *Lady Diana Spencer*, after Diana, who had become the Princess of Wales two years before it was built.

Running this locomotive is a joy. It is powerful, yet controllable. Throttle and blower levers are easily accessible on either side of the cab. The bypass valve is also readily at hand when wanted. The engine will creep down the track as long as you want it to, with the blower cracked, or it will tear around much faster than I am comfortable with. Running it at a prototypical speed is easy. Because of the sophistication of the entire system, the engine could easily be kept in steam all day long, pausing for water and fuel every half hour or so.

In addition to its sterling qualities as a runner, I think this locomotive marks a high-water point in Archangel production. It combines all of the positive qualities that made Archangel engines popular, with few of the negatives. It has all the features even the most die-hard steamophile could wish for, yet the engine is relatively tame in operation. And it faithfully captures the mass and bulk of the prototype while being graceful and elegant in motion.

The cab, while neatly laid out, is decidedly busy. In the centre, extending to the right, is the regulator lever. To the left of it is the blower valve. Just above the blower lever (far left) is the bypass valve. Toward the centre, immediately below the blower valve is the blowdown valve. The lubricator sits in the upper left corner of the cab.

Jack Wheldon's 'Charles Pooter'

ack Wheldon is a near-legendary name in the annals of small-scale live steam. He was a pioneer in the development of reliable, simple to operate, robust, no-fuss locomotives for use on narrow-gauge garden railways. His 'Charles Pooter' class is probably the culmination of his work and research.

In designing the Pooters, Jack wanted an engine with which anyone could achieve satisfaction – an everyman's locomotive. He named it after Charles Pooter, a character in George and Weedon Grossmith's 1892 book, *Diary of a Nobody*. (If you've seen the film *Topsy-Turvy*, about Gilbert and Sullivan, you know who George Grossmith is.) Mr. Pooter was an average fellow who represented the common man. Jack wanted this locomotive to be for him.

Jack advertised his engines in the model press and was soon overwhelmed with orders. He contacted Roundhouse Engineering about taking over the orders. I asked Roger

Loxley of Roundhouse about the Wheldon-Roundhouse connection. Here is his response.

"I met Jack in 1982, when 'Lady Anne' was first launched, and he contacted me to talk about a review of the engine for one of his regular magazine articles. We quickly became good friends, as we were of like mind and both developing a similar style of meths firebox. We shared ideas on small-scale live steam and had many, many long conversations and letters on the subject. I still have a thick file of all his correspondence, and interesting reading it makes, too.

"Jack had been advertising his 'Charles Pooter' locomotives in the railway press and had received about twenty orders in a very short time. Unfortunately, he could only produce them at the rate of two or three a year and felt rather awkward about the long waiting list that was quickly forming. He liked my work and we got on very well, so he asked me if I would

Opposite page: Daisy Mutler is one of Jack Wheldon's 'Pooter' class, which was intended to put powerful, reliable locomotives into the hands of the common person.

This page:
Right: The roof comes off for cab access. Controls are laid out simply and logically.

Lower: The engine features an unusual 'divided' valve gear, with the straight expansion placed towards the rear of the locomotive. The valve gear is controlled from the cab.

be interested in taking over the design as a Roundhouse model. I was eager to expand my fledgling company and quickly agreed.

"I spent several weeks 'productionising' his design and all the customers on his waiting list were contacted to see if they were happy with the idea. All were pleased to accept the change, especially as it meant that they would get their engines much quicker. At this point Barry Vaughan joined me at Roundhouse to cope with the sudden increase in work load.

"Pooter was introduced into the Roundhouse range in 1984 and was finally discontinued in 1990. The Roundhouse version went through a few minor changes over the years; e.g., the original tinplate bodies became etched brass, round spectacles later became square, and the Hackworth valve gear went through a couple of redesigns.

"There were two other variations: 'Mr Merlins Pooter,' produced for Tom Cooper in 1986 and 1987, and 'Erica', produced from 1988 to 1989. Both used the Pooter chassis/boiler with a different-style body.

"Although a good engine, the Pooters were never overly popular and only sold in relatively small numbers. The final tally would have been approaching two hundred engines. I can't give you exact numbers, though, as we didn't start assigning serial numbers until 1993."

The model
Only eight 'Pooters' were built by Jack. These were all meths fired. The engines were equipped with pot boilers and Jack's special firebox, which was designed to maximize efficiency of the fire while keeping the engine relatively cool.

The first four locos had slip-eccentric reversing while the latter ones had Jack's unusual Tayleur/Wheldon valve gear. This is a sort of divided Walschaerts. The idea was to place the expansion link as far as possible from the valve, obviating the need for a curved link. A straight link, as is on this engine, is easier to make and the reversing linkages are simpler, too.

My example is *Daisy Mutler*, named after another character in the book (whose last name was actually spelled MUTLAR) and is the fifth in the line of Pooters and the twenty-second engine produced in Jack's Burbage workshops. The engine is fitted with a vacuum tap – a valve on the backhead or (in this case) steam turret connected to a short length of pipe. At the end of a run, a rubber tube can be fitted to the pipe and the other end placed in a reservoir of water. When the valve is opened, residual steam bubbles into the reservoir. As the boiler cools, a vacuum is created that will suck water back into the boiler, thus refilling it.

Another interesting feature is the dummy drain cocks. Exhaust steam from drain cocks on British engines is traditionally jetted toward the front of the engine. On *Daisy Mutler*, two tiny lines are taken off the exhaust pipe from the cylinders and routed through the front buffer beam. As the engine travels, spurts of steam can be seen coming from these lines, giving an accurate illusion of open drain cocks.

Specifications

Builder: Jack Wheldon (UK)
Date built: 1983
Gauge: 0 (32mm)
Scale: 16mm
Boiler: Pot
Fittings: Safety valve, throttle, pressure gauge, vacuum tap/blowdown
Fuel: Alcohol
Blow-off pressure: 60psi
Cylinders: Two, double-acting D-valve
Reversing gear: Tayleur/Wheldon
Lubricator: Displacement
Weight: 7lbs 2oz
Dimensions: Length, 10¼in; width, 4¼in; height, 6¼in

Merlin's 2-6-2 Hunslet

Above: The engine's entire body slips off in a moment, exposing the radio gear and controls. This is a great aid to maintenance.

I n 1898 The Sierra Leone Government Railways, operating in the (then) British colony in West Africa, took delivery of its first 2-6-2 tank engine, built by Hunslet. The railway was built to 2ft 6in gauge, unusual for a national railway. The locomotive proved so successful that a total of thirty-two of them were ultimately built for the line, the last two in 1954. A similar locomotive, *Russell*, was built for the Welsh Highland Railway.

The Sierra Leone Government Railways were finally closed in 1974, at which time there were still five steam locomotives in operation, along with four diesels. One of the Sierra Leone locomotives, N° 85, is preserved in Britain on the Welshpool & Llanfair Railway. It is this engine that Merlin has reproduced in miniature.

The model

Merlin's model is a fair representation of this attractive prototype. It has some unusual and innovative features.

This engine was designed by Colin Cooper, son of Tom Cooper. The body of the locomotive, including smokebox, side tanks, and cab, lifts off the working chassis as a single unit, being held in place only by gravity. This engine is radio controlled, as were all of Merlin's engines of this type. The electronics and batteries are carried in the right side tank. The large butane tank is housed in the left.

As with most R/C locomotives, this one uses two channels – one for the throttle and one for reversing. The reversing servo is near the front of the left side tank. A linkage connects it to levers that move the radius rods. The servo controlling the throttle is opposite, on the right side. This is connected to the throttle via a very long arm that extends over the electronics compartment.

This example is fitted with a pressure gauge and safety valve. Others had water glasses

Left: Merlin's Sierra Leone Hunslet is an attractive and unusual locomotive. While the detail level is low, the proportions capture the essence of the prototype.

(there were several changes and modifications made to this engine over its production life). The throttle is unusual for a couple of reasons. One is that it is integral with the lubricator. Another is that it does not employ a needle valve to control the steam. Instead, it has a rotating plate with holes in it that, when the throttle is open, align with holes in the throttle body. When closed, the plate rotates so that the holes are not in alignment, blocking the steam passages.

The chassis is fairly straightforward. The engine shown here is an earlier example that was made with remaining Beck piston-valve cylinders, which the company had acquired in 1981 when Beck went out of business. Valve gear is dummy Walschaerts. Drive wheels are regaugeable, but the lead and trailing bogies have to be replaced if the gauge is to be changed.

The backhead is fitted with a pressure gauge. The large gas tank is on the left. Across the footplate from it is the lubricator/throttle assembly.

The detail level is relatively low. Prototype photos show a variety of details (on various engines) that might be incorporated into this model. These include a double, 'tropical' roof and strap-iron pilots on both ends.

This engine is a good performer. It has the typical roar of a single flue, gas-fired boiler. Because of the nature of the throttle, speed control is very touchy but, with practice, you can get good control out of it. Reversing is no problem, and the engine is a smooth runner.

Specifications

Builder: Merlin Locomotive Works (UK)
Date built: Circa 1983
Gauge: 1 (45mm)
Scale: 16mm
Boiler: Single flue
Fittings: Safety valve, pressure gauge
Fuel: Butane
Blow-off pressure: 40psi
Cylinders: Two, double-acting piston valve
Reversing gear: Dummy Walschaerts
Lubricator: Displacement
Weight: 10lbs 8oz
Dimensions: Length over end beams, 12in; width, 4⅜in; height, 6⅜in

Roundhouse Engineering's *Dylan*

Roundhouse Engineering of Doncaster, England, must certainly be the most well-known manufacturer of 16mm scale, live-steam locomotives for gauge-0 and gauge-1 track today. The company, under the direction of Roger Loxley, began production in 1982 with *Victoria*, a model of a profoundly ugly tram engine from the Plynlimon & Hafan Railway. Later that same year, *Dylan* (named after Roger's dog) emerged.

This is an attractive freelance locomotive. It has small, dummy coal bunkers ahead of, and on either side of, the cab. Forward of these is a dummy saddle tank. A variety of colours was available, including red, green, black, and brown, and all engines were lined out at the factory.

Dylan is a mechanically simple engine. The boiler is a plain, externally-fired pot heated by a four-wick alcohol burner (all Roundhouse engines were alcohol fired in those days). An ample fuel tank is carried beneath the footplate and there is a large, uncovered filler hole in the cab. Although this wide opening makes filling a simple matter, it sometimes catches fire, especially in warm weather, adding interest to the run.

The spartan backhead includes a throttle valve and a pressure gauge. A good-size lubricator stands on the footplate and there is a built-in servo bracket in the cab. The engine could

Dylan is an attractive, well proportioned, freelance locomotive. The small tender was an optional extra when the engine was first introduced.

be radio controlled (throttle only) with relative ease. The steam line to the cylinders includes a superheater coil above the fire. Reversing is provided by slip eccentrics, the motion being carried through the outside frames by unusual horizontal rocker arms, a Roundhouse signature.

A four-wheel tender was offered as an optional extra. The front wall of the tender has holes for the on-off switch of a radio and servo wires to the loco. *Dylan* was finally withdrawn from production in 1994.

In operation, the engine is everything a garden railroader could want. It is easy to run, powerful, and will run for half an hour or more unattended. With this engine, the tone was set for the production of Roundhouse's future line of locomotives. Solid engineering and near-absolute reliability became the company's hallmarks, and remain so today.

Motion is brought through the frames to the valves by an unconventional horizontal rocker arm. The rocker is attached to a part of the frame that has been bent down 90°.

The cab roof and back sheet comes off as separate pieces, sometimes when the engine is running. This feature was changed in later locos. The plain backhead has a throttle valve and a pressure gauge. A generous opening for filling the alcohol tank, while convenient, also promotes cab fires.

Specifications

Builder: Roundhouse Engineering Company (UK)
Date built: 1984
Gauge: 1 (45mm)
Scale: 16mm
Boiler: Pot
Fittings: Throttle, pressure gauge, safety valve
Fuel: Alcohol
Blow-off pressure: 60psi
Cylinders: Two, double-acting D-valve
Reversing gear: Slip eccentrics
Lubricator: Displacement
Weight: 5lbs 2oz (locomotive only)
Dimensions: Length over end beams, 11⅞in (sans tender); width, 4⅜in; height over stack, 5⅛in

Archangel's coal-fired *Jack*

The prototype of this attractive locomotive was built by WG Bagnall in 1914 for the Cliffe Hill Mineral Railway in Leicestershire, which was begun in 1896 and closed in 1946. The railway served granite quarries in the area, some of which were reputed to have been in operation on and off since Roman times.

From the information I was able find, the line had two 0-4-2Ts, one built in 1911 (*Mary*) and one built in 1914 (*Jack*). Both were scrapped in 1957. *Jack* is a fairly typical industrial engine without much to distinguish it, aside from pleasing proportions.

The model
Archangel's model, too, has pleasing proportions. It has an open cab and working side tanks connected by a balance pipe, with a hand pump in the left one. There is a second pump under the right-side tank that is actuated by a linkage to the crosshead. This functions the same as an axle pump, adding water to the boiler while the engine is in motion.

Frames are made of steel. Plain drivers are turned from solid steel bar, while the trailing wheels are brass.

The open cab gives easy access to the controls. Fittings include a safety valve under a brass dome, a throttle, blower, whistle, and pressure gauge, plus a bypass valve for the crosshead pump. The only thing lacking is a water glass.

The boiler is a locomotive-type with five small flues and a larger superheater flue. There is no smokebox door *per se*, but the whole front pops off for cleaning and maintenance. The fire door in the cab can be opened by pulling a chain and, being spring loaded, closes by itself. An opening gate in the

Top Right: The busy and not particularly well ordered cab. The knob at the right is the bypass valve from the crosshead pump. The whistle is that cylinder sticking up on the left. A gate in the back sheet provides direct access to the firebox.

Lower right: Slip eccentrics on the rear axle provide direction control. Note how far the valves are from their cylinders.

Left: This is quite a small locomotive to be coal fired. However, it is no problem to keep in steam and is easy to control. Note the crosshead pump below the side tank.

Specifications

Builder: Archangel Models (UK)
Date built: 1984
Gauge: 0 (32mm)
Scale: 16mm
Boiler: Locomotive type
Fittings: Safety valve, blower, whistle, pressure gauge, bypass valve, crosshead pump, hand pump
Fuel: Coal
Blow-off pressure: 50psi
Cylinders: Two, double-acting D-valve
Reversing gear: Slip eccentric
Lubricator: Displacement
Weight: 5lbs
Dimensions: Length over end beams, 10¼in; width, 3⅞in; height, 5⅜in

back sheet gives easy access to the fire door with a shovelful of coal. The ashpan can be dropped by removing a single screw. The grate is also held in place by a single screw.

Cylinders are outside the frames, while the valves are inside, unusually positioned a fair distance in from the cylinders. The engine is reversed via slip eccentrics, the eccentrics being on the rear axle.

As coal-fired engines go, this one is relatively easy to run. Once it is burning anthracite and pressure is up to near blowoff, the fire can be steadily maintained by adding a shovelful or two of coal every four or five laps. The crosshead pump is turned on as needed. The engine performs very well and is powerful for its size. But despite its complexity, it is an excellent garden-railway locomotive and it smells just right.

Left: This locomotive captures much of the charm of the prototype. An interesting feature is that the cylinders are not placed directly beneath the stack, as is usual.

Lower: An unusual device is this offset, Goodall-type filler valve on the side of the boiler. The steam dome is made of sheet metal. It comes off to reveal the safety valve, throttle valve, and a tiny lubricator.

the model does manage to capture some of the flavour of the original.

This is a fairly simple engine, but it has some interesting features. It's gas fired, with a large tank suspended beneath the cab roof. Access to the filler valve is through the roof. The throttle is under the steam-dome cover, actuated from the cab via a long rod. Also in the steam dome is the safety valve and an odd little displacement lubricator. On the left side of the boiler, near the top, is a Goodall-type filler valve. There's no water glass, so filling the boiler while under pressure is a matter of trial and error.

One of the most interesting features of this model is its prototypically correct Koppel valve gear. Externally, this resembles Hackworth, but has no sliding link. Instead, it has a series of levers (concealed by the dummy side tanks) reminiscent of Baker valve gear. This is controlled from the cab by a simple control arm that competes for space with the gas-supply line.

The valve gear resembles Hackworth but is actually Koppel. Unlike Hackworth, it has no sliding links. Change of direction is accomplished by levers that, unfortunately, are hidden behind the side tank.

With the dome removed, the throttle-lubricator-safety-valve assembly is visible.

igiau was built by the German firm of Orenstein & Koppel in 1912 as works Nº 5668. The little engine weighed 6.1T and was built to run on 600mm track (23.62in). It was evidently purchased new by someone called Charles L Warren, and passed through several hands over the years including, among others, Aluminium Corporation Ltd, Penrhyn Slate Quarries, and Alan Bloom's Bressingham Gardens. The engine is alive and well today, restored and working at the Bredgar & Wormshill Light Railway in Britain.

The model

As with many Archangel models, this one is a rough approximation of the prototype. Its wheels are solid, where the prototype's are spoked. The cab side sheets are a little different, as is the slant of the cylinders. However,

The large (for such a small engine) gas tank is suspended from the cab roof. The touchy gas-control valve is right next to it.

Specifications

Builder: Archangel Models (UK)
Date built: Mid 1980s?
Gauge: 0 (32mm)
Scale: 16mm
Boiler: Single flue
Fittings: Safety valve, throttle, Goodall-type filler valve
Fuel: Butane
Blow-off pressure: 45psi (estimated)
Cylinders: Two, double-acting D-valve
Reversing gear: Koppel valve gear
Lubricator: Displacement
Weight: 2lbs 14oz
Dimensions: Length over end beams, 8in; width, 3¼in; height, 5⅝in

Creekside Forge & Foundry's Baldwin 0-4-0ST

Although American in appearance and manufacture, the locomotive's Mamod antecedents are clearly visible. The engine had an unusual boiler, though. Hot gases escaped through large holes in the dome tops.

There are no controls in the cab – only the Mamodesque water glass. The knob below it is the cap on the fuel tank.

Sometime in 1983 I began corresponding with Carlos Grundhoeffer of Palmyra, New York. Carl wanted to develop a steam locomotive along the lines of the (then) new Mamod, but featuring better construction and American styling. His letters over the next couple of years make fascinating reading, as they chronicle the development of a new steam locomotive, including all the trials and errors, frustration, failures, and ultimate success of the project.

Carl was a reclusive fellow. He lived (so I was told) in an abandoned pickle factory. He had no phone. To speak to him, I had to call a friend of his down the road. This good person would then drive to Carl's place and bring him back so that he could call me.

The first operating prototype reached my hands in early August, 1984. I had just completed my first garden railway (all thirty feet of it) and it was on this line that the initial tests were made. I ran the locomotive several times with varying loads, noting the results, which I communicated to Carl. He offered suggestions and ideas for changes, many of which were ultimately incorporated into the production models. It was about this time that he also settled on a company name: Creekside Forge & Foundry.

The locomotive, which became known as the Creekside Baldwin, finally reached the market early in 1985, selling for $150. Demand was high but production was low. Availability was a problem from the outset. Carl was a perfectionist and nothing left the factory that wasn't top notch. Production problems continued to haunt him and the locomotive ultimately faded from the scene only a year or so later, leaving many disappointed potential customers. I'm guessing that only about thirty engines were made. Carl's letters indicated his intention of producing a whole range of gauge 0 and 1 locomotives in a variety of configurations. It's too bad that the frustrations of bringing a single one to reality proved so draining.

The model

As mentioned above, the Creekside Baldwin is based on Mamod technology. It has two, double-acting oscillating cylinders controlled by a conventional rotary valve located between the frames, under the smokebox at the front of the engine. The boiler features a water glass similar to Mamod's and, like the Mamod, it has no lubricator. It was offered in both gauge-0 and gauge-1 versions.

The Creekside's boiler, though, was a departure from the Mamod's. It is an unusual design and might even be considered internally fired, even though the fire is beneath it, as with a pot boiler. The boiler has a longitudinal, vertical slot from top to bottom, wider at the bottom. Inside this slot are two water tubes and what amounts to a superheater tube.

The burner is a more-or-less traditional alcohol burner, except that the wick tubes are thin rectangles and use a ceramic-fibre-sheet material called Fiberfrax for wicking. The burner keys into the frame at the front end and can be quickly removed by unscrewing a nut inside the cab. There is also a screw-on cap on the alcohol tank.

The lever in front of the smokebox controls both speed and direction. Cylinders had Russia-iron covers.

Specifications

Builder: Creekside Forge & Foundry (US)
Date built: 1985
Gauge: 1 (45mm)
Scale: 1:24
Boiler: Semi-internally fired
Fittings: Safety valve, water glass
Fuel: Alcohol
Blow-off pressure: 10 psi
Cylinders: Two, double-acting oscillators
Reversing gear: Rotary valve
Lubricator: None
Weight: 2lbs 5oz
Dimensions: Length over end beams, 9¼in; width, 3½in; height, 5¼in

Specifications

Builder: Cyril Clarke (UK)
Date built: Mid 1980s
Gauge: 0 (32mm)
Scale: 16mm
Boiler: Pot
Fittings: Safety valve, water glass, blow-down valve, pressure gauge, check valve
Fuel: Butane
Blow-off pressure: 60psi
Cylinders: Two, double-acting D-valve
Reversing gear: Abbreviated Walschaerts
Lubricator: Displacement
Weight: 9lbs 6oz
Dimensions: Length over frames, 13in; width, 4⅛in; height, 5⅝in

This model is an accurate representation of Campbeltown & Macrihanish's *Atlantic*. It has a pot boiler fired by gas burner. The engine was built for radio control but was converted to manual by the author.

*A*tlantic is based on a locomotive once owned by the 2ft 3in gauge Campbeltown & Machrihanish Light Railway, which ran in Scotland from around 1906 to 1932. *Atlantic* was ordered from Andrew Barclay & Sons in 1907 and was the last locomotive the railway purchased. It was virtually identical to *Argyll*, purchased from the same company a year earlier. Both engines were used for passenger service and coal hauling, which was the principle freight carried by the line.

The model

This model was scratchbuilt by Cyril Clarke. In cooperation with a friend, Peter Brookbank of Rugby, he completed a number of pairs of locomotives, including *Russells*, C&M 0-6-2s, and Indian 4-6-0 tender locos. This loco is one of the pair of C&M 0-6-2s.

The locomotive is nicely made and was neatly painted and lined out by David Hardy. It is a pot boiler, with a gas burner similar to an internal-flue-poker burner, but mounted under the boiler. The gas tank is carried in the bunker. Gas flow is controlled by a valve on top of the tank that must be actuated with a screwdriver. The engine, including the cylinders, was constructed entirely without castings.

The double-acting cylinders are controlled by the usual D-valves. These are run by an abbreviated Walschaerts-type valve gear. Reversing is accomplished via a lever in the cab. The model has disc drivers, whereas the prototype had spoked wheels. This is not too noticeable, since the wheels are inside the frames. The only noticeable major deviation from the prototype is the fact that the model has a centre-buffer/coupler at each end, while the prototype had a pair of buffers with chopper couplers.

Boiler fittings include a pressure gauge, a water glass, a safety valve, and a check valve for feedwater, which is supplied through an Enots-type fitting below the left-hand cab door. The lubricator is in the right-hand side tank and can be accessed by removing the cap atop the tank. Both side tanks are stuffed with insulating material. The roof is removable for access to the cab.

The engine was originally designed for, and fitted with, radio control. I prefer manually controlled locomotives, so I removed the R/C gear. This was a simple task for the throttle, but not so for the reverser, since there was no proper reversing lever. The reversing gear worked off a rotary crank that was actuated by the motion of the servo mounted in the cab. Without having to rebuild the entire system, I was able to fit a manual rotary lever in the cab that took the place of, but functioned in the same way as, the servo. The engine is a good performer and a strong hauler.

The cab is spacious and well laid out. The gas filler valve is in the bunker, as is the control valve, which must be operated with a screwdriver.

Merlin's 'Matterhorn' 0-6-0T

Batteries are housed under the footplate. The rotary reversing valve can be seen at the front of the engine, between the cylinders.

'Matterhorn' was an attempt by Merlin to tap into LGB's then growing market. The engine is intended to look German.

Merlin Locomotive Works, the brainchild of Tom Cooper, started life around 1981. Over the years the company produced a wide variety of different locomotives, some quite charming and some more nondescript. Merlin's 'Matterhorn' leans toward the latter.

This 0-6-0T is a freelance model, made by Merlin as a somewhat unsuccessful attempt to tap into the LGB market with live steam. It is vaguely Germanic in appearance, with its boxy body, oval windows, and square sandbox astride the boiler. It has loop couplers that are compatible with LGB hooks, but otherwise mar the appearance of the engine.

The loco is gas fired, with the fuel tank residing under the roof. The filler valve is accessed through a hole in the roof and the control valve for the gas is inside the cab. A square displacement lubricator with a screw drain sits on the footplate in the right-hand door of the cab. The locomotive was offered only as a gauge-1 product. It was also offered with a whistle, although this example has none.

The engine is radio controlled, utilising a single servo to control both speed and direction through a rotary valve. The two, double-acting cylinders are controlled by piston valves, so they can be reversed by switching the admission and exhaust lines.

There is a banjo fitting on the backhead, to which both the pressure gauge and the steam line are attached. The steam line passes through the fire, providing some superheat, then goes directly to the rotary valve beneath the engine. Since there is no actual throttle to close, there is nothing to prevent the boiler from sucking oil back into itself when cooling. However, this does not seem to affect performance.

The radio's receiver is in the cab; the servo is also in the cab, below the receiver. This engine was designed specifically for radio control and would be difficult to convert to manual operation.

The knob that is accessible from the left side of the cab controls gas flow to the burner. The radio's on-off switch is in the door.

In the right-side door is the pressure gauge and the unusual square lubricator.

Specifications

Builder: Merlin Loco Works (UK)
Date built: Circa 1986
Gauge: 1 (45mm)
Scale: 1:22.5
Boiler: Single flue
Fittings: Safety valve, pressure gauge
Fuel: Butane
Blow-off pressure: 40psi
Cylinders: Two, double-acting piston-valve
Reversing gear: Rotary valve
Lubricator: Displacement
Weight: 7lbs 6oz
Dimensions: Length over end beams, 11in; width, 4¼in; height, 6⅝in

John Turner's *Caledonia*

The prototype of this three-foot-gauge 0-6-0T was built by Dubs of Glasgow and went into service at the Foxdale Lead Mine on the Isle of Man in December, 1885. It was named *Caledonia* and given the number '4.' *Caledonia* later served on the Manx Northern Railway, which was absorbed by the Isle of Man Railway in 1905. In 1895, the engine was used in the construction of the Snaefell Mountain Railway, a 3ft 6in-gauge line. Because *Caledonia* was 3ft gauge, a third rail had to be temporarily laid for it. *Caledonia* still exists today in running condition on the Isle of Man Railway.

The model

In 1981, a company in England called Model and Miniature Railways, run by a man called Kevan Winward, introduced a 16mm scale, 0-6-0T locomotive kit. The prototype was the Isle of Man's *Caledonia*, and, indeed, the kit was called *Caledonia*. This kit was put out under the name of Lindale. John Turner was the designer of this locomotive.

The Lindale engine was pretty plain. It had double-acting, slide-valve cylinders controlled by slip eccentrics and was alcohol fired. Body work was rudimentary, being made up of simple folded shapes. There was a throttle in the cab and another, which regulated the engine's exhaust, on the front of the smokebox. This second regulator was something of an innovation and it allowed the engine to run slowly, but under full power, even when running light.

The unpainted, screw-together kit was well designed and the engine was a smooth, powerful runner. Initial kits suffered problems with the wheels falling off and the zinc-alloy siderods disintegrating. Due to these problems, perhaps, as well as some others, the company lasted but a very short time.

Upon Lindale's demise, Mr. Turner took over the design and began producing the locomotives built up in a much more advanced form. He was a very slow builder, alas, so not many of his engines are around today. In addition to the *Caledonia*, he offered an 0-4-0 tender engine.

The engine in the photos (named *Punsholt*) is gauge 1 and is gas fired. Mr. Turner also made gauge-0 locomotives as well as meths-fired ones. The engine has a particularly good whistle, an effective exhaust regulator, and body work that is far better and more detailed than the plain Lindale bodies.

The locomotive features John Turner's original valve gear, which he calls 'a cross between Hackworth and Baker' and is not unlike that used by Koppel on their industrial engines. He wanted a valve gear that did not rely on a return crank, as he felt these would too easily slip out of adjustment, so he came up with his own. This gear proved to be excellent and was later adopted by Cheddar for their 16mm-scale locomotives.

Water is admitted through a filler plug under the lift-off dome. Steam is also taken from beneath the dome. There is a displacement lubricator near the smokebox, masquerading as a sand box.

The locomotive has a sophisticated fuel system. The engine must be laid on its side for gas filling (there was a fitting that allowed it to be filled while standing, but I have managed to

Specifications

Builder: John Turner (UK)
Date built: Mid to late 1980s
Gauge: 1 (45mm)
Scale: 16mm
Boiler: Single flue
Fittings: Throttle, exhaust regulator, safety valve, pressure gauge, whistle, blowdown
Fuel: Butane
Blow-off pressure: 50psi
Cylinders: Two, double-acting D-valve
Reversing gear: Turner valve gear
Lubricator: Displacement
Weight: 7lbs 7oz
Dimensions: Length, 12in; width, 4⅛in; height, 6¾in

Right: Punsholt (nee *Caledonia*) is a well-made locomotive with a lot of unusual features. The wheel on the smokebox door is actually the exhaust regulator, which facilitates slow running.

Lower: John Turner's unique valve gear has characteristics of Hackworth, Baker, and Koppel. The displacement lubricator sits above the cylinder. Notice that the blind driver is not actually resting on the rail.

mislay it). I had to make an adapter to mate with the valve on the tank. Gas transfer is much quicker than on most other engines, even given this loco's large tank.

In the cab is a diaphragm-type gas regulator and the delightful accessory of a second pressure gauge. This one reads up to 15psi and measures pressure in the gas line. John Turner designed this as a low-velocity system that would enable him to use a larger jet in the burner. The result is a very controllable, quiet fire that needs no adjustment as the engine heats up. The gas-line pressure gauge lets you know just what's happening – a marvelous system!

On the left side of the cab is the gas regulator, which ensures an even and constant flow of gas to the burner. Note the second pressure gauge, which monitors gas-line pressure. The whistle valve is atop the boiler.

Peter Angus's Overtype

Left: While an unusual type of engine, the overtype makes an ideal garden-railway locomotive. This is a well-proportioned and nicely finished example. Because of the simple gear arrangement, the mechanism operates in the opposite direction of the engine's motion.

Lower left: A double acting, D-valve cylinder from Roundhouse powers the engine. Mounted atop the pot boiler, the entire assembly gets very hot. Note the oil cups over the bearings on the jackshaft.

Lower right: The open cab makes access easy. The throttle lever is visible, with the blowdown valve below it. Immediately above the throttle lever is the handle for the lubricator cap.

Peter Angus has become well known for building one-off models of unusual locomotives. In more recent years he has built models of specific prototypes, as opposed to freelance engines, but in earlier days he did build some freelance models. The engine shown here is one of those.

Overtype locomotives – engines that had the cylinder(s) atop the boiler – were few and far between in the prototype world, but there were some. Aveling & Porter, the British manufacturer of steam tractors and road rollers, once applied their talents to the rails, coming up with some unusual engines.

The model
Peter Angus's engine is not a model of any specific prototype. Because of this, it has better proportions and is much more attractive than full-size overtypes. This example (works № 20) has a single cylinder atop the boiler that runs a crankshaft, to which is attached a sprocket that drives a chain to another sprocket on a jackshaft near the rear axle. On this shaft is a pinion, which drives a large external gear on the axle. The overall reduction is around 5.5:1, making the engine

a smooth, slow runner. The two axles are connected by conventional side rods.

Peter relies on other manufacturers for most of the working parts of his engines – gears, cylinders, fittings, etc – while he concentrates on the body work and the mechanics of getting everything to work together properly. He is a meticulous craftsman and all of his engines that I have seen run superbly. This locomotive utilises a Roundhouse cylinder, fittings, and other parts.

The single cylinder is placed very close to the crankshaft, giving the short drive rod a lot of angular motion. If the engine were in constant use, this would be a cause for concern and a source of wear. On the bright side, though, it makes for a compact and good-looking unit. A large brass flywheel gets the engine smoothly past the dead spots in the cycle. Reversing is accomplished through a slip eccentric. The boiler has the usual fittings.

Visually, this is a wonderful engine. It runs at a nice, slow speed, while its various parts up top frantically flail around. The unsightly drive chain is covered by a chain guard, which adds lots of character to the left side of the loco.

Specifications

Builder: Peter Angus (UK)
Date built: 1987
Gauge: 0 (32mm)
Scale: 16mm
Boiler: Pot
Fittings: Safety valve, throttle, pressure gauge, blowdown
Fuel: Alcohol
Blow-off pressure: 30psi
Cylinders: One, double-acting D-valve
Reversing gear: Slip eccentric
Lubricator: Displacement
Weight: 5lbs 8oz
Dimensions: Length over end beams, 8½in; width, 3½in; height, 6in

Wrightscale's 'Wren'

Above: In front of the smoke-box is the cap to the condenser. This device needs to be siphoned out prior to each run.

Left: Wrightscale's 'Wren' is a tiny gem of a locomotive. Despite its size, it is a fine runner and is easily controllable. Valves are governed by Hackworth valve gear.

Kerr, Stuart was a British manufacturer of industrial locomotives, first steam, then diesel. The company was in business from 1881 to about 1930. They offered locomotives to run on many gauges of track, from 1ft 6in through standard gauge. Stock designs were offered and the company published a catalogue with photos and specifications of the engines, similar to a model-train catalogue. The 'Wren,' at three and a half tons, was the smallest engine the company made at that time.

It's interesting to me how some companies just seem to get it right, aesthetically speaking. Kerr, Stuart is one of these, along with John Fowler and Hunslet. Kerr, Stuart's locomotives are extremely attractive. Virtually all have pleasing proportions and the little ones are charming. It's a shame that more have not been preserved, but it's nice that accurate models, like the one shown here, have been made available to carry on the tradition.

The model

Wrightscale, run by Malcolm Wright, started life in Oxford but later moved to Scotland. Like Kerr, Stuart, Wrightscale produces mostly models of smaller, industrial engines. His 'Wren' is exquisite. It has tiny cylinders, working Hackworth valve gear, and a gas-fired boiler. The gas tank is hidden in the back sheet, below the spectacles, and it is filled via an extension that comes up through the roof. The engine has two gas-control valves – one on the tank and one on the burner.

Also projecting through the roof is the throttle extension. This keys loosely into the throttle itself and can be disengaged and removed for display, if one wishes.

Atop the boiler is a working water tank with a line to the backhead. When the engine cools down, the valve on this line

(actually a vacuum tap) can be opened and the cooling boiler will draw the water in for the next run. Otherwise, the boiler must be filled by removing the safety valve (awkward). A displacement lubricator resides on the footplate and a condensate tank sits beneath the smoke-box, between the frames. This makes for a cleaner-running engine.

The model, like the prototype, is just plain cute. Wrightscale got the proportions right and the tiny, working details make this engine an accurate rendition of the prototype.

Tiny engines have a reputation for being fast runners, often out of control. Not so this one. While it certainly will run faster than you'd ever want it to, it will easily throttle right down to a walk, even running light. It is a pleasure to run and fascinating to watch. It's a true gem in the world of mini steam locomotives.

The gas tank is tucked inside the back sheet. Its two control valves can be seen here, as can the throttle extension, which protrudes through the roof. The lubricator sits in the doorway.

Specifications

Builder: Wrightscale (UK)
Date built: 1988
Gauge: 0 (32mm)
Scale: 16mm
Boiler: Single flue
Fittings: Safety valve, throttle, pressure gauge, vacuum tap
Fuel: Butane
Blow-off pressure: 40psi
Cylinders: Two, double-acting D-valve
Reversing gear: Hackworth valve gear
Lubricator: Displacement
Weight: 2lbs 12oz
Dimensions: Length over end beams, 6¾in; width, 2¾in; height, 5⅝in

The Lindsay Shay

A most unusual Shay, this one is a lefty. It originated in a set of frames that was drilled backwards. The meths-fired loco is one of only about twenty-two made (all the others were 'rightys').

Larry Lindsay, a New Zealander residing in Denver, Colorado, built his first Shay in 1986. His initial loco-motive utilised Mamod cylinders and a scratchbuilt, silver-soldered copper pot boiler. It had a four-wick burner (production engines had three) and was geared 28:10. On its inaugural run it performed well on a local garden railroad with three LGB flatcars in tow. It ran up hill and down dale, hardly varying in speed.

The next year, in conjunction with Mike Bigger of (then) Narrow Gauge Machining, Larry started work on a commercial batch. Some of the first of these locos were shown at the 1988 Garden Railway Convention in Denver. After building five or six engines entirely by hand (Larry did all the assembly work himself), Mike and Larry ordered the deck plates and fireboxes from a local sheet-metal company. Mike made the initial batch of wheels but later shopped them out to a screw-machine company in Michigan.

Larry and Mike worked together for about three years, dur-ing which time eighteen or nineteen Shays were produced. After they separated, Larry finished around three more, bringing the total count to perhaps twenty-two. With the exception of one or two 0-gauge engines, all were gauge 1.

The model

During the production of the Shays, Mike inadvertently countersunk one set of frames on the wrong side, resulting in a reversed set of frames. This engine, before it was even built, was offered to me. Always a fan of the odd and unusual, I accepted, and the locomotive was finished up as a left-hander (of which there were one or two prototypes). Aside from being a mirror image of other Lindsay Shays, this engine is exactly the same in all other features.

The locomotive features two, double-acting oscillating cylinders operating from a single port block. An external spring arrangement keeps the cylinders tight against the block. Reversing is effected through a traditional rotary valve mounted atop the motor unit. It is controlled by a reversing lever in the open cab.

The boiler resembles a traditional Shay T-boiler, but the 'T' part holds no water. It supports the rear of the longitudinal pot boiler and forms a sort of firebox around it. 'Porcupine quills' are fitted to the pot boiler to help draw heat into it. The firebox extends forward about half the length of the boiler and a three-wick burner is contained therein.

A large, cylindrical fuel tank is carried in the engine's bunker. This feeds a sump below the deck via a standard chicken-feed system.

The trucks are unusual in that they actually have inside frames. On the cylinder side of the engine, an auxiliary frame holds the gear assemblies. On the off side, the exterior frame is a dummy.

Since both speed and direction are controlled from the lever in the cab, the throttle is very touchy. It takes little movement to cause a great change in speed. However, the engine is controllable and will run for nearly thirty minutes before running out of fuel. A sewing machine comes to mind when describing this engine. The Shay has a silky action at prototypical speeds and is capable of hauling a reasonable train. These engines are much loved by their owners and are seldom seen on the second-hand market.

The boiler is an unusual pot with a dummy 'T' section added to the rear. This helps exhaust the hot gases. Inside the 'T' is a superheater coil. The actual firebox extends forward from the 'T.'

Specifications

Builder: Larry Lindsay (US)
Date built: 1988
Gauge: 1 (45mm)
Scale: 1:24
Boiler: Pot
Fittings: Safety valve, pressure gauge
Fuel: Alcohol
Blow-off pressure: 20psi
Cylinders: Two, double-acting oscillators
Reversing gear: Rotary valve
Lubricator: Displacement
Weight: 6lbs 2oz
Dimensions: Length over end beams,
14¼in; width, 3½in; height, 6¼in

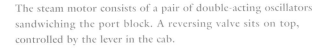

The steam motor consists of a pair of double-acting oscillators
sandwiching the port block. A reversing valve sits on top,
controlled by the lever in the cab.

A large meths tank sits in the coal bunker. The engine is fitted
with a pressure gauge, but little else. A single lever controls both
speed and direction.

155

Above: A reasonably accurate representation of a WW1 trench engine, this 2-6-2T is coal fired. The smokebox front pulls off for flue and smokebox cleaning.

Left: A throttle, blower valve, pressure gauge, whistle valve (upper right), and water glass fill the cab. The back sheet has been cut away for easier access to the fire door with a shovel of coal.

During WW1, the best way to get supplies to the troops and to move the wounded behind the lines quickly was via light, semi-portable railways. A vast network of these was built in France on both sides of the line. The British War Department ordered a large number of 2ft-gauge locomotives from US builders Alco and Baldwin. The Baldwins were mostly 4-6-0Ts while the Alco locomotives, of similar size, were 2-6-2Ts. After the war, many of these engines remained in France to help rebuild the country. One of this class survives today as *Mountaineer* on the Ffestiniog railway

Hugh Saunders' Alco 2-6-2T

The mechanical lubricator, a rarity in garden-scale locomotives, is driven by the motion of the expansion link.

(which really isn't very good) is located under the footplate on the left side of the locomotive. Cylinders are fitted with working drain cocks that can be turned on and off via a sliding plate beneath each cylinder. Condensate from the drain cocks is exhausted forward, as per British practice.

The best part, though, is that this engine is coal fired. It is fitted with a locomotive-type boiler with seven flues. The firebox, for an engine of this size, is quite large, making it relatively easy to keep a fire going. The smokebox front slides off, providing easy access to the large smokebox for cleaning out the ash and sweeping the flues.

Operating a coal-fired locomotive is a different experience from running any other type of steam engine. Even with the best of engines (and this one would certainly fall into that category), it takes much longer before you are ready to go and you must keep a constant eye on the fire, the pressure gauge, and the water level.

The engine is started on charcoal, then gradually changed over to anthracite. Side tanks are filled with water and the bypass valve is set at what you think will keep the boiler full, without overfilling it. It will need to be adjusted during the run. If water gets too low, you must pump more in by hand, but not too much, or you'll lose pressure and possibly your fire.

Meanwhile, you have to keep an eye on the fire, making sure that it is burning brightly and that the firebox is full. When adding coal, it must be carefully distributed over the grate to ensure even depth. If the fire gets too low or develops holes, you could lose it and be forced to retire in disgrace.

You must practice with this sort of engine to learn its ways so that, together, you can achieve the best performance. It's a gratifying experience to drive a tiny, coal-fired locomotive like this one.

in Wales and another is running in France on the Petit train de la Haute Somme.

The model

This locomotive is faithful to its prototype in proportion and major points. The detail level is relatively low (even boiler bands are absent) but mechanically the locomotive is first rate. The valve gear is superb – full Walschaerts, with each piece beautifully milled from the solid, not cut out of sheet metal. The only drawback is that it is operated by a screw reverser in the cab – a real nuisance, but probably prototypical. The engine sports a mechanical lubricator just forward of the cab and driven off the right expansion link.

Side tanks are functional and are joined by a balance pipe under the boiler. There is a hand pump in the left tank, tied into the engine's feedwater system. A second pump is driven from the middle axle via an eccentric and a scotch yoke. A bypass valve is activated by a handle in the cab.

The backhead is fully fitted, with a water glass, blower valve, throttle, pressure gauge, and whistle valve. The whistle

Both side tanks are functional. They can be filled through the hatch on either one.

Specifications

Builder: Hugh Saunders (UK)
Date built: 1980s
Gauge: 0 (32mm)
Scale: 16mm
Boiler: Locomotive type, unsuperheated
Fittings: Throttle, whistle, blower, safety valve, pressure gauge
Fuel: Coal
Blow-off pressure: 50psi
Cylinders: Two, double-acting D-valve
Reversing gear: Walschaerts
Lubricator: Mechanical
Weight: 8lbs 4oz
Dimensions: Length, 12⅞in; width, 4¼in; height, 6in

Specifications

Builder: Aster Hobby Company (Japan) for E.P. Lehmann (Germany)
Date built: 1989
Gauge: 1 (45mm)
Scale: 1:22.5
Boiler: Single flue
Fittings: Safety valve, throttle, pressure gauge, water glass
Fuel: Butane
Blow-off pressure: 45psi
Cylinders: Two, double-acting piston-valve
Reversing gear: Piston valve
Lubricator: Displacement
Weight: 7lbs 3oz (loco and tender)
Dimensions: Length over end beams (loco and tender), 17in; width, 4¼in; height, 5⅛in

Frank S is both colourful and well finished. It fitted right into LGB's visual program even though it was not well received by electric-train enthusiasts.

The prototype of this model was originally built by Henschel in 1941 for the Heeresfeldbahn (German military railway). It saw service on the Jüterog-Luckenwalder Kreiskleinbahn and on the island of Ruegen. In 1974 it was privately purchased, named *Frank S*, and was put to work on the Jagsttalbahn near Heilbronn/Stuttgart in Germany.

After 1992 it came to the Rügensche Kleinbahn on Ruegen Island in the Baltic Sea. Here *Frank S* and a similar engine, *Nicki S*, were rebuilt into a single engine, now called *Nicki-Frank S*.

The origins

In 1989, EP Lehmann (LGB) contracted with the Aster Hobby Company of Japan to produce a live-steam model of the *Frank S*. This was an interesting decision. At the time, the live-steam hobby had a foothold, but it was not large. Aster had been producing model steam engines since 1975 and had a good reputation. LGB had been producing large-scale electric trains since the late 1960s, also with a good track record.

Although the product resulting from this union was a good one, it was not that well received. There are a variety of possible reasons for this. One is that, while the engine looked a lot like – and was certainly compatible with – LGB's plastic trains, it was truly a different beast altogether. The average large-scale railroader at the time knew little of live steam, nor was he really that interested in it. Sales of the steam engine were not up to expectations and the locomotives were dumped on the market after only about a year, at a price far below the original.

A large number of *Frank Ss* were produced (3,028).

Unsightly and problematic control knobs for gas and steam hampered the engine's performance. Note the pressure gauge in the roof. The hole in the deck in the coal bunker was for water to surround the gas tank to keep its temperature up.

This number is in line with Aster's early production of their own engines until it became clear that selling that quantity of a specific engine would take a long time.

Perhaps LGB ordered this large number, expecting to sell them off much more rapidly than they were able to. After a time, a manufacturer must recoup costs, regain warehouse space, and move on. So, *Frank S* was remaindered and LGB never again entered the live-steam market.

The model

Frank S came packaged in a big, red box and it was supplied with a syringe, a screwdriver, a gas-jet cleaner, a plastic cup, a pair of cotton gloves, and a set of very complete instructions in German and English. Sadly, Aster's name was misspelled on the cover of the instructions ('Astor').

This was Aster's first piston-valve model, with direction controlled by a reversing block between the cylinders, actuated by a reversing quadrant in the cab. It is beautifully painted and came equipped with LGB-style loop couplers. There is a dead-leg displacement lubricator on the right-hand running board.

The boiler has a single flue and is gas fired. The gas tank is carried in the tender. There's a flexible hose between the engine and tender, and the gas jet is attached to it. The jet merely snaps into place in the flue when engine and tender are coupled. There's an inconveniently placed condenser in the smokebox that many people ultimately remove.

Fittings include a water window; a throttle; an interesting, external-spring safety valve; and a pressure gauge mounted in the roof, covered with a rubber cap that resembles a roof vent.

Control knobs on both the throttle and the gas tank are large and clunky. These were probably the biggest problem the engine had; they had built-in travel limits (usually insufficient) and, because of their internal O-rings, wanted to spring back to their former positions and wouldn't stay in place.

When in top form, the *Frank S* is an excellent performer. Its six-coupled chassis and short wheelbase also made it attractive to kitbashers, and a variety of interesting modifications have emerged.

Brandbright's GWR 0-4-2T

Left: **Brandbright's model of the GWR 14XX-class 0-4-2T captures well the essence of the prototype. The rear axle has a lot of lateral play for negotiating curves.**

Below: **The unusual drive mechanism incorporates two pair of cylinders, each pair working in tandem. This system is a great space saver. The rotary valve controlling speed and direction is at the front end of the locomotive.**

The Great Western Railway developed its 14XX-class 0-4-2T locomotives for rural branchline service. The engine was designed by CB Collett. Despite its slightly old-fashion appearance, the 14XX was, in fact, a relatively modern locomotive, being first brought into service in 1932. In all, seventy-five were built.

These engines were used on branch lines all over the GWR system, usually in push-pull service, often with just a single coach. There was a compartment at the far end of the coach from which the driver could control the engine – through both direct linkages and a system of signals to the fireman – on the return trip. Since these trains often provided the best link to the outside world, they were looked upon with some affection by the local residents, who usually bestowed nicknames on them. For instance, the train from Maidenhead (on the mainline) to Marlow was known as the 'Marlow Donkey.'

Many of this class of engine lasted until nearly the last days of steam in Britain. The remaining ones were officially withdrawn from service in 1965.

The model

In 1990, Brandbright Ltd. produced an interesting model of this small engine. In outline, it well captures the character of the prototype. The level of detail is good and the platework, assembled from brass etchings made from artwork by Donald Pearse, is festooned with rivets. It is nicely painted and crisply lettered.

Mechanically, this is an odd duck. It is powered by a four cylinder, oscillating steam motor. The motor, developed by Peter McCabe, was made by Ian Pearse. It has two small cylinders on either side of the port block that work in tandem, each pair driving a yoke that engages the crankpin. A small gear on the crank axle drives a larger one on the driven axle. The engine's frames are actually only cosmetic, as the axles are supported by a central frame that is integral with the steam motor. Reversing and speed regulation are via the sort of rotary valve customarily associated with oscillating engines and are controlled from the cab by a single lever. The trailing

axle is sprung and has considerable lateral play for negotiating tight curves.

The cab itself is cramped. On the left side is a small, vertically operated hand pump. You are supposed to fit a rubber tube from an outside water source over the inlet and pump the boiler up that way. However, there is no water glass, so you'd be hard pressed to know how much water to add. A valve on the right side of the cab opens and closes the line from the pump. A displacement lubricator sits right behind the left-hand door. It has a drain conveniently hidden (or inconveniently placed, depending on your point of view) behind the step.

The gas tank sits in the bunker, with an unobtrusive filler valve in the coal pile, just behind the cab. The control-valve stem protrudes from the right-hand door and must be operated with a screwdriver, as no handle is provided. The boiler itself is a traditional, centre-flue boiler.

As mentioned above, control is via a single lever in the cab, accessible through the removable roof. This is difficult to reach, especially when the engine is hot, and it tends to flop around. Although offered in a manual version, the locomotive was intended for single-servo radio control, which obviated the control problem. In all, only about a dozen of these models were produced.

The engine is a good runner, with an audible exhaust beat. Although its controls are awkward to deal with, once it's in motion, it goes well.

Specifications

Builder: Brandbright Ltd. (UK)
Date built: 1990
Gauge: 1 (45mm)
Scale: 1:32
Boiler: Single flue
Fittings: Throttle/reverse lever, hand pump, feed-line valve, pressure gauge, safety valve
Fuel: Butane
Blow-off pressure: 45psi
Cylinders: Four, double-acting oscillators, working two-and-two
Reversing gear: Rotary valve
Lubricator: Displacement
Weight: 6lbs 10oz
Dimensions: Length over end beams, 10¼in; width, 3⅜in; height over stack, 5⅛in

Miniature Steam Railways' 0-4-0

Miniature Steam Railways (MSR) is a little-known American manufacturer. The company existed in the 1980s and early 1990s under the leadership of Jim Wilson, of Dallas, Texas. Jim was both a steam fan and a toy-train enthusiast. He was, I feel, something of a genius at taking existing parts from different companies and combining them into entirely new products.

While I knew Jim, I didn't know him well, and so do not have a lot of background information. I met him a few times when he visited Denver. One of his early engines (though not produced commercially) was a live steam, Stirling-style 2-2-2 in N scale (1:160), inspired by the micro-miniature work of Australian, Arthur Sherwood, with whom he corresponded. This engine he brought to my studio one day in 1983. Jim had scratchbuilt an entire train set, including the locomotive and tender, three freight cars, and a loop track, all packaged in a beautiful presentation box. He set up the track on one of my work tables. The engine's boiler was ⅜in in diameter by 1¾in long. The tender served as both the alcohol tank and the burner. A wick tube extended forward from the front wall of the tender into the cab of the engine, putting the fire in the general proximity of the backhead.

Once the fire was lit, steam came up in about a minute. After giving the engine a nudge, the train ran smoothly for an astonishing twenty minutes or so, powered by one single-acting oscillator. The spring for the oscillator came from a lock tumbler, to give you an idea of its size. Jim had considered producing these sets for sale but, as far as I know, never did. I wonder where the original is today.

The model

Jim was interested in producing an American-style steam railway system similar to that of Mamod's in Britain. The commercial product that finally bore the name 'Miniature Steam Railways' was an amalgam of ideas and parts. Technologically, it was a Mamod locomotive, using a Mamod boiler, smokebox, backhead, and other parts. I don't know where the cylinders

The locomotive is powered by a pair of double-acting oscillating cylinders. These, in fact, were better than Mamod's of the time.

The pilot is a toy-train replacement part. Reversing is accomplished via a rotary valve, accessed in front of the boiler, as with a Mamod loco.

came from, as they don't look like Mamod's. The safety valve is Wilesco, as is the whistle. The sheet-metal work is original. I don't know who made the drivers. The pilot is a toy-train reproduction part.

In addition to the locomotive, MSR came out with some rolling stock. The pieces I have on hand include tank cars in two different liveries and a charming, manually operated crane and boom car. These, I believe, are mostly original to MSR, although some parts, including the very un-American buffers, were acquired from other steam-toy companies.

MSR also produced at least three examples of a steam roller that used Wilesco cylinders mounted vertically on one side, Shay style. Jim was also developing a diesel-outline locomotive that was to run on a Stirling hot-air engine. I know that he had at least one working prototype.

Shortly after I received my train (I don't recall exactly when), I received a call from Jim's friend Terry Shirley, telling me that Jim had died of a massive heart attack at the breakfast table one morning. He was only in his mid fifties. We have been deprived of an ingenious, creative, and industrious manufacturer. It would have been fascinating to see what he would have come up with had he been given the chance.

MSR's loco and tender is, in essence, an American Mamod. It utilises parts from several manufacturers as well as its own original parts.

Specifications

Builder: Miniature Steam Railways (USA)
Date built: 1990
Gauge: 1 (45mm)
Scale: 16mm (nominal)
Boiler: Pot
Fittings: Safety valve, whistle
Fuel: Dry pellets (Esbit)
Blow-off pressure: 10psi
Cylinders: Two, double-acting oscillators
Reversing gear: Rotary valve
Lubricator: None
Weight: 3lbs 4oz (loco and tender)
Dimensions: Length (loco & tender), 15¼in; width, 3½in; height, 5in

Robins Springs' Shay

I purchased this Shay (along with a similar, vertical-boilered model) from the obscure French firm of Robins Springs. I know little of the company itself. I usually keep all correspondence but in this case I somehow didn't. I was told that this was a father-son operation.

This is a good-sized locomotive, nominally to 1:20 scale, and is freelance in design. The engine employs an unusual, single-acting-twin steam motor with cranks set 180° apart. D-valves are run by standard eccentrics and the cylinders are non-reversing. The pistons are long and are connected directly to the drive shafts with wrist pins.

The drive train is typical for a Shay, with telescoping square shafts and nicely made U-joints. The gears, though, are another matter. Instead of proper bevel gears, these engines have tiny, ten-tooth pinions on the shaft and (approximately) forty-tooth, pressed-steel crown gears on the wheels. There is a small amount of adjustment in the journals to keep the

The Robins Springs Shay is a strange and unusual engine. It has two, single-acting fixed cylinders that are 180° opposed, so it's not self-starting.

gears properly meshed. Wheels are turned from steel bar and have relatively deep flanges.

A dead-leg lubricator sits in the cab. The boiler is gas fired. There is an inner barrel (the boiler proper) and an outer shell, with space between, similar to a Smithies boiler. A large, enclosed firebox below is lit from the off side.

A gas tank is carried in the coal bunker. There is not what we would consider to be a standard gas filler valve. Instead, there's a sort of odd, non-return valve with a ball in it. A screw-on cap actually keeps the gas from leaking out. This system works okay but is not ideal.

A toy-engine safety valve is fitted to the boiler. The steam line passes directly from the boiler to the cylinders, without benefit of a throttle. These engines are basic indeed. Workmanship varies from pretty good to pretty awful.

Operation of this engine tends to be problematic. The gas takeoff is evidently too low in the tank, allowing liquid butane into the burner until the level drops sufficiently. Once that happens, the fire settles down and burns well.

After a few minutes, steam starts to come out of the stack, as well as from a few other places it shouldn't. It is balky on starting but will finally run continuously and at a pretty good speed for a Shay. It is not uncommon for one or more of the gears to back off from its pinion, resulting in an unpowered axle. Despite this, the engine is a good runner. It runs loudly, with lots of mechanical noise, partly due to the indifferent fit of many of its components. With no throttle and no reversing, the best you can do is turn it on and stand back to enjoy the run.

Specifications

Builder: Robins Springs (France)
Date built: 1990
Gauge: 1 (45mm)
Scale: 1:20 (nominal)
Boiler: Enclosed inner boiler with protective shell and water tubes (similar to Smithies)
Fittings: Safety valve
Fuel: Butane
Blow-off pressure: 20psi
Cylinders: Two, single-acting D-valve
Reversing gear: None
Lubricator: Displacement
Weight: 2lbs 5oz
Dimensions: Length over end beams, 15½in; width, 4½in; height, 5⅞in

Where most Shay utilise bevel gears, this one uses less-than-satisfactory crown and pinions.

Mike Gaskin's *Ceylon*

Ceylon is a chunky, attractive locomotive. With the exception of its slip-return-crank valve gear, it is as fully configured as many much larger locomotives. The prototype had no tender.

This model is based on a Bagnall 0-4-0 tank engine built in 1906 for the 2ft 6in gauge Ceylon Irrigation Dept. The prototype had Bagnall-Price valve gear. As a tank engine, the prototype had no tender. The one on the model was added by Mike Gaskin and is based on those attached to the Mansfield-type 0-4-2s built for Egypt Sugar Factories in 1907.

The model

Mike Gaskin was one of the lesser-known British handbuilders. His output was limited, which makes his products all the more delectable when one comes along. His engines are workman-like and reliable and each has its own particular charm.

This is one of two similar locomotives that Mike made. The second engine does not have side tanks, but is otherwise close to *Ceylon*. *Ceylon* is fitted with a locomotive-type boiler containing seven tubes and one superheater flue. The smokebox front is not hinged – you just pull it off to clean out the smokebox and sweep the flues. There is a proper grate in the firebox, below which is an ashpan. These can be quickly dropped at the end of a run by undoing a simple latch. The four-wheel tender carries both coal and water, and is fitted with a hand pump. There is an axle pump on the engine's second axle, which is tied into a typical bypass system. The bypass valve is in the cab, as are the blower and throttle valves and blowdown. This engine is as fully featured as a small, full-size locomotive.

Reliable Roundhouse cylinders are used to power the engine. Valves are controlled via slip-return-crank valve gear (similar in operation to slip eccentrics). Workmanship is good throughout and this is a relatively easy locomotive to operate, with all controls readily at hand.

As coal-fired engines go, this is a fairly easy one to fire. It has a large, forgiving firebox. It's important to make sure the initial charcoal fire is burning well and that the firebox is full before adding anthracite to the mix. The changeover to coal can be done in a reasonable amount of time and the engine is then self-sustaining.

The boiler can easily be kept full via the bypass system, controlled by the valve in the cab. In a pinch, the tender pump can be used.

One funny thing about the engine is the dome, a standard Roundhouse unit, which is purely cosmetic. It is strapped to the boiler with a boiler band, like a birthday hat. And, like a silly hat, it sometimes goes astray, sliding to one side or the other, giving the engine a decidedly odd appearance.

The backhead is neatly arranged and complete. The throttle and blower levers (hidden by the roof) work off a manifold. The generous water glass has a blowdown on its bottom fitting. The fire door has plenty of room around it for access. On the right is the bypass valve.

Graham Stowell's *Irulan*

The prototype for this model was one of five engines built by Hunslet for the Lagos Steam Tramway. The originals pulled four-wheel carriages. The model, however, was not provided with couplers.

The model

This engine was built by Graham Stowell, of England, from a Mamod 0-4-0T. It is estimated that somewhere around 30,000 Mamod locomotives have been made, and a goodly number have been fodder for kitbashers' creativity. Such was the fate of this particular engine. Graham is a prolific builder and kitbasher, one with a peculiar turn of mind. Whimsy, often of a startling nature, is incorporated into much of his work. I suspect he was attracted to this particular prototype because of its own inherent whimsy.

Anyway, Graham built a beautiful little trailer out of wood and metal to go behind the engine, while modifying the locomotive to suit. The front of the trailer is supported by an interesting harness arrangement that hinges on the locomotive's frame above and between the drivers. The rear bogie is sprung. A proper alcohol burner replaced the horrible Mamod pellet burner, and the fuel tank is cleverly built into the trailer's bogie. An Enots valve is fitted to the engine so that the boiler can be refilled with a squirt bottle while the engine is under steam. There's a Mamod-type water glass in the back of the boiler.

The main body of the locomotive is painted a lurid blue, as were all of Graham's locomotives built around this time. Also, as with many of his other engines, it is named after some significant person, place, or thing from Frank Herbert's *Dune* series.

The performance of this locomotive is everything you'd expect from a Mamod. The motion of the pistons imparts a side-to-side 'boxing' or 'hunting' motion typically associated

Above: The all-wood trailer is a nice bit of coachwork.

Below: Mamod's pellet tray has been replaced by a meths burner fed from a tank incorporated into the trailer's bogie. A filler tube extends out the back.

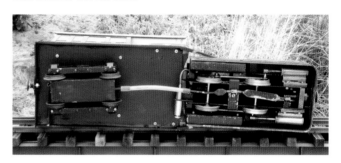

with small engines, particularly four-wheelers. This motion is small on the locomotive itself, but is magnified by the time it gets to the trailer, which bobs down the track in a most entertaining way. Water and fuel can be added to this engine at any time, so keeping it in steam indefinitely is easy.

Irulan is a more-or-less faithful model of a little tram that ran in Lagos, Nigeria. It started out as a run-of-the-mill Mamod.

Specifications

Builder: Graham Stowell/Mamod (UK)
Date built: 1991
Gauge: 0 (32mm)
Scale: 16mm
Boiler: Pot
Fittings: Safety valve, water glass, throttle/reversing valve, Enots water-filler
Fuel: Alcohol
Blow-off pressure: 15psi
Cylinders: Two, double-acting oscillators
Reversing gear: Rotary valve
Lubricator: None
Weight: 4lbs 2oz
Dimensions: Length, 13⅝in; width, 4in; height, 6¼in

Jetty's 0-4-0T

The Jetty Company of Japan was established in 1955 by Mr. M Hayashi. At that time the company produced model reciprocating racing engines. The company went on to develop small motorcycle racing engines and high-performance racing engines for automobiles (though whether for model or full-size cars is unknown). In 1977 the company began planning a line of model live-steam locomotives in 1:24 and 1:32 scales, though nothing evidently came of this.

Live steam was once again approached in 1989, with the design and development of a small 0-4-0T based on a Krauss (German) industrial locomotive. This project came to fruition in the locomotive shown here, although it seems never to have been put into actual production. In addition to this fixed-cylinder engine, Jetty planned a similar locomotive with oscillating cylinders as well as models of US and Japanese prototypes. There were also some rumblings of locomotives in 2½in gauge.

Jetty engines were to be sold through a marketing company, not directly. I suspect that this had something to do with the engines never seeing the light of day. With so many middle men, the ultimate retail price would have been prohibitive.

I never had any correspondence directly with Mr. Hayashi – only the marketing company. Unfortunately, this company had vastly inflated ideas about the size of the potential market for live-steam locomotives. The last communication I had with them was in 1996, at which time the release of the oscillating engine seemed imminent. However, I never saw it, if it was produced.

The model

The Jetty engines are neatly made with an absolute minimum of detail. They feature Smithies boilers that run on alcohol. The burner is integral with the fuel tank and consists of two large wicks that appear to be tightly coiled ceramic sheet. This is accessible through a door in the firebox. The fuel tank itself is filled with absorbent ceramic cotton.

Since the boiler is internally fired, a suction fan and blower are required and are supplied with the engines. Water can be added to the boiler through the safety-valve hole.

The cylinders are nicely made, with gland nuts on both piston and valve rods. The first sample I received was not reversible, the valves being driven directly by traditional return cranks. After some discussion with Mr. Hayashi (via the marketing company) a reversible model was produced. This incorporates a lever on the left-hand footplate that moves the radius rod up and down in a link, similar to the valve gear used by Roundhouse and others today. No lubricator is provided.

The locomotive is an indifferent performer. In the best of times it runs only adequately. The boiler never seems to have enough oomph to make the loco truly energetic. However, it would run languidly around for fifteen to twenty minutes, with the fire door cracked open.

Above: The backhead features only a throttle and a blower. Access to the burners is through the fire door, a nice touch. Burners appear to be coiled ceramic sheet.

Below: Although a simple engine, the Jetty 0-4-0T captures the character of the Krauss industrial locomotive that it models. This engine is reversible – the original model was not.

Specifications

Builder: Jetty Engines (Japan)
Date built: 1991
Gauge: 1 (45mm)
Scale: 1:22.5
Boiler: Smithies
Fittings: Safety valve, throttle, blower
Fuel: Alcohol
Blow-off pressure: 30psi
Cylinders: Two, double-acting D-valve
Reversing gear: Simple eccentric with link, controlled by lever on left-hand footplate
Lubricator: None
Weight: 3lbs 3oz
Dimensions: Length over end beams, 8½in; width, 3⅜in; height over stack, 5⅛in

Aster's C&S Mogul

Aster's rendition of the C&S Mogul accurately captures
the feel of the prototype. It is correct in all essential details.

Colorado & Southern's Nº 22 was one of a batch of sixteen identical Moguls purchased by the Union Pacific Railroad from Brooks in the early 1880s for its (then) Denver, South Park & Pacific Railroad in Colorado. In 1902, after some typical haggling and wangling, the 3ft-gauge railroad became independent, with a new name: the Colorado & Southern. The C&S was later acquired by the Chicago, Burlington & Quincy Railroad, but retained its own name until the end.

By the time the C&S came into existence, only two of the original sixteen Brooks engines remained: Nºs 21 and 22. By this time both had been extensively rebuilt, probably ending up with a fair number of parts from similar Cooke engines on them. Aster's model represents the locomotive toward the end of its life in the mid 1920s. It was scrapped in 1927.

The model
This model is a butane burner. The gas system has a couple of unusual features. The first of these is a sight glass (actually a little window) in the generous fuel tank in the tender. The gas (which is stored in its liquid state) is clearly visible, giving the operator an indication of how much is left. The other unusual feature is a secondary tank in the cab, between the gas-storage tank and the burner, which is also equipped with a control valve. This was evidently intended as a sort of buffer to even out the gas flow and make the burner more controllable. It turned out to be problematic and many owners removed it entirely, piping the gas directly to the burner in the usual way. The boiler is a conventional single-flue type with an internal poker burner.

The backhead has the usual fittings, including a throttle (controlled by a wheel instead of a lever), a pressure gauge, a water glass, and an awkwardly placed blowdown valve beneath the boiler, under the cab. There are two safety valves, one under the steam dome and one inside the cab. The latter vents through the cab roof via a silicone tube. The tender is fitted with a hand pump to keep the boiler topped up. The gas tank sits in the water reservoir to help keep the gas temperature constant, especially on colder days.

Cylinders are the typical double acting, slide-valve type. Reversing is accomplished by a single, simple eccentric for each valve, connected to an expansion link so that reversing can be controlled from the cab. (The prototype had Stephenson's link motion.) Motion is brought through the frames via rocker arms. A dead-leg lubricator resides on the pilot deck in front of the smokebox.

The model features the prototype's distinctive 'bear trap' spark arrestor and the interesting (dummy) air tank atop the boiler. Cab controls are accessed by removing the rear section of the cab roof.

With the back half of the roof removed, the backhead is accessible. On the left is the gas-control valve from the secondary tank. The large wheel in the centre is the throttle.

Specifications

Builder: Aster Hobby Company (Japan)
Date built: 1991
Gauge: 1 (45mm)
Scale: 1:22.5
Boiler: Single flue
Fittings: Safety valves (2), throttle, water glass, pressure gauge
Fuel: Butane
Blow-off pressure: 60psi
Cylinders: Two, double-acting D-valve
Reversing gear: Simple eccentrics with reversing links
Lubricator: Displacement
Weight: 14lbs 6oz (loco & tender)
Dimensions: Length (loco & tender), 24¾in; width, 4in; height over stack, 7¾in

Peter Fenn's Mt. Gretna 4-4-0

The Mount Gretna Narrow Gauge, an offshoot of the standard-gauge Cornwall & Lebanon, was a two-foot-gauge line in Pennsylvania. It was built to carry tourists to picnic sites and hiking trails and, later, National Guardsmen to their training grounds. The four-mile-long railroad owned a total of four locomotives. The first was a 0-4-4 Forney that proved unsuitable. The other three, constructed for the line by Baldwin, were smaller replicas of the 4-4-0 standard-gauge engines that ran on the Cornwall & Lebanon. The Mt. Gretna Narrow Gauge was the only two-foot-gauge US railroad ever to run 4-4-0 locomotives.

In 1986 I was approached by a man who lived in Pennsylvania and who had an interest in this railroad. He asked if there were any models of these obscure locomotives on the market. I assured him that there were not, so he asked if I could find someone to build some for him and coordinate and oversee the project.

I wrote to Peter Fenn of Wye Valley Model Engineering in Hereford (UK), with whom I'd had some correspondence and had visited on one of my trips over, to see if he was interested in the project. Peter, I knew, was a superb engine builder. Fortunately, he was interested, and we were away.

We decided on a scale of 16mm to the foot. Our client wanted the engines to be functional and to resemble the Mt. Gretna locomotives as closely as possible externally. He was not so concerned about the workings of the engine, so Peter and I decided that meths firing and slip-eccentric reversing would be the best way to go. I supplied Peter with what drawings and photos I could find of these locomotives, and he commenced.

I received periodic progress reports from Peter, which I forwarded on to Pennsylvania. As the project neared completion, the problem of paint and colours came up. Here, our client was able to supply all the necessary information, as he was involved in the local historical society and had done a lot of research in this area. Colour samples and diagrams were forwarded to Peter. I supplied Peter with full-size artwork for the lettering and lining on the loco, and he had dry transfers made. Finally, in 1991, the locomotives were finished and shipped. A total of five were made – three for the man in

The Mount Gretna Narrow Gauge was the only two-foot-gauge railroad in the US to use 4-4-0 locomotives. The colourful paint job seems correct and proper for a 19th-century tourist line.

Pennsylvania, one for me, and the fifth was purchased by an anonymous buyer. We were all delighted.

The model

This model is finished to a very high standard indeed. The multi-colour paint job is flawless and as authentic as possible. All important details are there.

The engine has an internally fired multi-flue boiler. On the backhead is a proper pull-out type throttle, along with a water glass with blowdown, pressure gauge, blower valve, and a bypass valve for the axle pump. There's a dead-leg lubricator on the right side of the cab. Cab fittings are laid out with a precision I've not seen elsewhere.

Slip eccentrics operate the valves. All axles on the locomotive (but none on the tender) are sprung. The springs are soft enough that they actually function in the way they were intended.

The tender carries water in the rear and fuel forward. A hand pump can be accessed through the water hatch. A small valve just behind the coal bunker operates the chicken-feed fuel system. Alcohol is added via a port in one of the tool boxes.

The meths burner utilizes three flat wicks with septums between to help direct the flames. In the upper left is the lubricator, disguised as an air tank.

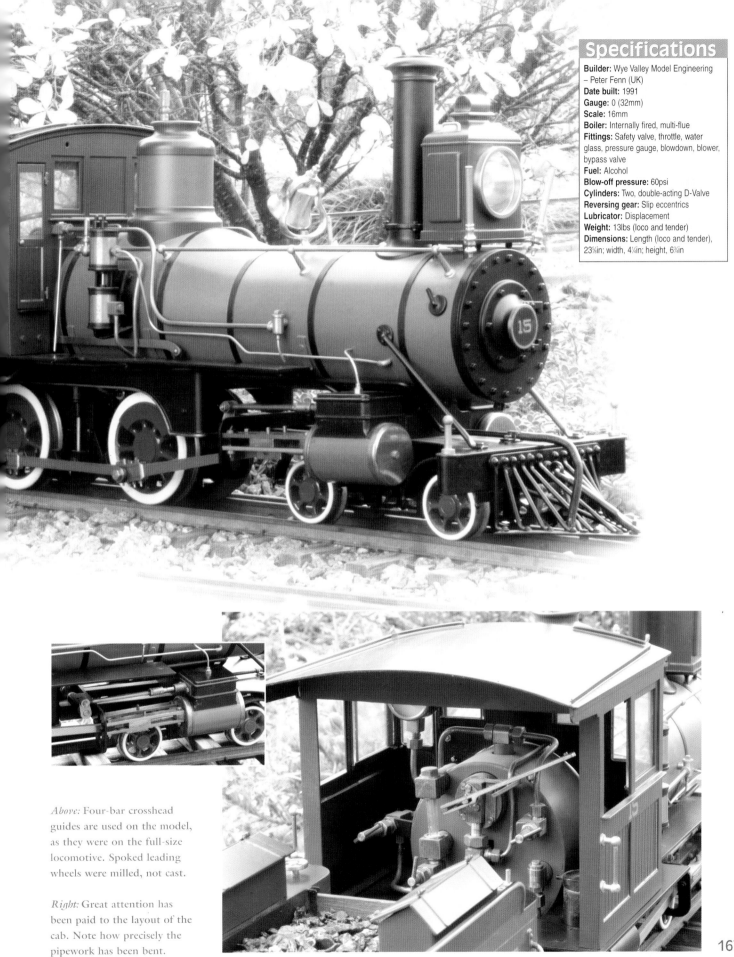

Specifications

Builder: Wye Valley Model Engineering – Peter Fenn (UK)
Date built: 1991
Gauge: 0 (32mm)
Scale: 16mm
Boiler: Internally fired, multi-flue
Fittings: Safety valve, throttle, water glass, pressure gauge, blowdown, blower, bypass valve
Fuel: Alcohol
Blow-off pressure: 60psi
Cylinders: Two, double-acting D-Valve
Reversing gear: Slip eccentrics
Lubricator: Displacement
Weight: 13lbs (loco and tender)
Dimensions: Length (loco and tender), 23⅝in; width, 4¼in; height, 6¾in

Above: Four-bar crosshead guides are used on the model, as they were on the full-size locomotive. Spoked leading wheels were milled, not cast.

Right: Great attention has been paid to the layout of the cab. Note how precisely the pipework has been bent.

Argyle's NA Class 2-6-2T

In 1897, the 2ft 6in gauge Victorian Railways of Australia solicited bids for a twenty-ton tank locomotive that could be run in either direction without having to be turned. While most locomotives in Australia at that time were British, Baldwin of Philadelphia won the bid for this one. The first two NA class, 2-6-2T locomotives, Nᵒs 1A and 2A were delivered in 1898. These would be the only NAs built in America. The remainder of the class, Nᵒs 3A through 17A, were built at the Newport Workshops of the Victorian Railways from 1900 to 1915, using Baldwin's design and patterns.

Today, engine 6A is preserved and running on the Puffing Billy Railway near Melbourne, along with other NA-class engines. This railway, which is part of the original line on which the NAs ran, was set up as a preservation society in 1955 and has become Australia's leading preserved railway.

The model

Argyle Locomotive Works (Gordon Watson) produces fine, sophisticated models, and this one is no exception. It is a beautifully detailed model that captures the soul of its proto-type. It has laser-cut frames (to resemble bar frames), sprung axles, cast stainless-steel wheels, and phosphor-bronze bushings at important wear points. Reversing is via full Stephenson's valve gear driven from the second axle and controlled by a reversing quadrant in the cab.

The cab roof lifts off for easy access to the controls. The boiler has a full complement of fittings, including a safety valve under the steam dome, set at 50psi; a water glass; a pressure gauge; a filler plug beneath the rear sand dome; and a blowdown valve. The engine has working side tanks connected by a balance pipe, so that only one

Lower left: Everything is readily at hand in the cab. The reversing quadrant is by the far door. Gas is carried in the tank in the coal bunker.

Lower right: The large steam dome conceals the safety valve, while the rear sand dome hides the filler plug (domes removed).

Opposite page:

Right: A large and elegant engine, this is a scale model of the famous NA-class locomotives of Australia.

Lower: This locomotive features full, working Stephenson's valve gear. Rods are made from castings.

tank need be filled. Water is pumped from the tanks into the boiler via an axle pump on the first axle. There is a bypass valve in the cab.

Butane is burned in the single-flue boiler. Gas is carried in a tank in the bunker at the rear of the engine. The displacement lubricator is beneath the smokebox on the righthand side.

The locomotive is elegant and stately in operation, though a lively engine. A good train will tame it, though. It has a loud chuff that can be heard all over the railway. Since it has an onboard pump, this engine can be kept in steam indefinitely. However, since it's gas fired, the fire must be shut down from time to time for refueling.

Specifications

Builder: Argyle Locomotive Works (Australia)
Date built: 1991
Gauge: 1 (45mm)
Scale: 15mm
Boiler: Single flue
Fittings: Safety valve, filler plug, throttle, water glass, pressure gauge, bypass valve for feedwater system
Fuel: Butane
Blow-off pressure: 50psi
Cylinders: Two, double-acting D-valve
Reversing gear: Stephenson's
Lubricator: Displacement
Weight: 9lbs 14oz
Dimensions: Length over body, 17in; width, 4¾in; height, 7⅞in

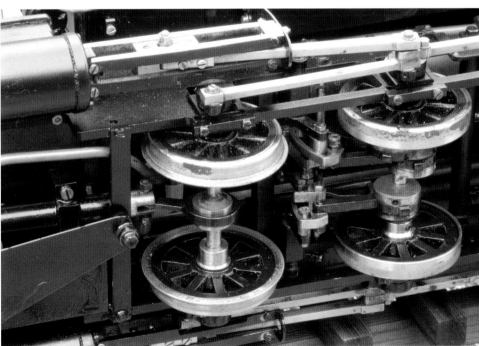

In this locomotive, Mike Gaskin not only captured the character of the prototype, but one of its most unusual physical attributes as well – its articulated chassis.

India's Matheran Hill Railway was built in 1905 to provide access to the resort of Matheran. It rises from Neral, near sea level, on the mainline near Bombay, to Matheran, elevation 2,500ft. The journey took about two hours. The line is twelve and a half miles long and has a ruling gradient of 1 in 30 (3.3%). There are many curves of 60ft radius and one as tight as 45ft. The consulting engineer was ER Calthrop, of Leek & Manifold fame, who specified 0-6-0T articulated locomotives with six-ton axle loading. Four locomotives were built to his specifications by Orenstein & Koppel in 1905-7. These engines had Klein-Lindner patented articulation.

With this type of articulation, the centre axle has sliding side-play while the outer axles have radial movement. All axles are linked so that one's motion affects the others. The trailing axle is behind the firebox, giving the engines a very long wheelbase. Externally, the engines do not appear to be articulated, as they have outside frames and, even on very sharp curves, it is difficult to see the sideways movement of the wheels and axles.

The four steam engines worked the line until the introduc-
tion of diesel power in 1956. The steam locos then worked with the diesels until the last was withdrawn from active service in 1982.

All four engines survive today. One is at the Museum in Delhi, one is at Bombay, and one resides at Matheran. The fourth was brought into the UK in 1987. It has been restored to service and is currently running on the Leighton Buzzard Light Railway.

The model
Mike Gaskin's Matheran 0-6-0T is a sophisticated locomotive. It has an alcohol fired, locomotive-type boiler with a metal arch in the firebox. There's a hand pump in the cab (with a large, removable handle), but no axle pump. Boiler fittings include a blower, a throttle lever accessible through the left-hand window, a safety valve, a water glass with blowdown, and a pressure gauge. The displacement lubricator is mounted in the cab, above the boiler – an unusual position. The roof is removable for access to the controls.

The engine has working side tanks linked by a balance pipe under the boiler. The hand pump draws water from the tanks

Specifications

Builder: Mike Gaskin (UK)
Date built: Circa 1991
Gauge: 0 (32mm)
Scale: 16mm
Boiler: Locomotive type with water tubes in the firebox
Fittings: Safety valve, throttle, blower, pressure gauge, water glass, blowdown, hand pump
Fuel: Alcohol
Blow-off pressure: 75psi
Cylinders: Two, double-acting D-valve
Reversing gear: Slip return cranks
Lubricator: Displacement
Weight: 7lbs 14oz
Dimensions: Length over buffer beams, 13¼in; width, 4¾in; height over stack, 5⅞in

There's a lot going on in the cab. On the far side is the hand pump with a removable handle. The lubricator sits atop the boiler.

With Klein-Lindner articulation, the centre wheelset can slide on its axle while the end ones pivot on theirs. All three work in harmony, enabling both model and prototype to negotiate very sharp curves.

and can be used for the initial filling of the boiler. Cylinders are conventional, double acting, D-valve, controlled by slip return cranks. Fuel is stored in a tank beneath the footplate that is filled via a pipe in the coal bunker behind the cab.

The most fun aspect of this model, though, is that it sports the same type of Klein-Lindner articulation as the prototype. The centre drum-axle can slide about ⅜in side to side on the inner driven axle. A spline transmits the power to the centre wheels. Wheelsets on the end drum axles are mounted on spherical bearings that are splined to inner axles, allowing them to pivot about their centre points. All axles are linked and work in concert with one another. This articulation allows the engine to negotiate remarkably sharp curves, given its long wheelbase (6⅝in).

The engine was formerly owned by DB Pinniger, who christened it *Sir Arthur*, in homage to Sir Arthur Heywood. Heywood is thought to have come up with the first radial-axle articulation, though his was for a 15in-gauge locomotive.

Control of this engine is quite good. Slow-speed running is no problem (nor is high-speed running!). However, it's an engine that cannot be left to its own devices. You must keep a constant eye on the water level and make sure the fuel is topped up as well. The loco can be kept in steam indefinitely.

Because it is a big engine with a narrow stance, and because of its suspension system (stability is mostly ensured by the arrangement of the centre axle), the loco has a strange rocking or waddling gait unlike any other locomotive I've seen.

171

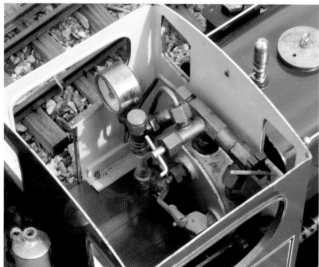

The cab is roomy and neatly laid out. An internal throttle has been fitted to the boiler. Note the polished cab floor. A hand pump is mounted to the floor on the right side, just out of sight.

Not a great deal appears to be commonly known about the prototype of this large saddle-tank locomotive. It was built by Hunslet in 1878 for the North Wales Narrow Gauge Railways as an outside-frame 0-6-4T, an unusual wheel arrangement. It was the largest of the locomotives built for this line.

The name *Beddgelert* is interesting. It means 'Grave of Gelert.' The story is a little long but, briefly, Gelert was a much-loved dog that was unjustly killed by its master, a Welsh prince, who believed that the dog had killed and eaten his infant child. When the child was found safe and it was discovered that Gelert had, in fact, killed a wolf that had tried to eat the child, the prince was filled with remorse and the legend was born.

The model

This engine, like virtually all of Hugh Saunders' work, is a fine, well-made model. It has a relatively high amount of detail and is nicely finished and lined out. It has two, double acting, D-valve cylinders that are reversed by slip eccentrics. Valves are inside the frames. Drive axles are unsprung, but the trailing bogie, which bears some of the engine's weight, is sprung and the wheels are equalised within a secondary

Specifications

Builder: Hugh Saunders (UK)
Date built: Early 1990s (?)
Gauge: 0 (32mm)
Scale: 16mm
Boiler: Single flue with firebox and water tubes
Fittings: Safety valve, throttle, blower, whistle, check valve, water glass, pressure gauge, hand pump
Fuel: Alcohol
Blow-off pressure: 40psi
Cylinders: Two, double-acting D-valve
Reversing gear: Slip eccentrics
Lubricator: Displacement (two)
Weight: 8lbs 6oz
Dimensions: Length, 13in; width, 4in; height, 5⅜in

Left: Beddgelert is a large and handsome narrow-gauge locomotive. The saddle tank is functional and the forward sand box on either side is actually a cylinder lubricator.

Top right: The water can on the coal pile conceals the fuel valve. The bucket on the right is actually the fuel filler plug.

Lower: Inside the cab is the unusual-but-handy feature of a gauge glass for the fuel tank. The clear, plastic tube has been stained by the colorant put into the meths.

frame, so all four feet are always on the rails. The rods are beautifully made, being machined from the solid as opposed to stamped from sheet or plate.

Cab fittings include the throttle, blower, pressure gauge, water glass, and whistle valve. The nearly useless whistle itself lives under the right-hand footplate. The engine's safety valve is under an ornate dome, with dummy safeties outside it.

A working saddle tank sits astride the boiler and there is a hand pump in the cab, with a removable handle, to keep the boiler topped up. The tank has a balance pipe to equalise the water level in both sides. The boiler has a (dry) firebox and a large, single flue. There are cross tubes in both the firebox and the flue to increase the heating area and water capacity. The burner is Hugh Saunders' standard box-type alcohol burner, perforated with air holes. It must be lit through the fire door in the cab. Fuel is stored in the rear bunker, under the coal load in a chicken-feed tank.

This locomotive has some unusual features. There are a pair of displacement lubricators, one on either side, disguised as sand boxes. Each feeds one cylinder. The fuel tank has the welcome amenity of a sight glass in the cab. The filler cap for the fuel tank is disguised as a bucket. You stick a screwdriver into the bucket to engage the slot at the bottom. The fuel-control valve is under a liftoff water can. To gain access to the burner, the rear bogie slips right off. A spring helps to hold it in place while the engine is in operation.

The underbelly. The rear bogie has been unclipped, but is still attached by the spring to the buffer beam. Burner and fuel line are clearly visible, as are the eccentrics and the rods to the valves. Note the profiling of the side rods.

Trams by D&M Horovitz

Left: This pair of tiny tram engines emerged as the result of a father-daughter project when the daughter was twelve years old. Each engine has a pot boiler and one, single-acting cylinder. The one closest to the camera was built by Dori.

Lower: A compound-gear train provides the engine with low speed and adequate power. The boiler is fired by a single wick.

When my oldest daughter, Dori, was twelve, she decided she wanted to build a live-steam locomotive from scratch. She was a determined child, so I agreed to design a simple engine. I decided to build one alongside her, to show her what to do, but she had to do all of her own work. This included learning how to use precision measuring instruments, doing her own math, and learning how to use a lathe and the necessary hand tools.

The agreement was that we would build our engines in phases. If she got tired of the project, she could quit, but only at the end of whichever phase we were working on at the time.

The first section to be completed was the actual steam motor, which we were able to operate with a tire pump. After this, work progressed steadily and enthusiasm remained high. One of the final major jobs was making the boiler. The parts were cut out of copper and silver-soldered together. Dori and I helped one another do this two-person job. After one or two reheats, we both had steam-tight boilers.

Once the chassis were complete, we put everything together for the first steam test. Up until now, I had only hoped it would work. This was the moment of truth. Dori

got hers together first, late one spring evening, and we went out to the track to test it. She filled the lubricator with steam oil, the boiler with distilled water, and the fuel tank with alcohol. She lit the fire and we waited. After six or seven minutes, the safety valve began to sputter. Dori was a little leery of the thing, so I gave the flywheel a flip, and the engine was off. Performance far exceeded expectations, and it ran for a good long time. I quickly finished mine up and it also passed the test.

After this came the more tedious work of making the cosmetic body parts. A lot of this was done with hand tools and it was at this point that Dori's interest began to flag. However, the National Garden Railway Convention (in Washington DC in 1992) was coming up, and we discussed the possibility of running our engines there together. This lit the fire again, and we finished up the project, each of us completing a tiny, functioning live-steam locomotive. And we did run them at the convention that year. Dori received a lot of praise from the other live steamers in attendance, as well as a second-place ribbon in the scratchbuilding contest, which made the entire project more than worthwhile.

The model

As mentioned above, this is a simple engine. It has a transverse pot boiler fired by a single-wick burner. The boiler is plumbed into a small displacement lubricator, from where it goes to the steam motor. This is a single-acting oscillating cylinder geared to the axle around 17:1. Side rods connect the driven axle to the other one. There is no throttle or reversing gear.

Brass wheels from Delton Locomotive Works were used. These were rebushed and fixed to the axles with set screws. Construction, except for the boiler, is almost entirely of brass.

Specifications

Builders: Dora & Marc Horovitz (US)
Date built: 1992
Gauge: 1 (45mm)
Scale: 15mm
Boiler: Pot
Fittings: Safety valve
Fuel: Alcohol
Blow-off pressure: 20psi
Cylinders: One, single-acting oscillator
Reversing gear: None
Lubricator: Displacement
Weight: 1lb 15oz
Dimensions: Length, 5¼in; width, 3¼in; height over the stack 6½in

Archangel's Cyprus Government Railway 2-6-0

The prototype of this model was built for the Cyprus Government Railway by Nasmyth Wilson in 1904. The 2ft 6in-gauge railway there was introduced by the British in 1905 and it lasted until 1951. Nº 21 had a sister engine (Nº 22), built at the same time, and another (Nº 23) assembled later from parts. These engines were built originally with round-top boilers, but were later converted to Belpaire fireboxes. Archangel's model is of the original design.

The model

This engine is a pip! It was made late in Archangel's day in the sun, after Stewart Browne had moved to Wales from High Wycombe. I've been told that it was a one-off. I don't know exactly when it was made – probably in the early to mid 1990s. Earlier Archangel engines often had the date of manufacture stamped on the frames somewhere, but this one does not. With no extant prototype against which to compare it, I cannot comment on its fidelity. However, as a model locomotive, it has a lot to recommend it.

The engine has sprung first and third axles, while the second, driven axle is rigid with the frames and has blind drivers (one driver is fully blind, while the other still has the vestiges of a flange). Side rods are articulated and nicely shaped. Valves are driven by full Walschaerts valve gear (have a look at the combination lever), with each of the components made by hand from steel plate. The valve gear is controlled by that most inconvenient of appliances, a screw reverser in the cab.

The dome lifts off to reveal the water-filler plug, and the stack slides off for no apparent reason. A displacement lubricator resides on the deck in front of the smokebox, with a drain beneath, behind the leading wheels. The steam dome sports a Salter-style safety valve and a dummy whistle.

The backhead contains a throttle, a pressure gauge, and a water glass with a blowdown valve – a nice feature. The gas tank rides under the roof, with access to the filler valve through a hole in the roof. An unsightly silicone hose connects the tank to the gas jet.

Sadly, the tender, though well made, is purely ornamental. It would have been nice if it carried at least the fuel, to get the gas tank away from the heat of the boiler. The drawbar is simply a long screw that loosely connects the engine and tender, with a brass spacer between to prevent them getting too close to one another – crude but effective.

Above: Full Walschaerts valve gear, reversed by a screw reverser in the cab, controls the valves.

Right: The cab is fairly spacious and the throttle is easily accessible. The gas tank is slung under the roof; the control valve and silicone supply line appear to be afterthoughts.

Left: This is an attractive model with pleasing proportions. It has a distinct colonial look about it, with its four-wheel tender and slatted pilot.

Specifications

Builder: Archangel Models (UK)
Date built: Early to mid 1990s
Gauge: 1 (45mm)
Scale: 16mm
Boiler: Single flue
Fittings: Safety valve, throttle, pressure gauge, water glass with blowdown
Fuel: Butane
Blow-off pressure: 50psi
Cylinders: Two, double-acting D-valve
Reversing gear: Walschaerts
Lubricator: Displacement
Weight: 7lbs 12oz (loco and tender)
Dimensions: Length over end beams (loco and tender), 17⅝in; width, 4⅝in; height, 6⅜in

Martin Sheridan's Hunslet

The Hunslet Engine Company, of Leeds, England, was founded in 1864. Over its long history, it provided a vast array of industrial locomotives to companies around the world. One of its best-known designs is the diminutive 0-4-0 saddle-tank locomotives designed to work in the slate quarries of Wales and, thus, became known as quarry Hunslets. A large number of this type of engine was manufactured in different classes (according to weight) and a surprising sampling still exists, many in operation.

Gertrude worked at the Penrhyn Quarry as one of the 'Large' class, having been delivered there in 1909. It has an open cab and was worked by one man. The engine's working life was spent at the quarry. In 1960 it was withdrawn and shipped to Canada, where it is still on display at the Ontario Science Centre. The Hunslet Engine Company is still in business today and has actually begun offering brand-new quarry Hunslets again.

The model

Martin Sheridan's *Gertrude* is a faithful model of the prototype. The detail level is exceptionally high. In ⅞in scale, this is a large model.

Gertrude has a near-scale backhead. There is an internal throttle with a beautifully crafted lever, two whistles (one dummy and one working), a pressure gauge, and a blower valve. A small, vented brass dome conceals the safety valve. There's a hand pump with a removable handle to the left of the boiler, as well as an axle pump on the driven axle. The bypass valve is just below the saddle tank on the right side. A dummy brake column stands by the right side of the boiler.

The saddle tank is functional and there's a balance pipe between the two sides. The supply line for the axle pump comes off the balance pipe.

A locomotive-type boiler with a wet-leg firebox is mounted to the chassis. The removal of a single pin allows the grate

Martin Sheridan's quarry Hunslet is an excellent model of an iconic prototype. Its locomotive-type boiler will burn either coal or meths.

and ashpan to drop out as a single unit. The boiler has eight flues; there is no superheater on this engine. The smokebox door is held closed with a proper two-handled dart – lovely! There are two sliding panels on the back sheet to facilitate firebox access. Firing tools are carried in brackets mounted to the left side of the saddle tank. While the engine burns coal, it was also provided with a meths burner that fits into the firebox.

The engine is reversed by Stephenson's valve gear. There's a reversing lever in the cab with a working locking handle. The engine can be run in full gear or it can be notched up in either direction. The chassis is fully sprung, though the leaf springs are dummies.

A large displacement lubricator with a drain is concealed beneath a plate just below the smokebox door. On the left side of the firebox is a screwdriver-actuated blowdown valve.

The level of finish on this engine is as high as the craftsmanship that went into the construction of it. The flawless black paint job has been lined out by hand in blue. This locomotive is a joy, accurately portraying the work horses of the quarries.

Cab controls are near scale in proportion. Note particularly the throttle and reversing levers. The pump handle on the left side slips off.

Right: Full working Stephenson's valve gear characterises this locomotive. The axle pump can be seen in the middle.

Specifications

Builder: Martin Sheridan (UK)
Date built: 1993
Gauge: 1 (45mm)
Scale: ⅞in
Boiler: Locomotive type with wet-leg firebox
Fittings: Safety valve, water glass, pressure gauge, blowdown valve, blower, whistle
Fuel: Coal or alcohol
Blow-off pressure: 75psi
Cylinders: Two, double-acting D-valve
Reversing gear: Stephenson's
Lubricator: Displacement
Weight: 11lbs 14oz
Dimensions: Length over end beams, 13⅞in; width, 5⅜in; height, 8⅜in

Aster's 'Grasshopper'

Left: Perhaps Aster's most unusual engine, the 'Grasshopper' is a model of the Baltimore & Ohio *Atlantic*. It was supplied with the coach. The plug in the side of the boiler is a level plug.

Right: The walking beams are attached to the top of the boiler, one on either side of the stack. Between them is the safety valve. Piston valves are between the cylinders. The handrail is laser-cut steel.

I n the earliest days of railroading, around the 1830s, locomotives were still being developed and there was no standard form. It was not uncommon for railroads to come up with their own designs and, back then, the Baltimore & Ohio was one of the leading railroads in the US. In 1832, Phineas Davis created *Atlantic* for the B&O. The engine had a vertical boiler and twin, vertical cylinders, each of which powered an overhead walking beam that was, in turn connected to a geared jackshaft via rods. The jackshaft was then geared to the axle. It was these walking beams atop the engine that gave the engine the nickname 'Grasshopper.'

The coal-burning locomotive was so successful that the B&O built twenty more to a similar pattern. The original *Atlantic* faded from history about 1836, but in 1893 the B&O rebuilt a similar engine, the *Andrew Jackson*, to resemble the *Atlantic*. This became a B&O 'heritage' locomotive and was exhibited at various important exhibitions. It currently lives at the B&O Railroad Museum in Baltimore. It is this rebuilt locomotive that Aster has modelled.

The model

The 'Grasshopper' is a real departure for Aster in many ways. It is the earliest locomotive they have ever modelled; it is, mechanically, perhaps the most unusual; it was supplied unpainted; and it was supplied with a coach!

The model is equipped with a vertical, internally fired boiler with four flues. It burns alcohol, which is carried in a tank beneath the footplate. The burner has four small wicks that correspond with the flues. A suction fan is required to get steam up.

Fittings are minimal and include a safety valve, a check valve on the side of the boiler for external filling, and a level plug on the other side. There's an additional plug atop a stubby tube on top of the boiler. This tube amounts to a steam dome, as the steam takeoff pipe is within it. There is no pressure gauge or water glass. (The prototype didn't have these amenities, either, we are told in the model's instructions.)

Like the prototype, the model is equipped with a pair of vertical cylinders mounted over one axle. These are controlled by piston valves. In the time-honoured tradition of piston valves, reversing is accomplished via a rotary valve, which also serves as the throttle. Extensive use of banjo fittings is made for steam connections. These, while perhaps a little unsightly, are easy to produce, simple to assemble, and reliable in use.

The piston rods are connected to walking beams, the ends of which are attached to the top of the boiler. The other ends are connected, via shafts, to the cranks on the geared jackshaft ahead of the front axle. This shaft is geared to the axle to power the engine. Strangely, this engine is geared up, whereas most geared locos are geared down, making an already fast-running engine even faster. Since the other axle is unpowered, this engine could technically be called an 0-2-2T.

Interestingly, the locomotive came with a period coach – actually a stage coach on a railroad chassis. This coach is well below Aster's usual standard. Its body is made entirely of etched brass sheet and die-crunched plywood. The chassis is better, being all brass and incorporating an interesting suspension system.

This engine is a smooth runner, though it tends to be fast. It would benefit from a proper throttle. With its primitive feedwater system, it is possible to keep it in steam indefinitely.

The cranks power a large gear, coupled to a smaller one on the axle, thus increasing the wheel velocity and making this engine a speedy runner.

Specifications

Builder: Aster Hobby Company (Japan)
Date built: 1994
Gauge: 1 (45mm)
Scale: 1:32 (nominal)
Boiler: Vertical, multi flue
Fittings: Safety valve, filler plug, check valve
Fuel: Alcohol
Blow-off pressure: 45psi
Cylinders: Two, double-acting piston-valve
Reversing gear: Rotary valve
Lubricator: Displacement
Weight: 2lbs 2oz
Dimensions: Length over end beams, 6in; width, 3⅛in; height, 5⅝in

Prescott Engineering's *Robin*

Prescott Engineering was founded in 1994 by John Prescott. The company offers essentially one engine in a couple of variations. *Robin* is an attractive model of a typical British industrial locomotive. While it does not represent any particular prototype, it has many of the characteristics of the small engines that a variety of manufacturers supplied to commercial firms around the world.

A short but large-diameter boiler gives the engine a pleasing 'chubby' look. The boiler has a single flue and is fired by butane. Gas is carried in a tank under the cab roof. To fill it, you slide back a hatch on the roof to reveal the filler valve – a nice touch.

The gas-control lever protrudes from the front wall of the cab, just beneath the roof. While this sounds a little clunky and toylike, the valve is small, nicely made, and in keeping with the other fittings on the engine. I don't find it obtrusive. Boiler fittings include a safety valve under the lift-off brass steam dome, a throttle, a pressure gauge that you must read through a cab window, and a fitting for filling the boiler under pressure. A displacement lubricator sits next to the left side of the boiler. An allen key is required to open the drain plug.

Side tanks are dummies, as are the filler hatches atop them. Bodywork, according to the manufacturer's literature, is made primarily of nickel silver, not the customary brass or steel. Sheet-metal work is neat and cleanly done, with no rivet or other added detail. This is a plain, workmanlike locomotive.

The chassis is unsprung and all axles are bushed in the frames. The tiny cylinders have outside valves controlled by Hackworth valve gear. This is operated from the cab by a lever that locks into forward, neutral, or reverse positions. End beams are fitted with sprung (outside springs!) centre buffers. Lamp irons adorn the smokebox and back sheet.

Once the engine is prepared for operation, the gas valve is opened and a match placed near the stack. The fire catches at once. For a single flue, gas-fired boiler, this one is remarkably quiet in service.

This is a very lively locomotive and is a challenge to run light. It does much better with a train – preferably a heavy one. Then it settles down quietly to its work with no more histrionics.

Left: To gain access to the gas-filler valve, you slide back the roof vent. Gas is controlled by the valve on the front of the cab.

Right: Hackworth valve gear controls the valves on this little engine. Construction is neat and to a high standard.

Above: While not a model of any specific prototype, *Robin* shares characteristics with numerous small industrial locomotives.

Below: The gas tank is mounted beneath the roof, above the boiler. The pressure gauge, with its back to the camera, faces out the front window. The engine is remarkably quiet in operation for a gas-fired locomotive.

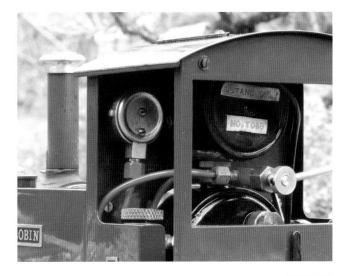

Specifications

Builder: Prescott Engineering – John Prescott (UK)
Date built: 1994
Gauge: 0 (32mm)
Scale: 16mm
Boiler: Single flue
Fittings: Safety valve, pressure gauge, throttle, filler fitting
Fuel: Butane
Blow-off pressure: 45psi
Cylinders: Two, double-acting D-valve
Reversing gear: Hackworth valve gear
Lubricator: Displacement
Weight: 3lbs 12oz
Dimensions: Length over end beams, 7⅜in; width, 3¾in; height, 5¾in

A 15in-gauge 0-4-0T for gauge 1

This 15in gauge, might-have-been engine is square and chunky. It's simple and straightforward in design and construction.

Specifications

Builder: Narrow Gauge Machining (US)
Designer: Marc Horovitz
Date built: 1994
Gauge: 1 (45mm)
Scale: 1⅛in
Boiler: Pot
Fittings: Safety valve, throttle, pressure gauge, blowdown valve
Fuel: Alcohol
Blow-off pressure: 50psi
Cylinders: Two, double-acting D-valve
Reversing gear: Slip eccentric
Lubricator: Displacement
Weight: 9lbs
Dimensions: 10¼in long x 5in wide x 9⅛in tall

Ever since I was a child, I've been interested in railways of the smaller variety. In Frederic Shaw's *Little Railways of the World*, I discovered 15in-gauge lines. I was especially interested in the British lines, particularly the Romney, Hythe & Dymchurch and the Ravenglass & Eskdale. I later learned about Sir Arthur Heywood, who proposed the notion that 15in gauge was the smallest practical gauge for a full size, narrow-gauge railway. Sadly, he built only two lines to this gauge; his own experimental Duffield Bank Railway and, later, the Eaton Hall Railway for the Duke of Westminster. He called these 'minimum gauge' railways and wrote a fascinating treatise on the subject.

For me, as well as many others, 15in became a sort of magical gauge. I never really considered modelling 15in gauge equipment until I met Mike Decker many years ago. Mike is a strong proponent of this gauge and is an authority on Sir Arthur Heywood's railways. Mike began producing castings for 1⅛in-scale models of 15in-gauge equipment to run on gauge-1 track. (Gauge 1 actually works out closer to 14.2in, but this is close enough for most modellers.) I purchased some wheelsets from Mike, along with some pedestals and couplers, and began building my own 15in-gauge equipment in gauge 1.

However, I had no locomotive. I had neither the time nor the inclination to build a scale model of any of Heywood's engines, attractive though they might be. I had in mind a freelance engine, something with relatively simple valve gear and a pot boiler that wouldn't take a long time to build.

Enter an old friend, Mike Bigger, of (then) Narrow Gauge Machining. I discussed the idea with him and we agreed that if I designed the engine and provided him with a complete set of drawings, he would build a small batch of them. The locomotive shown here is of that batch.

The model

On this engine, a simple pot boiler, fired by a four-wick alcohol burner, supplies the steam. The backhead is fitted with a standard needle-valve throttle, a pressure gauge, and a blowdown valve. Cylinders are controlled by D-valves and reversing is via slip eccentrics. The engine has outside frames and counterweights. The eccentrics are on the rear axle and drive rocker arms to the rear. The rockers were placed to the rear to leave as much room as possible for the fire-box. The fuel tank is at the very back, under the footplate.

A firebox, based on Jack Wheldon's principles, is concealed in the dummy side tanks. Blow-off pressure is around 50psi. Drivers are solid disks and are made to the same profile as the wheels Mike Decker provided. No castings are employed in this locomotive.

The locomotive stands a scale 6ft tall, or nine real inches, making it half again taller than, say, a 16mm-scale engine. A mammoth, polished-brass dome sits astride the boiler, as is only right. The locomotive's proportions are decidedly different – sort of squat and chunky – giving the engine and its train a unique character

The rocker arms were placed behind the driven axle instead of ahead of it to make room for the firebox. This necessitated a very long valve rod.

HB Models' Taff Vale 4-4-0T

The Taff Vale 4-4-0T is a simple but attractive locomotive. Note the ornamental skirts over the leading wheels.

Specifications

Builder: HB Models (UK)
Date built: Circa 1995
Gauge: 1 (45mm)
Scale: 1:32
Boiler: Pot
Fittings: Safety valve, throttle
Fuel: Alcohol
Blow-off pressure: 45psi
Cylinders: Two, double-acting D-valve
Reversing gear: Slip eccentrics
Lubricator: Displacement
Weight: 3lbs 14oz
Dimensions: Length, 11⅛in over end beams; width, 3⅜in; height, 5¼in

The prototype of this locomotive ran on the standard-gauge Taff Vale Railway, a large coal-hauling line that operated in South Wales from 1841 to 1922, when it became part of the Great Western Railway. (As an interesting aside, IK Brunel, the great engineer of the GWR, also laid out the Taff Vale.)

The model

This model, made by HB Models (Harold and Barbara Denyer), is a simply built, smooth-running engine. It's a small locomotive with large drivers, an unusual combination.

The locomotive features an alcohol-fired pot boiler running off a three-wick burner. Meths is stored in the usual

The inside valve and outside cylinder can be seen in this photo. The leading bogie is set up much like that of a toy locomotive. The actual frames do not extend forward to the front beam.

place under the footplate. The rectangular, box section, wick-feeder tube also provides a little additional storage. The burner must be removed from the engine for filling, as the filler cap is concealed in the bunker when in place. There is a vent tube at the rear, which could be used as a filler, if you are adventurous. Since there's no overflow pipe, there's no way of knowing if you've got enough (or too much) spirit in the tank. The alcohol could overflow, engulfing the engine in a pool of flaming meths, which is usually something to be avoided.

The backhead is quite bare, with only the throttle for adornment. The hand-done lining adds to the appeal of the engine.

There are two fixed cylinders outside the frames, controlled by D-valves inside. Valve gear is slip eccentrics on the leading, driven axle, so you must first push the engine in the direction you wish it to go to set the valves. There is an opening smoke-box door, behind which is the displacement lubricator. You have to stand the engine on its rear end to replace the oil.

Boiler fittings include only a throttle and safety valve. The backhead is very bare, with just the throttle. In some respects, the engine is almost toylike, despite its scale proportions and excellent workmanship.

With its big drivers, this can be a speedy engine. However, it's easy to throttle down and it will run sedately, even without a train. It will easily pull three or four coaches, running unattended for around twenty-five minutes.

Mike Gaskin's 4-8-2

This impressive locomotive has the proportions of a full-size miniature engine (if that makes sense). Built to the scale of 1in = 1ft, it runs on scale 15in-gauge track (0 gauge).

A roof extension comes off to facilitate cab access. The fire in the locomotive-type boiler must be lit through the firebox door. The white box is the lubricator. That round handle in the lower right is the bypass valve.

Capt. JEP Howey and Count Zborowski of Poland. Sadly, the Count was killed in an auto race before the railway was even begun, so Capt. Howey proceeded alone. He signed on Henry Greenly as Chief Engineer, and the first section of the diminutive line opened in 1927.

The RH&D is a miniature railway, using one-third-scale models of full-size engines to haul its trains. It is still in operation today and owns several steam locomotives, most designed by Greenly and built by Davey Paxman. Two, *Hercules* and *Samson* (both built in 1927), are of the 4-8-2, or Mountain, wheel arrangement. All of the other large engines are Pacifics, with 4-6-2 wheel arrangements.

The model

The engine examined here is N° 23 from Mike Gaskin's Caterham Works. While not a scale model of either of the Romney Mountains, it is definitely patterned after them, sharing their proportions. This gives it a most unusual

The Romney, Hythe & Dymchurch Light Railway is probably the best-known 15in-gauge line in the world. It runs between Hythe and Dungeness, a distance of fifteen miles or so, near the southeast coast of England. It was the brainchild of two famous auto racers of their day –

Specifications

Builder: Mike Gaskin (UK)
Date built: 1995
Gauge: 0 (32mm)
Scale: 1in = 1ft
Boiler: Locomotive type
Fittings: Safety valves (2), water glass, pressure gauge, blower, bypass valve, throttle, check valve
Fuel: Alcohol
Blow-off pressure: 50psi
Cylinders: Two, double-acting D-valve
Reversing gear: Slip return cranks
Lubricator: Displacement
Weight: 14lbs 8oz
Dimensions: Length overall, 27½in; width, 3½in, height, 4⅝in

scale/gauge combination. It is a ½-scale (1in = 1ft) model of a ⅛-scale model, and it runs on 32mm (0-gauge) track.

Nº 23 is a sophisticated locomotive. It has a locomotive-type boiler with seven flues and a superheater tube. It is fired by a two-wick alcohol burner that includes a stainless-steel arch. The fire, which is otherwise inaccessible, must be lit through the fire door. Fittings include a pair of safety valves, a water glass, a pressure gauge, a blower, a bypass valve, a throttle, and a check valve. The water glass is one of the thinnest I have seen, and therefore cannot be relied on. An extension to the cab roof comes off for easier access to the controls.

There is an axle pump on the second driven axle, with the usual bypass system. The tender holds both water and fuel, and there is a hand pump in it as well. The pump handle is carried in special brackets atop the tender. The fuel-control system is fairly primitive. A plastic tube emerges from the bottom of the fuel tank and runs back to a sump. A device that clamps the tube is built into the bottom of the tender to restrict the flow of alcohol to the sump. From there the line runs forward to the burner. It's a strange system, but it works okay.

Mr. Gaskin made liberal use of epoxy, both to seal places where pipes emerged from tanks (but not on the boiler) and to attach cosmetic bits. Some of these joints, particularly the smaller cosmetic ones like the handrail stanchions, have failed.

Cylinders are the standard D-valve type, controlled by slip-return-crank reversing. The springing, axle boxes, etc. on the

Valve gear and rods are made mostly from small-section bar stock. The mechanical lubricator on the footplate is a dummy, but it is tied into the valve gear and adds a little extra action.

trailing truck are attached to the frame and are dummies. The trailing truck itself is pivoted and swings between the frames.

In operation, the locomotive has a soft but deep-throated chuff, due to the large smokebox. With the cab-roof extension off, the throttle is easily accessible. The engine is responsive to the touch and it runs elegantly and smoothly. It's great watching those eight drivers revolve and all those red rods flail around.

Deryck Goodall's *Usk*

Usk (named after a Welsh river) is a charming interpretation of the deWinton quarry engines. The prototype engines have been mentioned elsewhere in this book (see page 124 on Maurice Cross's deWinton).

The model

This model is a tiny thing, neatly made in a workmanlike manner. It uses a Mamod flatcar as its chassis. The wheels appear to be Mamod as well, but have been rebushed with brass bushings and are now secured to the axles with set screws. The engine is 0 gauge at present but, thanks to the set screws, could be regauged to N° 1.

Alcohol is the fuel of choice for *Usk*, and a fuel tank is carried below the footplate at one end. A single, annular-ring burner heats the internally fired vertical boiler. The top of the boiler (effectively the smokebox front) comes off, revealing a central flue surrounded by eight additional flues. The boiler is fitted with a proper exhaust nozzle as well as a blower. Other fittings include a water glass, safety valve, pressure gauge, filler valve, and throttle.

The steam motor is a single, double-acting oscillator that drives a flywheel. This is geared to the axle about 4:1 through an idler gear. The idler enables the motor to rotate in the same direction as the wheels. Reversing is accomplished through the usual rotary valve, this one mounted on the motor. A displacement lubricator between the throttle and the cylinder keeps the piston well oiled.

I built a traveling/display case for the engine that holds it securely enough for it to be packed in checked baggage. The engine's compact size makes it a good choice to take when luggage space is at a premium.

Above: The boiler top lifts off, revealing the nine flues. The throttle is to the right of the boiler, while the lubricator is on the left. A rotary valve mounted on the port block controls the direction.

Left: Usk, patterned after the deWinton quarry engines, is an interesting locomotive with a lot of amenities. It utilises a Mamod flat car as its chassis. Paint on the back sheet was damaged by fire resulting from a leaky fuel tank.

Specifications

Builder: Deryck Goodall (UK)
Date built: Circa 1996
Gauge: 0 (32mm) (regaugeable)
Scale: 16mm
Boiler: Vertical
Fittings: Safety valve, pressure gauge, water glass, blower, throttle, filler valve
Fuel: Alcohol
Blow-off pressure: 50psi
Cylinders: One, double-acting oscillator
Reversing gear: Rotary valve
Lubricator: Displacement
Weight: 2lbs 11oz
Dimensions: Length, 6⅜in; width, 3⅛in; height, 6in

The locomotives of the HK Porter company are known for their pleasing proportions and they are popular subjects for modellers. The company began business in 1866, initially incorporated as Porter & Smith, and is still in business today, although they made their last locomotive in 1950. The company produced a wide variety of (primarily) industrial locomotives, including their line of tiny 0-4-0s, which were usually operated by one man. Porter constructed locomotives in both standard and narrow gauges, and their engines were used all over the world.

The model

Larry Herget has made some delightful little steamers over the years. Most use double-acting oscillating cylinders and are simple to run. *Slug* is one of a pair of Porter 0-4-0s he built in 1997. Like many of Larry's engines, this one is geared,

using Zebco fishing-reel gears. The single cylinder is hidden in the smokebox, transmitting its power to the lead axle via a helical pinion engaging a crown gear. The two outside cylinders are dummies, as is the headlight.

Slug's drivers are reproduction toy-train wheels. The dummy saddle tank lifts off to reveal a filler plug and the safety valve. The backhead is well equipped, lacking only a pressure gauge. A large water glass makes checking the water level easy.

The locomotive's boiler is externally gas fired. Flame shields protect the fire from prevailing gales. There's a large fuel tank in the cab that is filled through a hole in the roof. A displacement lubricator also sits on the cab floor; its drain plug protrudes from the engineer's side of the cab. The engine is equipped with link-and-pin couplers.

Slug is not reversible. Being a geared loco, it is a powerful engine for its size. It will run for twenty-plus minutes unattended. There's a Goodall-type boiler-filling valve in the top of the cab so the engine can be kept in steam indefinitely. It's a fun loco and a pleasure to run.

Above: Larry Herget's *Slug* is a charming caricature of a Porter 0-4-0T. The engine is gas fired and is powered by one, double-acting oscillator in the smokebox.

Left: The helical pinion and crown gears that power the engine came from a fishing reel. Drivers are toy-train reproduction parts.

Top right: The backhead is simple and well organized. The throttle and the water glass are the primary fittings. The tall gas tank on the left is fillable through the roof.

Lower right: The tank and dome slide off to reveal the safety valve and filler plug.

Specifications

Builder: Larry Herget (US)
Date built: 1997
Gauge: 1 (45mm)
Scale: 1:20.3
Boiler: Pot
Fittings: Safety valve, displacement lubricator, throttle, water glass, Goodall water-filler valve
Fuel: Butane
Blow-off pressure: 20psi
Cylinders: One, double-acting oscillator
Reversing gear: None
Lubricator: Displacement
Weight: 3lbs 8oz
Dimensions: Length over end beams, 7½in; width, 4in; height, 6⅜in over the stack

Charles Mynhier's 0-4-0

An engine like no other, this massive 0-4-0 appears to be hewn from the solid and, in fact, it largely was. It is made mostly of plate and bar, usually steel or stainless steel.

Left: Propane, kept in this stainless-steel tank, powers the engine. The brass artifact on the tender deck is an adapter for gas filling.

knows machinery and he knows materials and his locomotives reflect this knowledge.

Charles built the engine reviewed here as a project locomotive for *Steam in the Garden* magazine. The engine is *heavy*, weighing in at over eighteen pounds, which is a lot for an 0-4-0 running on gauge-1 track. To say that it is solidly constructed would be an understatement in the extreme. (Example: How does one pick up an eighteen-pound engine? The builder recommends by the handrails!)

Most of the sheet-metal work is ¹⁄₁₆in steel plate, bead blasted and chemically blackened, but there is quite a bit of ¹⁄₄in plate in there as well. All of the shiny parts are stainless steel. The fastener of choice is a socket-head cap screw, with which the locomotive is festooned. The only major commercially made parts are the tender trucks, which are from Accucraft.

The engine's frames are machined from the solid, as are the drivers. Rods have a satisfying, prototypical thickness to them. Cylinders were made from cast-iron bar and the pistons are fitted

Charles Mynhier's locomotives are unlike any others I've ever encountered. Like an artist, he has developed a personal style in locomotive design and construction. This style is based both on an eye for aesthetics and decades of experience as a professional mechanical engineer. He

Specifications

Builder: Charles Mynhier (US)
Date built: 1997
Gauge: 1 (45mm)
Scale: 1:24
Boiler: Single flue
Fittings: Safety valve, water glass, throttle (in steam dome), filler valve
Fuel: Propane
Blow-off pressure: 30psi
Cylinders: Two, double-acting D-valve
Reversing gear: Abbreviated Walschaerts
Lubricator: Displacement
Weight: 18lbs 8oz
Dimensions: Length over all, 18½in; width, 4⅜in; height, 6in

with Viton O-rings. A flow-through displacement lubricator, made from a CO_2 cartridge, sits to the right of the boiler. All of this combines to give the locomotive both a unique appearance and unique operating characteristics. More on that later.

A copper boiler with a single flue is fitted. The gas supply and air-mixing chamber enter the side of the burner instead of the rear. There is a water glass on the backhead and a filler valve, safety valve, and throttle on the steam dome. Valve gear is an abbreviated Walschaerts type, which can be actuated from the cab or by a secondary lever on the footplate ahead of the cab.

The engine burns propane. *Don't* try this at home. This locomotive has a specially designed, stainless-steel tank that is built to withstand the substantially higher storage pressures of propane, and it is well away from the heat of the boiler. A special filler-adapter screws onto the tender's footplate for storage. To use it, you unscrew the adapter, then screw it onto one of two Schrader valves on the removable gas tank in the tender. The other end of the adapter can then be inserted into a standard propane bottle, and the tank filled. The other Schrader valve must be opened briefly from time to time when filling the tank to bleed it.

Because of its massiveness, it takes a bit to get the cylinders warm enough for the engine to go. Once they are warm

The frame is a solid billet of steel. Socket-head screws are commonly used on this locomotive. They look strangely correct.

enough, the locomotive runs well. It is a quiet locomotive overall. You can hear the burner, but it is not the offensive roar that you get with some gas-fired locomotives.

This is not what you would call a snappy engine. When the throttle is opened, it doesn't bolt away. It will start slowly and accelerate reasonably to its top speed. Like all of Charles's engines, this one can be run at a steady crawl with a heavy load, a characteristic most often associated with geared locomotives.

An unusual 0-4-0

This relatively small locomotive by an unknown builder has just about every accoutrement that an engine can have.

This model is one of the more unusual locomotives I have run across. I've no idea who built it or when it was made. The person I acquired it from knew nothing of the engine's history.

The engine appears to be entirely scratchbuilt to a freelance design. Its proportions are squat and stubby, which appeals to me. The tender is nearly a cube. The loco has an internally fired Smithies boiler and a two-wick alcohol burner. Fuel is carried in a removable chicken-feed tank at the rear of the tender. The balance of the tender is available for water. There is a hand pump in the water tank as well as a takeoff for the crank-driven pump on the locomotive.

On the backhead is a throttle valve, a blower valve, a water glass, and a tiny pressure gauge, tucked up under the half roof. Attached to the frame on the right side, below the cab, is a pump driven by an eccentric crank on the rear driver.

There is no bypass system. So, when the engine is in motion, water is constantly being pumped into the boiler.

This engine has only one working cylinder. There's a single (slip) eccentric on the forward axle that drives both valves via a rocker arm. The fact that there is only one powered cylinder escaped my notice when I first examined the engine, and I couldn't figure out how the builder intended the loco to run when both valves moved with simultaneous motion. Then the penny dropped. The valve rod on the unpowered (left) side moves only for show, and, in fact, would be out of sync with the piston if that cylinder was powered. Also, the lube line to that cylinder

Above: The underside is almost as busy as the top side. The single eccentric can be seen on the leading axle. Two round wicks fire the Smithies boiler.

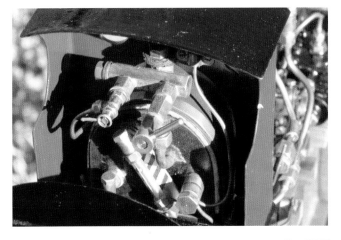

Specifications

Builder: Unknown
Date built: Unknown
Gauge: 1 (45mm)
Scale: 16mm
Boiler: Smithies
Fittings: Safety valve, throttle, pressure gauge, blower, water glass, blowdowns (2)
Fuel: Alcohol
Blow-off pressure: 60psi
Cylinders: One, double-acting D-valve
Reversing gear: Slip eccentric
Lubricator: Displacement
Weight: 9lbs 8oz (loco and tender)
Dimensions: Length (loco and tender), 15in; width, 4⅝in; height, 6¼in

Centre: The backhead includes a throttle, blower, pressure gauge (under the roof), water glass, and check valve. The striped panel behind the glass aids in water readings.

Lower: A pump mounted under the cab is powered by an eccentric crank on the rear axle.

is a dummy, even though it appears to be plumbed into the lubrication system.

The lubrication system is independent of the steam feed to the powered cylinder. A large displacement lubricator resides under the cab on the left side. There is a small-diameter line to it from the boiler, passing through a valve. On the downstream side is another valve. There's also a drain plug in the bottom of the lubricator. The oil line feeds oil into the top of the steam chest.

The locomotive is gauge 1. All wheels are retained on their axles with set screws, even though the engine cannot be regauged (there's too much stuff in the way). Water and fuel lines from the tender are stiff plastic, which I feared would hamper the engine on curves, but this did not happen.

Workmanship is agricultural at best, with tool and file marks everywhere on the unpainted parts. The engine was heavily painted with a brush. This is at least its second coat. Individual parts tend to be large and coarse.

There are other oddities about the engine as well. For instance, on the left side, the main rod is not retained on the crankpin. There's an obtrusive blowdown valve on the right side and another, less obtrusive one, on the water glass. The chimney leans slightly to the rear while the steam dome, which conceals a filler plug, leans slightly forward. All of this gives the engine a slightly cartoonish character that I find pleasing.

Archangel's Darjeeling Class B 0-4-0T

The Darjeeling Himalayan Railway (DHR) opened in July of 1881, traveling from Siliguri to Darjeeling, which lies about three hundred and seventy-five miles north of Calcutta. The railway was built to haul tea and tourists, and was a great success from its opening day. However, the route that it traveled was tortuous. With grades as steep as 6% and curves as sharp as sharp as 57ft radius, the 2ft-gauge line traverses some of the most spectacular scenery anywhere.

The first locomotives on the DHR were small 0-4-0s, which proved unequal to the demands of the line. The next engines, the Class B models, developed by Sharp Stewart of Manchester, proved to be just what was required. It is these Class B tank engines that are still in use today, though in sadly diminished numbers. There were thirty-four of them built between 1889 and 1927. Today, only a dozen or so remain functional.

Sharp Stewart's Class B engine is one of the most distinctive and easily recognizable locos ever made, with its coal bunker atop the boiler in front of the cab and the unusual collar tank forward of the bunker. Two heavy rerailing poles were standard equipment on these engines. Surprisingly, each engine had a standard crew of five men! There was the driver and the fireman; a fellow who sat atop the coal pile, whose job it was to push the coal toward the fireman; and two men who sat on the front end beam, whose task it was to drop sand (by hand) onto the rails when ascending, to maintain traction.

The model

Stewart Browne of Archangel made just a few models of this locomotive – perhaps only seven or eight over the years. This example is an impressive engine that fully captures well the essence of the prototype.

The engine is painted green (an earlier livery that I find more pleasing than the current blue) and is nicely lined out in black and red. The steam dome lifts off to reveal a filler plug. Under the dummy water hatch is a Goodall-type filler valve. A displacement lubricator sits on the left side of the boiler, in front of the cab. The gas-control valve occupies the same position on the other side.

Backhead appliances include a throttle, a water glass (with a blowdown valve), and a pressure gauge. A reversing quadrant stands next to the right-hand cab wall. Prototype builder's plates adorn the exterior cab sides, while Archangel's own plate sits above the boiler inside.

The prototypically inclined cylinders are controlled by Walschaerts valve gear. All the motion work is steel and is well made. All the important details are present, save the rerailing poles, which have evidently been lost, but the brackets are there.

This engine was formerly owned by Rob Bennett, of Home & Colonial fame. When I received it, it was in good mechanical shape, but had seen a great deal of use. The back rail of the cab was gone, which I replaced (it still needs paint), and some of the ornamental coal has disappeared along the way (which I have not yet replaced). Coal is glued to a removable screen that covers the twin gas tanks. These tanks can be filled with or without removing

DHR locomotives are some of the most distinctive anywhere. Archangel's model captures the prototype well. On the prototype, the distinctive brass pipes on either side of the smokebox communicate between the collar tank and the flat tank carried under the cylinders (dummies on the model). The brackets on either side of the collar tank held large rerailing poles (missing here).

Proper Walschaerts valve gear and inclined cylinders help to make this a most unusual locomotive.

the screen. The front wheel-guard rail, below the coupler, is also missing. The smokebox front simply clips into place and is easily removable for fire lighting. This locomotive is a superb runner, easily controllable and powerful.

The open back makes controls readily accessible. The bowed back rail is a replacement, still waiting for paint.

Specifications

Builder: Archangel Models (UK)
Date built: Circa 1998
Gauge: 0 (32mm)
Scale: 16mm
Boiler: Single flue
Fittings: Safety valve, throttle, water glass with blowdown, pressure gauge, Goodall-type filler valve
Fuel: Butane
Blow-off pressure: 60psi
Cylinders: Two, double-acting D-valve
Reversing gear: Walschaerts
Lubricator: Displacement
Weight: 6lbs 8oz
Dimensions: Length, 13⅛in; width, 4⅛in; height, 5⅝in

Wrightscale's War Department Baldwin 4-6-0

In 1916 and 1917, the British War Department took delivery of a large number of sixty-centimetre gauge, pannier-tank 4-6-0 locomotives, designated class 10-12-D. These were built in the US by Baldwin and were to be used behind the lines on the Western Front in France to help keep the troops supplied and transport the wounded. After the war, surviving locomotives went to different small railways around the world. A few are still with us and are preserved today on railways primarily in Britain.

The model

Wrightscale (Malcolm Wright) produced a beautiful, highly detailed scale model of this locomotive. Without looking into the cab, there is little to give away that fact that this is a live-steam model.

The engine is gas fired and has a single-flue boiler. Gas is carried in the right-hand pannier tank. The gas line is plumbed to a valve under the coal bunker and then to the burner. The control knob projects vertically through the coal bunker. Near the gas valve, also in the coal bunker, is a water inlet, through which water can be injected into the boiler with a syringe or squirt bottle. A dead-leg lubricator is housed in the left pannier. Boiler fittings include a safety valve in the steam dome, a pressure gauge, throttle, check valve, and a water glass.

Reversing is provided by full Walschaerts valve gear. All of the components are beautifully to scale, small and delicate. Axles ride in individual axle boxes, which are stiffly sprung. The bar frames, dummy springing, and brake gear all look just right. There's an abundance of rivet detail in all of the right places. The only thing missing is cab-window glazing.

The locomotive is controlled by radio, most of the components of which have been well concealed. The receiver is in the cab next to the boiler. The throttle servo is tucked up under the cab roof. In the bunker is the reverse-gear servo and two AAA battery packs. It's all pretty crowded, but it works.

In steam, the locomotive performs as well as it looks. Once the condensate has cleared, it responds readily and willingly to the sticks on the radio transmitter. Slow-speed running is no problem, nor are smooth starts and stops. This is a beautiful model of an interesting prototype.

Above: It would not be difficult to mistake this locomotive for its full-size prototype. Almost every detail has been included and it runs as well as it looks.

Left: The cab is crowded with steam appliances and radio gear. Because there is a servo mounted to the ceiling, the pressure gauge must lie on its side.

Opposite: Underneath, the engine looks much as would the full-size article. This locomotive has been signed, numbered, and dated, as should all engines be – but, alas, few are.

Specifications

Builder: Wrightscale (UK)
Date built: 1998
Gauge: 0 (32mm)
Scale: 16mm
Boiler: Single flue
Fittings: Safety valve, water glass, pressure gauge, check valve, throttle
Fuel: Butane
Blow-off pressure: 50psi
Cylinders: Two, double-acting D-valve
Reversing gear: Walschaerts
Lubricator: Displacement
Weight: 6lbs 10oz
Dimensions: Length over end beams, 11⅝in; width, 4¼in; height, 6in

Denis Jukes' *Gelert*

Specifications

Builder: Denis Jukes (UK)
Date built: Circa 1998
Gauge: 0 (32mm)
Scale: 16mm
Boiler: Wrighton
Fittings: Safety valve, pressure gauge, blower, throttle, check valve
Fuel: Alcohol
Blow-off pressure: 60psi
Cylinders: Two, double-acting D-valves
Reversing gear: Slip eccentrics
Lubricator: Displacement
Weight: 9lbs
Dimensions: Length overall, 12½in; width, 4in, height, 4⅝in

For an 0-4-2T, this is a large locomotive. The model is sophisticated and must be closely attended while running.

This is a model of *Gelert*, a relatively modern locomotive, built in 1953 by the British firm of WG Bagnall for the Rustenberg Platinum Mines in South Africa. It was one of four, similar, two-foot-gauge locomotives supplied. The engines were used to haul platinum ore from the mines to the reduction plant.

In 1980, when the two-foot-gauge line had been replaced by a larger gauge, this locomotive (along with a sister engine) was purchased by the Welsh Highland Railway (WHR). It sat for many years awaiting restoration, which was finally completed in 1992. It was then that it received the name *Gelert*.

The model

The builder of this model is Denis Jukes, a retired metallurgist who has since passed on. The engine is well constructed and

captures the proportions of the prototype nicely. It incorporates a number of unusual features. The engine is alcohol fired using a chicken-feed system. The tank, which resides in the bunker, slides right out. With the valve closed, it can be filled outside the engine, then just dropped into place. Feed and vent tubes protrude from the bottom of the tank into a sump, when in position. The burner has two good-size wicks.

The boiler is internally fired and appears to be of the Wrighton variety. It has a proper firebox connected to a single, large flue with cross tubes. The smokebox door has a working dart (the twin handles on the front), which is a nice feature. One handle loosens the latch, while the other disengages it, allowing the door to be opened.

All the valve-gear parts are hand crafted to a high standard, as is the entire locomotive. There is not a lot of detail, as the engine was evidently designed more for work than show.

The backhead has the usual fittings, along with an unusual lubricator setup. There is a separate line from the turret to the exceedingly large lubricator, with a control valve. From there, a lubricator line travels forward and connects with the steam line before the cylinders. The steam line passes through the fire for superheat, so I gather the lubricator setup is an attempt to deliver oil to the cylinders after the steam has passed through the superheater, so that carbonization of the oil does not occur. In any event, it works well.

There is a Goodall-type filler valve under the cast-aluminum dome for replenishing the boiler. Side tanks are dummies.

Because of the massiveness of the cylinders, the engine tends to be slow off the mark, needing a fair amount of encouragement before it heats up enough to travel alone. Once it does, though, it's a good runner and a satisfying engine to run.

The fuel tank comes out for refuelling away from the engine. A tilting cab roof makes controls easily accessible.

Berkeley Locomotive Works' 'Cricket'

The 'Cricket' is a well-made locomotive with pleasing proportions. This one is the only two-cylinder example made. The smokebox front was lost – the replacement in the picture is unlike the original.

The builder of the 'Cricket', Michael O'Rourke, a.k.a Berkeley Locomotive Works, discovered an advertising illustration for a small, geared, contractor's locomotive manufactured by the John F. Byers Machine Co. of Ravenna, Ohio, in John H. White Jr.'s *A Short History of American Locomotive Builders*. The little engine seemed to him to be a perfect candidate for an inexpensive, entry level, American outline, live-steam locomotive for the garden-railroad market.

There were no drawings or illustrations of the prototype available at the time, except for the advertising drawing that appeared in the book, so the design was extrapolated from the ad. Thus, 'Cricket' was largely an interpretation of the engine rather than a model. It was posited that the engine was driven by a single vertical steam engine – a stock item in the Byers catalogue – with a flywheel on the fireman's side. If true, this arrangement would have allowed the engine to be driven to a job site, the wheels disconnected from the drive train, and the unit used as a power source for a hoist, sawmill, or other device through a belt drive from the flywheel.

This, in fact, was not the case. More-recently revealed drawings from *Engineering News* of 1896, discovered by Mr. O'Rourke, show the engine as having two vertical engines – one port and one starboard – and no flywheel, thus precluding its use as a movable power source.

The locomotive was evidently not a best seller for Byers, as it never appeared in any known Byers catalogues and probably no more than a half dozen engines were ever built.

The model

I acquired this locomotive from its original owner, for whom the engine was made by Berkeley Locomotive Works. Mr. O'Rourke was in the habit of customizing his engines according to the customers' wishes, and so it was in this case. This is the only two-cylinder 'Cricket' ever produced.

The engine has a pair of single-acting cylinders set 180° apart. Because they are single acting, the engine still requires a flip of the flywheel to get it going. Cylinders are controlled by Teflon piston valves. The engine is reversed via slip eccentrics mounted between the counterweight and the frame on either side. Because of the cylinder on the flywheel

side, there is a sort of auxiliary frame to help support the axle to which the flywheel is attached.

The engine is fired by butane gas. The boiler is a T-boiler, the 'T' being a standard bit of plumbing. This engine is fitted with every conceivable fitting, including a safety valve, pressure gauge, water glass, blowdown valve, Goodall valve (under the ornate, lift-off dome), and a Mamod whistle without its lever. It has a bell, dummy wing tanks with cast-brass fillers, and wooden end beams.

When I acquired the engine, it was missing its bell, smokebox front, and exhaust lines from the cylinders to the stack. Berkeley provided me with a new bell and I made new exhaust lines out of copper tubing. I also made a new smokebox front unlike the standard (missing) 'Cricket' smokebox.

In operation, the engine is smooth, controllable, and powerful for its size. Its gearing lets it travel at a realistic speed and it's a pleasure to run.

An unusual T-boiler powers the engine. This one is fitted with all of the amenities, including an ultra-small pressure gauge. The gas tank is on the left.

The flywheel side of the engine. The 'T' part of the boiler is a standard plumbing fitting.

The drive shaft, with its pinion, is actually concealed behind the jackshaft with the two large gears. Note the auxiliary frame supporting the flywheel shaft.

Specifications

Builder: Berkeley Locomotive Works (US)
Date built: 1999
Gauge: 1 (45mm)
Scale: 1:20.3
Boiler: Single flue
Fittings: Safety valve, throttle, water glass, pressure gauge, whistle, blowdown valve, Goodall valve
Fuel: Butane
Blow-off pressure: 35psi
Cylinders: Two, single-acting piston-valve
Reversing gear: Slip eccentrics
Lubricator: Displacement
Weight: 4lbs 12oz
Dimensions: Length, 7in; width (over flywheel), 4⅝in; height, 6⅛in

Aster's USRA Mikado

In 1918, because of WWI, the US government took control of all American railroads. The agency that managed them was the USRA, or the United States Railroad Administration. During the two years of its existence, the USRA was responsible for designing several classes of locomotives. Most of these proved to be excellent designs that were popular with the railroads that used them.

Two classes of Mikado (2-8-2) were produced, light and heavy. Of the light Mikados (which Aster modelled), six hundred and twenty-five were built during the war and about the same number of copies after the war. In all, over fifty railroads used these engines.

The model

This locomotive is alcohol fired, the fuel being carried in the tender. Alcohol is fed to a three-wick burner in the firebox through a traditional chicken-feed system. Backhead fittings include a throttle, blower valve, pressure gauge, water glass, and a check valve for filling the boiler with an external pump. Reversing gear is Walschaerts valve gear, controlled from the cab. A pair of safety valves are mounted atop the boiler. The design of the engine is simple and direct, making it reliable and easy to operate.

The boiler is a type B, as designed by John van Riemsdijk. It's a copper barrel with fire tubes that penetrate the flue sheet at the front end of the boiler. At the rear, they curve down and exit the boiler barrel into an external firebox. This type of boiler is both efficient and relatively simple to build, and Aster had used it before on locomotives.

The engine's big failing, as supplied, is that it didn't come with a pump. Locomotives of this sophistication usually have at least a hand pump in the tender and, often, an axle pump with a bypass system as well. In an effort to keep costs down,

Above: Aster's USRA Mikado typifies American locomotive construction in the early years of the 20th century. The model conveys the bulk and proportions of the prototype.

Left: With the cab-roof extension flipped up, controls are more accessible. Note the long lever handles for the throttle and blower. The water glass is prominent in the centre.

Opposite: As this engine has outside valves and gear, the underside is relatively plain. Note the eccentric on the second axle, ready for an after-market water pump.

these were omitted from this model, although an eccentric for an axle pump was included on the second axle. The axle pump was available separately.

This engine was re-released in 2000 in Southern Railway (US) green, complete with both pumps and additional details (at greater expense). In all, four hundred of the USRA Mikado were made – two hundred and sixty in black and one hundred and forty in green.

I purchased mine as a kit. Aster's kits are always good, but I thought this one exceptionally so. Although still a fairly complex locomotive, the kit went together easily and smoothly. Construction problems were minimal. The engine is adequately detailed, but isn't loaded with a lot of delicate parts. I consider this an asset, as the engine can be easily handled without risk of knocking anything off.

Once the condensate has cleared, this engine is a strong, smooth, steady runner. With the addition of a pump, it could be kept in steam indefinitely.

Specifications

Builder: Aster Hobby Company (Japan)
Date built: 1999
Gauge: 1 (45mm)
Scale: 1:32
Boiler: JvR type B
Fittings: Safety valves (2), throttle, blower, water glass, pressure gauge, check valve
Fuel: Alcohol
Blow-off pressure: 60psi
Cylinders: Two, double-acting D-valve
Reversing gear: Walschaerts
Lubricator: Displacement
Weight: 15lbs 8oz (loco and tender)
Dimensions: Length, 30¼in (loco and tender); width, 4in; height, 6¼in

Larry Herget's ⅞in-scale Dunkirk

This model is clearly patterned after a four-wheel, seven-ton locomotive built by the Dunkirk Iron Works (Dunkirk, New York). Only about three engines of this type were ever made, to 3ft and standard gauge, in 1882. They appear to be the first locomotives produced by the company, which was founded in 1865 to make boilers and stationary engines. The company's output of locomotives was quite small, and they evidently didn't produce any more after 1894.

The model

As a model, this engine has a number of remarkable features, not the least of which is its scale. The scale of ⅞in = 1ft, running on gauge-1 track, makes this a 2ft-gauge model. Models in this scale, while still easily manageable, are big!

The engine's body is made entirely of wood and it lifts off the chassis for access to the mechanics. A tall, vertical boiler with three fire tubes sits near one end of the engine. It is fitted with a throttle, a pressure gauge with an attractive flange around it, a water glass, a safety valve, and a Goodall-type filler valve. The boiler is held in place simply by gravity. When the steam line is disconnected and the exhaust line released, the boiler pops right out. The steam lines are all lagged with cotton shoe laces!

The boiler is alcohol fired with a three-wick burner – one wick under each of the vertical flues. An enormous meths tank supplies the burner with fuel via a chicken-feed system.

A chain drives one axle while side rods power the other. The three-wick burner, connected to the sump, is visible here.

Specifications

Builder: Larry Herget (US)
Date built: 1999
Gauge: 1 (45mm)
Scale: ⅞in = 1ft
Boiler: Vertical with three flues
Fittings: Safety valve, throttle, water glass, pressure gauge, filler valve
Fuel: Alcohol
Blow-off pressure: 40psi
Cylinders: Two, double-acting oscillators
Reversing gear: Rotary valve
Lubricator: Displacement
Weight: 4lbs 14oz
Dimensions: Length over end beams, 10½in; width, 4¾in; height, 9¼in

This tank, too, is held in place mostly by gravity. It is removed by just lifting it out.

Two, double-acting oscillating cylinders, controlled by a rotary reversing valve between them, provide the power. Pistons turn a shaft on which is a sprocket that engages a ladder chain. This, in turn, drives another sprocket on the axle. There is some gear reduction, but not a lot – perhaps 1.5:1.

The exhaust line returns to the stack, but is divided on its way there. Some of the exhaust is ported out the side of the engine near the bottom. The idea here is that the heavier steam oil will go out the bottom and only clean steam will be exhausted from the stack. This seems to work, as the roof remains clean at the end of a run. The locomotive's wheels are toy-train reproduction wheels with the flanges turned down.

A variety of cosmetic details festoon the engine: hooks and chains, tools, a lantern, a brake wheel, a water bag for the crew, and an axe in a special bracket on an outside wall. Link-and-pin couplers are fitted to the end beams. The engine came with a pair of workman-style coaches – spare and uncomfortable. Together, they make a pleasing train.

This is a fun, easy-to-run engine. It is smooth and reliable and the controls are readily at hand. With the filler valve on the boiler and the alcohol-feed system, the engine could be kept in steam all day long.

Above: This ⅞in scale engine is based on a Dunkirk logging locomotive, but with a few liberties taken. Running on gauge-1 track, it represents a two-foot-gauge engine.

Right: The wooden body lifts off to expose the works. The three-flue boiler and meths tank are likewise easy to remove. The engine is powered by a pair of double-acting oscillating cylinders and chain drive.

Accucraft's *Ruby*

Specifications

Builder: Accucraft (China)
Date built: 2000
Gauge: 1 (45mm)
Scale: 1:20.3
Boiler: Single flue
Fittings: Safety valve, throttle
Fuel: Butane
Blow-off pressure: 20psi
Cylinders: Two, double-acting piston valve
Reversing gear: Piston valve
Lubricator: Displacement
Weight: 5lbs 8oz
Dimensions: Length over end beams, 8⅞in; width, 3⅞in; height, 5¾in

Ruby is based on a typical Baldwin industrial locomotive. It was the first mass-produced starter engine for the American market.

The cab lifts off completely. Two knobs control gas to the burner and steam to the cylinders. The side tanks can also be removed without affecting performance.

Eccentrics on the rear axles drive the piston valves. Rocker arms bring the motion outside. Reversing is accomplished through another piston valve, visible between the cylinders.

Accucraft of China is one of the newest live-steam manufacturers on the scene. The company has made an impression internationally and, as this is written, has offerings for the US, UK, and German markets. The company's products have steadily improved over the years. Today they are generally good, reliable locomotives.

Ruby, introduced in 2000, is important because it is the first modern, mass produced, starter engine made especially for the American market. It was intended to satisfy several requirements. The engine needed to: have a low price; be easy to operate and be a reliable runner; be non-intimidating to the beginner, yet offer enough to attract those who already have some steam experience; be easy to maintain; be a plausible (in appearance) locomotive; be easy to cosmetically alter or kitbash; and be radio controllable. It is felt that the engine has satisfied all of these requirements.

This is not to say that it is flawless, however. Like the Mamod, it has stimulated a certain number of after-market products, both functional and cosmetic. These include new and better cylinders and safety valves, all-wood cabs, and Forney conversion kits, to name a few.

Ruby was patterned after Baldwin-locomotive practice, though is not a model of any specific engine. It needed certain things to look typically American, including bar frames (at least in appearance), a US-style smokebox, and proper spoked wheels. As produced, the cab lifts entirely off, exposing the simple backhead. The side tanks are purely cosmetic and can also be removed without affecting the performance of the engine in any way. What's left is a basic American running chassis, upon which owners can (and have) build any sort of superstructure. *Ruby* modifications are legion.

Ruby spawned two close variations: *Ida*, a saddle-tank version, and *Mimi*, a 2-4-2 tender version. The basic unit is the same in these engines.

Ruby has a single flue, gas-fired boiler, with the gas tank in the cab. A large displacement lubricator sits in front of the tank. On the right side of the cab is a reversing lever. The engine has two piston-valve cylinders. Valves are run off eccentrics on the second axle, with the motion being brought through the frames via rocker arms to the valves. Reversing is accomplished through the use of another, identical, piston valve in a valve block between the cylinders. The lever in the cab controls this valve.

The safety valve is under the steam dome. Beneath the sand dome is a large filler plug for the boiler. A throttle knob is on the backhead. As supplied, the engine is fitted with link-and-pin couplers.

This locomotive has provided the starting point for hundreds of American live-steam enthusiasts. It has also provided the basis for numerous creative modifications that have further broadened the hobby.

Rishon Locomotive Works' 'Coffee Pot'

Right: An unusual model of an unusual prototype, this 'Coffee Pot' is gas fired with a single-flue boiler. The wooden coach has only a rear bogie and is articulated with the engine.

Lower right: With the roof off and the coach gone, the back-head is exposed. The wire and plug come from the electronic water-level sensor. It plugs into the coach, where a red LED flashes to warn of low water.

The prototype for this model was a railmotor – essentially a steam-powered bus on rails – built for the South Australian Railways (SAR) in 1906. It was built in England, the locomotive part by Kitson and the trailer by Metro Carriage & Wagon Co. The engine was a 2-2-0 well tank (water was stored in a 'well' between the frames). Two of these 3ft 6in-gauge units were built for the SAR, one to operate in the southeast and one to run on the northern line. It is the northern-line's unit that has survived.

Inside valves and slip-eccentric reversing are features of this engine. It is a simple, basic locomotive.

The Commonwealth Railways took over the line in later years, although this did not affect the railmotor, which continued its daily duties. At that time, it was given the classification NJAB1, but was already known to the populace as the 'Coffee Pot,' an appellation it has carried ever since.

It was withdrawn from service in 1932 and stored until 1960, when it was placed on display at Alice Springs. In 1975 the engine was acquired by the Pichi Richi Railway and restored, going back to work on that line in 1984.

The model

Rishon Locomotive Works (Paul Trevaskis) built this model of the 'Coffee Pot.' While not an exact-scale model of the prototype, it has most of its important features, including a stubby locomotive and an attractive wooden coach, both in the correct proportions.

The engine is gas fired, with a single-flue boiler. It is fitted with a throttle, a pressure gauge, a Goodall-type filler valve, and an unusual feature – an electronic water-level sensor. The cab lifts off for access. A displacement lubricator sits on the footplate ahead of the cab on the right side.

The water-level sensor consists of a probe in the boiler with a lead coming out. Another lead is soldered to the

boiler. These leads go back into the coach where, through some electronic witchcraft, they are connected to a red LED in the front wall of the coach. A switch under the coach activates the unit, which is powered by four AA batteries. When the water gets low, the LED will start blinking.

The engine is a 2-2-0, with the cylinders placed behind the leading axle. It has inside valves that are reversed by slip eccentrics (the prototype had Walschaerts gear).

The coach has only a rear bogie. The front end has a deck that extends into the cab and actually becomes the footplate of the locomotive. It has a pin at the front end that rests in a hole in a cross member of the locomotive's frame. A rudimentary interior is provided in the coach, which has centre-access doors.

Specifications

Builder: Rishon Locomotive Works (Australia)
Date built: 2000
Gauge: 1 (45mm)
Scale: 1:20.3
Boiler: Single flue
Fittings: Safety valve, throttle, Goodall-type filler valve, pressure gauge, electronic water-level sensor
Fuel: Butane
Blow-off pressure: 40psi
Cylinders: Two, double-acting D-valve
Reversing gear: Slip eccentrics
Lubricator: Displacement
Weight: 9lbs 4oz (with trailer)
Dimensions: Length (including trailer), 23½in; width, 5in; height, 6¾in

Denver 0-4-0T

In the year 2000, members of the Denver (Colorado) Steam Group decided that we would like to have a project locomotive to build. We wanted an engine that would be largely scratchbuilt, with just a few purchased components. The object of this exercise would be to raise the general level of metalworking capabilities of club members.

We decided that the engine should be buildable with only a small lathe (Taig, Sherline, Unimat, etc.) and drill press as the main power tools. Its design would need to be as simple as possible but (ideally) something interesting and something that would lend itself to modification by the builder, if so desired. It had to be made with common, readily available tools and materials.

A design committee was formed, consisting of Jim Reyer, Ken Orme, and myself. With the above mandate firmly in our grasp, we set off.

The model

We ultimately arrived at a design that pleased us all. It is an overtype engine (the steam-engine part is on top) with a simple pot boiler. The engine drives a primary shaft with a pinion gear on it, which drives a larger gear on a secondary shaft, providing an initial gear reduction. The secondary shaft carries a small ladder-chain sprocket that powers a larger sprocket on the locomotive's rear axle, providing a second reduction. The overall reduction is around 6:1. The two axles are linked with additional chain and sprockets inside the frame.

The frame is made of a piece of 1½in-square aluminium tubing with one side cut off to form a U-shaped channel. Axles are made from stock rod and the wheels are purchased. The frames are slotted for the axles, which go in from the bottom and are held in place by retainer bars.

A piece of 1⅝in-OD copper tubing forms the boiler. Two standoffs soldered to the bottom are used to attach it to the aluminum frame. Two bushings on the top are used as motor mounts. Also on top of the boiler are a stud over which the smokestack fits, a safety-valve bushing, and a steam-takeoff bushing.

The engine is alcohol fired by a traditional three-wick burner. The fuel tank is carried beneath the cab.

Dummy side tanks, easily folded up from sheet brass, serve as the firebox and are insulated with Fiberfrax, a refractory material, which helps to hold in some of the heat. The tanks are not physically attached to anything, but are trapped in place when the boiler is installed.

The lubricator is a standard displacement type, hung off the steam line aft of the boiler. The entire lubricator body unscrews from the steam line, facilitating emptying and filling. The safety valve is a purchased product.

The frame of the steam motor itself is a piece of 1in-square steel tubing, again with one side cut off to form a channel. The three of us who built engines each came up with different motor designs. Ken and I used a single-acting oscillating cylinder, while Jim designed a more complex double-acting engine. All of the engines work well. In each, steam is exhausted to the stack.

The locomotive is finished off with a rudimentary plantation-style cab made of two brass rods and two pieces of sheet metal. It comes right off for access to the backhead. My engine is pictured here.

Specifications

Builder: Marc Horovitz (US)
Date built: 2001
Gauge: 1 (45mm)
Scale: 1:20.3 (nominal)
Boiler: Pot
Fittings: Safety valve
Fuel: Alcohol
Blow-off pressure: 40psi
Cylinders: One, single-acting oscillator
Reversing gear: None
Lubricator: Displacement
Weight: 2lbs 6oz
Dimensions: Length over end beams, 6⅝in; width, 3⅜in; height over stack, 6⅛in

Denver, an overtype locomotive, is powered by a simple chain drive to the axle. While not the most attractive engine in the world, it is easy to build and has served as the starting point for many aspiring engine builders.

With the cab removed, the works are fully exposed. The engine has one, single-acting oscillator that is geared to the jackshaft with the sprocket. The lubricator hangs off the steam line behind the boiler.

The Lizard Valley's monorail engine

While the model shown here is a freelance locomotive, it is built on prototype practice. Charles Francois Marie-Therese Lartigue, a Frenchman, came up with the concept of this monorail system. The railway has a single supporting rail atop a series of A-frames, with stabilizing rails on either side. Several Lartigue monorailways were built in various parts of the world. Some were animal hauled and some were hauled by electric locomotives.

Only a couple of steam-powered monorailways were built to this system, the most famous being the Listowell & Ballybunion Railway in Ireland. This railway had three Hunslet-built 0-3-0 tender engines designed by Anatole Mallet, of compound, articulated-locomotive fame. The tenders on the L&B engines had steam boosters to help them up hills.

The railway hauled both freight and passengers between Listowell and Ballybunion, a distance of some nine-and-a-half miles. There were a number of obvious drawbacks to the system, not the least of which was the track, which essentially formed a fence nine-and-a-half miles long. Grade crossings were problematic, as were diverging tracks and just getting passengers to the other side to help balance the coaches. This latter problem was solved by the expedient of a sort of stair car that was coupled into the middle of trains. It gave people a way of more conveniently crossing the track.

What to me is the most amazing thing about this unique railway, though, is that it lived and worked for nearly forty years, serving well both of the communities it connected. Part of the line is being restored today, but with a dummy steam engine, alas.

The model

As mentioned above, this model does not replicate the L&B (or any other) full-size locomotive. It was built for my own Lizard Valley Steam Monorail Company and is named *Iguana*.

Iguana is an 0-2-0T, with a pair of gas fired, single-flue boilers. Each side tank conceals a gas tank, and there's a control valve and filler valve on top of each. The boilers, although

202

Specifications

Builder: Marc Horovitz (US)
Date built: 2003
Gauge: None (monorail)
Scale: 15mm
Boilers: Single flue
Fittings: Safety valve, throttle, pressure gauge, filler plug
Fuel: Butane
Blow-off pressure: 40psi
Cylinders: Two, double-acting oscillators
Reversing gear: Rotary valve
Lubricator: Displacement
Weight: 4lbs 8oz
Dimensions: Length, 8in; width, 6in; height (including track), 8⅜in

Opposite: Iguana has a pair of gas-fired boilers connected by a balance pipe in the cab. Fuel is carried in the side tanks, each tank supplying its own boiler.

Right: An open cab makes access to the controls easy. The balance pipe with its manifold in the middle spans the divider between the boilers.

Lower: A pair of double-acting oscillators drive a geared jack-shaft, which turns a larger gear and the wheels. The top of the angled side rod can be seen on the large gear's crank.

fired independently, are connected by a balance pipe at the rear. In the middle of the balance pipe is a manifold that contains the throttle and a pressure gauge. Since the boilers form, in essence, a single pressure vessel, only one has a safety valve. The other has a plain filler plug.

The engine is powered by a pair of double acting, oscillating cylinders that drive a jackshaft with a pinion on it. This drives a large gear with a 5:1 ratio. Cranks on the large gear's axle are connected to cranks on the drivers' axles with side rods shaped like a 'V' on its side. The cylinders exhaust to the stacks.

Iguana is stabilized by a pair of spring-loaded horizontal wheels that bear against the side rails of the track. These are hidden behind the side tanks.

The locomotive runs surprisingly well. It can be radio controlled (throttle only), and I have videotape of it with a short train running back and forth along the line. Sadly, about a third of the track was crushed during the winter of 2006-07 by the weight of snow and ice upon it. As of this writing, it has not been rebuilt.

Regner's model has all the character of a typical Krauss industrial locomotive. Steam lines from the steam dome are dummies, as are the safety valves atop it. The high level of detail adds to the engine's presence.

The 'Stainz' locomotive was made famous to large-scale modellers by LGB's production of it in plastic in untold numbers. The prototype, named *Stainz*, was the second of four engines made by Krauss in 1892 for the Styrian Regional Railway. Styria is a state in Austria and Stainz is a province within it. Of the four locomotives built for the railway, only *Stainz* survives.

The model

Strictly speaking, this is not a model of *Stainz*, being N° 1, not N° 2. They are basically the same engine, but there are some detail differences. Regner's engine is a scale model. The detail level is high and the spirit of the prototype has been accurately captured.

This engine, which I built from a kit, has lots of interesting features. It is gas fired, with a single-flue boiler. The cab is equipped with a throttle valve, pressure gauge, and water glass. The boiler has a feedwater system that involves a check valve and vertical filler pipe on the left side of the engine. On the prototype, this same pipe would have been used to fill the well tank in the locomotive's frame, so its use as a filler on the model is prototypical. To fill, you have to use a syringe or squirt bottle to overcome the boiler's pressure.

There's a large gas tank in the cab that provides over half an hour of running time. The filler valve is not of the self-bleeding type. I found that to fill the tank, the control valve must be cracked a little.

On the right side of the boiler is a lubricator disguised as an air pump. It is equipped with a feed-control. The safety valves on the steam dome and all the plumbing to the cylinders are dummy. The actual safety valve sits immediately behind the steam dome, while the steam line is internal. The front axle is sprung while the rear is fixed. The engine is fitted with LGB-style loop couplers and was obviously intended for use with LGB rolling stock.

Cylinders have D-valves controlled by Allan valve gear, which is unusual for a model locomotive. This is similar to Stephenson's gear but with straight links and a different lever system for changing gear. Like Stephenson's though, there are two outside eccentrics on either side.

Another unusual feature on this engine is working drain cocks. These were intended to be radio controlled, as was the entire locomotive, but I chose to build it as a manually controlled engine. Because of that, I had to modify the lever that actuates the drain cocks so that it was accessible from without, but not visually obtrusive.

This engine is a strong runner, although the burner is troublesome. I suspect that this may be altitude related, as I live a mile above sea level. This would not be the first engine to come my way that suffered from altitude sickness.

Above: Allan valve gear is featured. Like Stephenson's, it has two outside eccentrics. The leaf springs above the front axle are functional.

Left: The cab roof lifts off for access. Controls are neatly laid out and readily to hand.

Specifications

Builder: Regner (Germany)
Date built: 2005
Gauge: 1 (45mm)
Scale: 1:22.5
Boiler: Single flue
Fittings: Safety valve, water glass, pressure gauge, check valve, throttle
Fuel: Butane
Blow-off pressure: 45psi
Cylinders: Two, double-acting D-valve
Reversing gear: Allan valve gear
Lubricator: Displacement
Weight: 7lbs 4oz
Dimensions: Length over end beams, 9⅛in; width, 4⅜in; height, 6¾in

David Hick's 'Cranmore' Peckett

Above: The 'Cranmore' Peckett is an attractive little locomotive. David Hick's rendition of it captures all of its charm and personality.

Top right: With the back sheet removed, the neatly laid out cab is easily accessible. The removable gas tank sits against the left-hand wall.

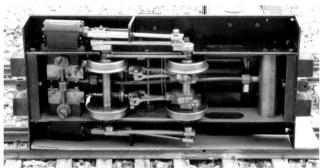

Full, working Stephenson's valve gear drives the inside valves. Each rod is milled from the solid and is beautifully profiled.

Peckett & Sons, Ltd, was a small (relatively) British builder of industrial locomotives of many different sizes and gauges. The 'Cranmore' class was one of the smaller ones, a diminutive 0-4-0 saddle tanker with Stephenson's valve gear.

The model

David Hick produces some of the finest model locomotives I have seen. His 'Cranmore' Peckett is a finescale model of the original.

This is a gas-fired locomotive with a single-flue boiler. The gas tank is connected to the burner by a piece of silicone tubing. The tank, which sits next to the left side of the boiler, is held in place only by gravity. It must be removed for filling.

Boiler fittings include a safety valve, an internal throttle, and a pressure gauge. There's an enormous (for this engine) displacement lubricator under the footplate, with a filler plug in the floor of the cab. The safety valve, which is concealed beneath the slip-off steam dome, is removed to fill the boiler. Since there is no water glass or provision for filling the boiler under pressure, the engine must be shut down after each run to prepare for the next.

This tiny locomotive has full, working Stephenson's valve gear, driving inside valves. This is controlled by a beautifully made reversing lever in the cab, which locks into position as would a full-size lever. When it's in forward gear, the handle is near the front cab wall and is difficult to grasp with full-size fingers. The back sheet, held in place by a clip under the roof, pops off for removing the gas tank and filling the lubricator.

The saddle tank is not functional on this engine. The smoke-box door opens with a proper dart with two handles. Front and rear buffer beams are fitted with wooden dumb buffers.

Both the workmanship and the finish on this engine are to an exceptionally high standard. All rods and links are nicely

profiled from solid stock. Valve-gear components, while very small, are robust and intended for hard work. The paint finish, including the superb hand lining, is top notch, down to the fine red line at the bottom of the engine's frames.

The smokebox door is secured with a proper dart.

Specifications

Builder: David Hick (UK)
Date built: 2005
Gauge: 0 (32mm)
Scale: 16mm
Boiler: Single flue
Fittings: Safety valve, throttle, pressure gauge
Fuel: Butane
Blow-off pressure: 45psi
Cylinders: Two, double-acting D-valve
Reversing gear: Stephenson's valve gear
Lubricator: Displacement
Weight: 3lbs 14oz
Dimensions: Length over end beams, 7⅜in; width, 3⅛in; height, 5⅜in

205

A pair of tram engines

The two trams at home on the Ogden Botanical Railway. These engines were purpose built for the line and have served it well.

For many years, our Ogden Botanical Railway had no engines of its own, even though it had played host to countless guest engines. I wanted to come up with a standard design that would fit the character of the OBR – at least as it was in my own mind. It is a small railway that serves just two or three communities, hauling both passengers and light freight. Since the line is essentially level, large or heavy locomotives are not required. Also, since the length of the mainline is not excessive, smaller, lighter engines would serve just fine. Locomotives that were relatively simple in design and construction were also desirable. Tram engines, always a personal favourite, seemed to fit the bill just fine, so a basic design was embarked upon.

This design embodies an open, box-like cab. A transverse pot boiler, fired by two wicks, sits in the middle. A steam motor occupies the space at one end, while the other end is open from the floor up. A displacement lubricator sits between the boiler and the steam motor. Beneath the footplate, at the end opposite the steam motor, is the fuel tank. Frames are brass and body work is steel, riveted wherever feasible and bolted where it needs to come apart. Roofs are removable for internal access by the extraction of pins at either end. Externally, the two trams that have so far been built are quite similar. Internally, they differ considerably.

Nº 1

The first tram was built with one, single-acting oscillating cylinder. It is non-reversing and the steam motor is geared to the axle via a 4:1 reduction through a compound gear train. The other axle is driven via conventional siderods. Exhaust from the motor is piped directly to the stack, which comes up through the middle of the roof.

This engine is a prodigious user of steam oil, much of which ends up on the engine's roof after a run. Also, the engine, on a calm, cool day, has the unexpected but appealing characteristic of leaving a trail of perfect smoke rings behind it as it travels, something that I've never seen any other locomotive do. It runs pretty smoothly, but makes quite a bit of noise.

Nº 2

Based on the success of Nº 1, and given the fact that the OBR now had at least one locomotive it could call its own, the pressure for additional engines was somewhat lessened. Sometime later, design work commenced on another, more sophisticated version.

I developed a two cylinder, double-acting steam motor that was based on another locomotive that I had built. It has a rotary reversing valve atop the motor. This is basically a stand-alone unit that can simply be dropped into place in a chassis.

The motor is plumbed into the boiler (via the lubricator) in the usual way. However, I didn't want another engine that slobbered all over itself like the last one, so I added a condenser between the exhaust port and the stack. The oil-laden exhaust steam goes first to the condenser, where the oil drops out and falls to the track through a hole in the bottom, while the remaining steam is exhausted through the stack.

This engine is also geared to the axle, this time 2:1. It is self-starting and runs smoothly and quietly. Because of this, it has been deemed the passenger engine.

Left: Nº 1 (top) is non-reversing and runs on just one, single-acting oscillator. Exhaust is piped directly to the stack. Nº 2 reverses via a rotary valve and has a pair of double-acting oscillators. Exhaust is piped to a condenser that separates out the oil.

Right: Tram Nº 1 (top) is geared to the axle 4:1 via compound gearing. Nº 2 is simply geared 2:1.

Specifications

Specifications: Nº 1
Builder: Marc Horovitz (US)
Date built: 2004
Gauge: 1 (45mm)
Scale: 15mm
Boiler: Pot
Fittings: Safety valve, throttle
Fuel: Alcohol
Blow-off pressure: 30psi
Cylinders: One, single-acting oscillator
Reversing gear: None
Lubricator: Displacement
Weight: 3lbs
Dimensions: Length, 7⅛in; width, 3⅜in; height, 6in

Specifications: Nº 2
(only differing specifications listed)
Date built: 2006
Cylinders: Two, double-acting oscillators
Reversing gear: Rotary valve
Weight: 3lbs 2oz

Index